# Terrorism, R

# Terrorism, Rights and the Rule of Law

## Negotiating Justice in Ireland

Barry Vaughan and Shane Kilcommins

WILLAN
PUBLISHING

Published by

Willan Publishing
Culmcott House
Mill Street, Uffculme
Cullompton, Devon
EX15 3AT, UK
Tel: +44(0)1884 840337
Fax: +44(0)1884 840251
e-mail: info@willanpublishing.co.uk
website: www.willanpublishing.co.uk

Published simultaneously in the USA and Canada by

Willan Publishing
c/o ISBS, 920 NE 58th Ave, Suite 300
Portland, Oregon 97213-3786, USA
Tel: +001(0)503 287 3093
Fax: +001(0)503 280 8832
e-mail: info@isbs.com
website: www.isbs.com



First published 2008

Hardback
ISBN 978-1-84392-265-0

Paperback
ISBN 978-1-84392-264-3

British Library Cataloguing-in-Publication Data

A catalogue record for this book is available from the British Library.

Project management by Deer Park Productions, Tavistock, Devon
Typeset by PDQ Typesetting, Newcastle-under-Lyme, Staffordshire
Printed by T. J. International Ltd, Padstow, Cornwall

# Contents

# Introduction

> I have been restless at the curious blankness with which men from other social disciplines face any legal matter or any talk of law. Of all the social disciplines it stands most isolated. My own guess is that that [sic] is because the law-men mainly think doctrine and talk a language which runs in terms largely of correct doctrine – which is to exclude communication and contact with any premises except the premises of correct doctrine. But underneath all doctrines there lie problems, and those problems seem to me a proper study for all men of the social disciplines, and an illuminating one ... For the store of record, of knowledge, and of light which the law-men have heaped up has no business to be kept locked away from the other social disciplines. Traffic in ideas, like traffic in goods, runs best when there are return-loadings ... The social disciplines are due to discover that modern work in the legal field is not only a market for their product but a rich productive area. One thinks of ancient mines, once worked and valued, since lost, now relocated – and waiting. (Llewellyn 1940: 1357)

Commentary on our times suggests that we live in a uniquely insecure age, beset by terror at a global level through the actions of Al Qaeda and their associates and at a local level where anti-social behaviour of some diminishes the quality of life of many citizens. Responses vary but many comprise strategies that restrict the freedoms of those suspected of such actions in a way that cuts against the grain of normal protections.

The two disciplines that may be most profoundly affected by these developments and that have most to offer in terms of reasoned commentary upon them are those of criminology and law. Criminology teaches us especially about how the coercive arm of the state can be used to incapacitate those deemed suspect; law tells us about the legal mechanisms through which this social paralysis of opponents can be achieved. These are useful lessons but taught separately can lead us astray. Criminology's emphasis on how state powers can be turned against suspects can too easily lead to predictions of a maximum security society in which individual liberty is curtailed. Law's analysis of legal frameworks and decisions can omit the wider social importance of such activities, content to establish that decisions accord with precedent and process.

As a criminologist and lawyer, we believe that combining insights from both disciplines helps to avoid these errors. Criminology can learn from law by attending to individual case law through which judges can resist the machinations of governments intent on increasing the reach of the state. The specificities of legal reasoning and the process of judicial interpretation continues to be influenced by assumptions and values – which are entrenched in various constitutional and human rights provisions – that emphasise the primacy of the individual often over broader collective goals or policies. Such decisions can preserve the rule of law and prevent state rule descending into rule by law, legislation that has been faithful to democratic process but nullifies many rights. The internal logic of law must therefore remain an important consideration when contemplating broader socio-political forces. But law too can learn from criminology by thinking critically about the wider social significance of judicial decisions, acts of parliaments or delegated powers granted to organisations or individuals.

Trading ideas across disciplines, we argue that the future is neither as bleak as criminologists are inclined to think nor is it as simple as attesting to the growth of more laws. Judges do resist the siren-call of counter-terrorism by insisting that due process must be followed and that a certain level of equality is maintained between citizen and state; of course, due process is often relaxed precisely to defend the state against terrorism and judges have been complicit in this. Many criminologists and lawyers are inclined to put due process on a pedestal and refuse to countenance any change to it; criminologists do so because of their perennial suspicion of the state and lawyers because of their ahistorical approach to legal systems. We try to be more nuanced, arguing that due process has suffered as counter-terrorism strategies have permeated the 'ordinary' criminal justice system yet it also has been justly amended to include identities and interests that have been unfairly glided over. Law's importance in regulating lives is increasing yet the social and political implications of this and its impacts on people's rights are rarely debated. The rule of law is threatened not only by terrorism but also by law enforcement through regulatory agencies which threatens to wrench law away from public accountability. We hope that this book makes some effort in broaching these matters for public debate.

Although this book is the culmination of a dialogue between law and criminology, its emergence depends on broader social influences. We are grateful for the valuable suggestions provided by colleagues, especially Andrew Ashworth, Caroline Fennell, David Gwynn Morgan, Siobhan Mullally, and Dermot Walsh. Barry would like to thank his wife Olga for all her assistance. His first book coincided with the birth of their first son, Conor, and this volume has been entwined with the birth of their second, Darragh. Newborns are no longer a prerequisite for the appearance of any future volumes. Shane would like to thank Maria, Kate and Jack for providing ample distraction in the writing of this book.

## Chapter 1

# Ending or extending the long nineteenth century of criminal justice?

The history of events: surface disturbances, crests of foam that the tides of history carry on their strong backs. A history of brief, rapid, nervous fluctuations, by definition ultra-sensitive; the least tremor sets all its antennae quivering. But as such it is the most exciting of all, the richest in human interest, and also the most dangerous. We must learn to distrust this history with its still burning passions, as it was felt, described, and lived by contemporaries whose lives were as short and as short-sighted as ours. It has the dimensions of their anger, dreams, or illusions ... a world of strong passions certainly, blind like any other living world, our own included, and unconscious of the deeper realities of history, of the running waters on which our frail barks are tossed like cockleshells. A dangerous world, but one whose spells and enchantments we shall have exorcised by making sure first to chart those underlying currents, often noiseless, whose direction can only be discerned by watching them over long periods of time. Resounding events are often only momentary outbursts, surface manifestations of these larger movements and explicable only in terms of them. (Braudel 1973: Preface)

### Understanding the present

It is a common conceit of the current era to believe that we are living in unique times, that present circumstances have thrust us away from previous habits and towards practices that are foreign to us. Currently, politicians are telling the public in many countries that the new forms of terrorism that have arisen since 9/11 demand responses that may cut into previously untouched freedoms. Furthermore the relationship between citizen and state may have to be reordered to cope with the risks to security that this new terrorism poses. And states may have to impose unusual restrictions on citizens' movements and routines and dissolve some of the protections that have previously been afforded to suspects.

Many criminologists are somewhat jaundiced about these claims, not because they disagree with the notion that there has been a break with the past, but because they locate it elsewhere. Many of the techniques now being utilised against terrorist suspects – racial profiling, scrutiny of financial records, extended periods of detention – have previously been used against criminal suspects so it has proven quite easy to redeploy them in a different direction. For criminologists, the great transformation has been the onset of an overt punitiveness directed against offenders that is barely concerned with the rights of convicted criminals and insouciant about the protections afforded to suspects. Rehabilitation of offenders and respect for due process values seem like archaic sentiments that have little purchase upon the contemporary predicaments troubling the public. Once the political centrality of addressing people's concerns by governing through crime (Simon 2007) has been established, the idea of 'governing through terrorism' (Mythen and Walklate 2006) meets little resistance since people have become used to governments capitalising on their public anxieties.

These two accounts, which might respectively be characterised as a war on terror and a war against crime, share several similarities. They emphasise the need for governments to take decisive action against those suspected of committing prohibited actions and are sceptical about the legitimacy of the protections afforded to these suspects. Instead, greater powers should be granted to investigative agencies to determine whether suspects have actually committed alleged actions, and these agencies should face fewer constraints on their powers. To adapt Herbert Packer's famous couplet, the values of crime/terror control are stamping that of due process into the ground. Packer likened the operation of the first value to an assembly line that produces guilty pleas as expeditiously as possible; due process is more like an obstacle course that sets up many barriers and obstacles for law enforcement officials to overcome before a conviction can be secured. The increasing primacy granted to crime/terror control means that governments are more willing to infringe supposedly inviolable rights in the pursuit of some supposed greater good like public security and bend the activities of customarily autonomous actors, like the police and courts, towards the ends of terror or crime control.

The impact of the war on crime that has been going on for some time (Garland 2001; Simon 2007) and the predicted long war on terror (Rogers 2006) seems to be squashing the values of due process in many western democracies. It does not seem too fanciful to enquire if their character as liberal jurisdictions is being radically transformed. The United States has been trying to create a 'new legal regime' with respect to the Guantanamo Bay detainees that 'renders quaint' international rules such as the Geneva Convention (Sands 2005). The British government has introduced detention without charge for 28 days, a doubling of the previous period (although senior police figures were clamouring for 90 days). Alarm has been pronounced over the departure from the rule of law that anti-terrorist measures like this represent (Blick and Weir 2005) but as John Lea (2005) points out, this departure from due process has been prefigured by advances made against those suspected of organising the drugs trade. Both sets of measures are a response to the perceived difficulties of obtaining information about either terrorist or serious criminal activity and react by revoking vital aspects of procedural justice.

If we are to come to some understanding of the significance of executive encroachment upon the rule of law, then we require an account of the development of what has quaintly come to be called the rule of law that is associated with the development of modern states: publicly promulgated and enforced law that circumscribes the arbitrary power of the executive and state and affirms the equality of every citizen within that state. Stating matters in so cursory a fashion risks obscuring how some of the key features of the rule of law – non-arbitrariness, publicity, etc. – only developed gradually. Moreover, it might seem to efface how this notion was realised differently in particular national contexts or, more radically, ignore claims that arbitrariness is at the heart of state power through the power to invoke exceptions. These counter-arguments shall be considered but, for now, we think it sufficient to highlight the prominence given to the rule of law within contemporary jurisdictions so that it can help decipher some of the most momentous changes affecting modern states.

## The rule of law

Although the emergence of the notion of the rule of law and, more importantly, the practices associated with it shall be dealt with more extensively in Chapter 3, it is important to outline its precept and influence. Although it has a long lineage, it is still worth considering A. V. Dicey's account in *Law of the Constitution* (1959), not only because he popularised the notion but also because he is thought to have illustrated the vulnerability of the rule of law to governmental decree.

Dicey outlined three main facets of the rule of law. He outlined the first through the principle that:

> no man is punishable or can be lawfully made to suffer in body or goods except for a distinct breach of law established in the ordinary legal manner before the ordinary Courts of the land. In this sense the rule of law is contrasted with every system of government based on the exercise by persons in authority of wide, arbitrary, or discretionary powers of constraint. (Dicey 1959: 188)

It is easy to forget just what a revolution in justice this entailed. Requiring that people only be punishable via courts and through clearly enunciated offences presupposes some system of due process that was inconsistent not only with the arbitrariness of the sovereign but also with how communities would dispense justice. Rejecting a presumption of innocence, local communities often put the onus upon suspects to refute the charges laid against them. Wresting control of justice away from communities required the state to establish some kind of monopoly of justice via the deployment of state-employed justice personnel.

Besides due process, one of the other noted features of the rule of law is the idea of legal equality (Allan 2001), Dicey's second characteristic of the rule of law. We ordinarily associate the rule of law 'not only with predictability but also with a roughly equal treatment of social groups' (Holmes 2003: 21). Agents of the state should not be exempt from the kind of justice that keeps the ordinary citizen within its reach: 'every man, whatever be his rank or condition, is subject to the ordinary law of the realm and amenable to the jurisdiction of the ordinary tribunals' (Dicey 1959: 193). Law enforcement officials have often displayed a tendency to elevate themselves above the rule of law, often for the sake of a supposedly 'noble cause' such as catching criminals. Arrogating to themselves such power is partly explicable by their perception that they are above or beyond the rule of law themselves, even though they maintain they are in service to it. The effectiveness of the rule of law is judged not only by the extent to which arbitrary state power is hemmed in but also the frequency with which it is investigated when it breaks free from these procedural confines. For the rule of law to function, it must be capable of calling justice to account. Supporting the rule of law may mean the criminal justice system is itself overseen and regulated. The extension of the rule of law is one aspect of a process of democratisation that entails 'increases in the breadth and equality of relations between governmental agents and members of the government's subject population' constituted through '*protected consultation*' (Tilly 2004: 13–14, italics in original). Citizens should be able to indicate when the state has exceeded its powers and expect effective review and redress.

Extending the rule of law beyond mere predictability to encompass equality may have important ramifications for the machinery of justice that the state sets up. Establishing some system of procedural fairness meant that the state largely took control of the investigation of crime and the adjudication of punishment away from local communities. A criminal justice system may extend its reach as events that were once viewed as harms become labelled as crimes and susceptible to investigation and prosecution by the state. Although this is often portrayed as an effort to reassure an anxious public that the state retains its capacity to protect, it may be the case that the state is responding to pleas from people to take action against the ills that afflict them. Dicey believed that legal equality had been pushed to its 'utmost limit' (1959: 193) in the England of his day.

Michel Foucault had a more nuanced view. In describing the departure from arbitrary sovereignty as a form of government, he spoke of how this movement was challenged by 'tolerated illegalities', defined as 'the non-observance of the rule' (1991: 82), in which both upper and lower strata of society indulged. Groups defended their own interests and often the state was not concerned to intervene even though these groups were breaching the rule of law. The extent to which illegalities are now tolerated may be constricting in contemporary societies. There has been a noticeable growth in the regulation of contemporary capitalist societies (Moran 2003; Braithwaite 2005) and it is a mistake to view this effort at control as being restricted to a 'punishment of the poor' project (Braithwaite 2003). Instead, the state is intruding upon areas where regulation was provided by organisations producing the good in question or else was largely absent. Examples in Ireland of the state establishing agencies to deal with these areas would include the Competition Authority and Environmental Protection Agency, among others. Both of these organisations, like many other recently established regulatory agencies, have been set up, either directly or indirectly, as the result of deepening European integration.

As a result, regulation as a kind of self-provided 'club-government' (Moran 2003) has been in comparative decline as the state has demanded that organisations submit themselves to external review and audit. But when we talk of the state, it is important that we do not present it as some sort of monolithic entity. Proceeding in this way gives us too unilateral a view of control or regulation, leading us to believe that we can chart its ascendancy or fall in some clear linear fashion and causing us to overlook the variety of ways in which it can be undertaken and the diversity of organisations that are controlled. The state may become both the recipient of regulation and its initiator. It might be better to speak of a 'disaggregated' state (Slaughter 2004) whose actions, in the pursuit of justice, are irreducible to a single modality of control or a single form of production, however loosely combined, as with the traditional criminal justice system of police-courts-corrections. Some organisations may seek to negotiate or institute a process of dialogue with those whose actions they oversee, the so-called 'responsive regulation' paradigm. The outcome is a form of disaggregated justice as many organisations are free to prosecute cases as they see fit without any reference to a central decision-maker, such as a chief prosecution service. In fact, while the traditional agencies of the criminal justice system are subject to increasing forms of control and oversight, newer forms of policing may slip free from these bonds.

If acknowledging the onset of a disaggregated state helps us to chart a route beyond dystopian visions of control, it casts up some significant impediments in the path of democratisation to which the rule of law contributes. Construing this path as a deepening process of protected consultation jars with the state maintaining minimal public involvement in the process of criminal justice. Considering that the state felt it necessary to move away from a system of localised justice in establishing general rule, this initial stance was not surprising. But it should make us wonder whether this 'hands-off' strategy is now appropriate. Welcoming the prospect of greater public involvement should not mean conceding the last word to the general populace in matters of justice. The rule of law has to mean a protection from arbitrary action from both the state and the general populace. Similar issues about the inadequacy of consultation arise when we consider the emergence of disaggregated justice, since it is commonly acknowledged that these kinds of non-elected regulators suffer from problems of legitimacy and accountability (Maher 2006). Although they often justify themselves in terms of effectiveness or output legitimacy (Majone 1998) – they get the job done – their lack of national public or political input lends them an apparent air of a democratic deficit. In some respects, we need to rethink the relationship of the rule of law with national sovereignty given that we can no longer endorse, as did Dicey, the notion of parliamentary sovereignty.

Qualifying Dicey in this respect does not negate the relevance of parliament for promulgating or weakening the rule of law (and given we are speaking of Westminster-style systems of government that has characterised state rule in Britain and Ireland, in effect this means the executive). Dicey is often construed as proposing that parliament has absolute sovereignty so that 'no person or body is recognized by the law of England as having a right to override or set aside the legislation of Parliament' (1959: 40). Not only does Dicey seem to elaborate some version of parliamentary supremacy, he also admitted that 'there are times of tumult or invasion when for the sake of legality itself the rule of law must be broken' (1959: 412). Yet this bleak interpretation cannot be supported as Dicey did not believe government had complete freedom to legislate as it wished. He counselled that 'Powers, however extraordinary, which are conferred or sanctioned by statute, are never really unlimited, for they are confined by the words of the Act itself, and, what is more, by the interpretation put upon the statute by the judges' (1959: 413–14).

What we might call the judicial *habitus* (Hutton 2006) holds executive power in check especially since it is the product of thousands of individual decisions and built up over many generations. Dicey did not believe rights were bestowed or abrogated as a result of legislation passed by parliament thanks to the third distinctive feature of the rule of law. Instead, he argued that 'the general principles of the constitution (as for example the right to personal liberty, or the right of public meeting) are with us as the result of judicial decisions determining the rights of private persons in particular cases brought before the Courts' (1959: 195). Since rights, for Dicey, grew in a common-law fashion as accretions on previous decisions, they and their form of redress became implanted in the minds of people and judges: even though the 'Habeas *Corpus* Acts declare no principle and define no rights, but they are for practical purposes worth a hundred constitutional articles guaranteeing individual liberty' (1959: 199). Dworkin (1982) makes a similar point about judicial decision-making being indebted to and constrained by the past. Every judge regards himself as 'a partner in a complex chain enterprise' in which the conventions of the past structure the practice of judicial decisions. Ireland differs from Britain as it is governed through a written constitution, which although still dependent for their interpretation on the kind of incremental decision-making that Dicey described, gives rights a surer foothold.

Some contemporary theorists like Agamben (2005) take the opposite view and claim that in the present age of terror law has been suspended and replaced by a juridical void, a black hole from which all pretensions to legality are expelled. Alternatively, accounts derived from the work of Carl Schmitt (1985) emphasise that in time of emergency, the sovereign sheds any pretence of being constrained by law and instead deploys it against designated enemies. The sovereign's acts may be legal in a thin sense in that they have been ratified by a political process. In these circumstances, 'rule by law' has subjugated the 'rule of law', a strategy that may thrust people into a legal grey zone with few rights of redress. Yet this very much depends on the judicial *habitus* and whether judges are emboldened to challenge the executive in its attempts to rule by law. We wish to show that the notion of the rule of law, which contains within it the 'compulsion to legality' (Dyzenhaus 2006a), offers sufficient resources to contest the executive yet is also ambiguous enough to offer the executive a legal veneer for its actions.

## The present influence of the long nineteenth century

This kind of double-edged narrative can only be understood from within a historical narrative as the rule of law orientates judicial decision-making but is also constituted and developed by it. To paraphrase the historian Eric Hobsbawm, we need to understand the long nineteenth century of criminal justice as exemplified through the rule of law. Hobsbawm (1962, 1975, 1987) coined the phrase to designate the epoch 1789–1914, during which the capitalist system reached its potential. Similarly, we believe that our analysis has to trace the development of the rule of law over a similar period of time so that we can draw out its present configuration and assess what protections are being weakened as well as fortified.

Once we admit that the rule of law has grown as a result of a myriad of small accretions of judicial decisions and case law then this indicates a problem of writing a coherent history. Like many other criminologists, we are concerned to comprehend the most significant contemporary changes occurring in law and criminal justice. This so-called 'history of the present' devotes itself to explaining these changes rather than offer an exhaustive portrayal of the past through some sort of all-encompassing historical narrative (Garland 2001). And yet these changes can only be properly assessed by an understanding of the forces of history that block them, in this instance the judicially embedded rule of law. So our narrative has to include both coherence and possible discontinuity and this is difficult to achieve. It is common to write a criminological history segmented into relatively coherent eras – classic liberalism, penal-welfarism, punitiveness, etc. – each of which enjoys a rise and decline as one succeeds another. This kind of history discounts the messiness of the present by neglecting how the influence of the past persists. It focuses on contemporary events that pulse away in the media and drive political responses of expediency. In so doing, two kinds of methodological error are committed. There is too much emphasis given to short-term events with an accompanying neglect of, adapting Braudel (1973), *la longue durée* of legal time as revealed by judicial commitment to the rule of law as it unfolds across several generations. And the second oversight is to privilege the talk and policy discourse of self-styled political actors who seek to change the criminal justice system and to neglect those who pitch their decision-making in a lower key or else refer mainly to the individual case before them rather than make pronouncements to society.

We do not pretend that the judiciary represents some kind of impregnable redoubt in which civil liberties are always secure. Judges can and do defer to the executive, often on the positivistic grounds that the law is simply legislation that the government has succeeded in having enacted. But not only do judges exhibit a capacity to establish due process principles, they also resist their attempted attenuation by government. We will try to show this dual process at work, deference to and rejection of government initiatives, mainly with reference to developments in Ireland. The legal history and practice of Ireland is of more than parochial interest since it has seen continuous struggle between the rule of law and states of exception, beginning with the period under the colonial power of Britain up to contemporary times as it struggled with paramilitary groups that originated in the Northern Ireland conflict. We hope to show how the colonial past might prefigure what is currently happening in the present, as John Braithwaite (2003: 9) has suggested.

Focusing on the perpetual dissonance between the administration of justice based on the rule of law and responding to the turbulence of colonial rule by the invocation of emergency powers avoids the problem of positing one dominant penal paradigm that squashes resistance. Instead, there is essential opposition within the dispensation of justice because of the contested nature of the nation-state. The defence of the state seemed to demand special powers to defend it, under both British colonial rule and Irish self-government. Even after Ireland gained its independence from Britain, the disputed nature of the settlement meant that many disaffected people questioned the legitimacy of what they called a 'partitionist' state (since the Irish government accepted that the six counties in Northern Ireland would remain part of Britain) and tried to overthrow it. But even while Ireland relied on emergency powers to suppress paramilitary activities, it also developed its own written constitution in 1937 that guaranteed certain rights for Irish citizens. Although the Irish judiciary only began to explore the implications of these rights for the criminal process in the 1960s, they further strengthened the rule of law in Ireland by curtailing some of the questionable discretionary practices of the police. The dialectic between the rule of law and emergency powers pulsed again with the onset of paramilitary-related violence in Northern Ireland and its overspill into the Republic of Ireland. The Irish police became more results-oriented yet this created scandals that pulled the government into reforming control of the police and checking their behaviour.

This process has been augmented by the increasing influence of supranational conventions and norms such as the European Convention on Human Rights (ECHR). This cosmopolitan discourse of rights provides a resource for agitating for greater oversight and regulation of state agents. Their deployment makes it more difficult for the state to resist these overtures but the implantation of cosmopolitan rights often depends on a change in a national setting, in this instance a gradual cessation of paramilitary conflict in Northern Ireland. Consequently, the trump card of state security was diminished and the protection of human rights as a primary rationale for policing was elevated in both parts of the island of Ireland. The Irish state has established an ombudsman commission for the state police as well as an inspectorate and other review units (Vaughan 2005). In so doing the Irish state has acknowledged the validity of a cosmopolitan discourse of rights and confirmed Braithwaite and Drahos' view (2000: 3–4) of states as rule-takers rather than solely as rule-makers.

Parallel with these developments, a range of legislation has been passed granting more power to Gardaí [police] to detain suspects for longer periods of time and prescribing mandatory sentences for particular offences. Walsh (2007: 58) suggests that these novel powers 'are eating away at the due process foundations which have secured a reasonable balance between the state and the individual in criminal justice matters for generations'. In a Diceyean vein, Walsh (2007: 58) suggests that this damage is being 'inflicted in a piecemeal fashion through a rapid succession of separate enactments'. But this staccato style of law-making issues, in part, from the executive's exasperation with the judiciary as they frustrate the government's designs, such as refusing to impose mandatory sentences. There is a legal dialectic at work which is often overlooked when commentators talk of the suspension of law (Agamben 2005). They neglect how the judicial *habitus*, in its constant re-articulation of the rule of law via individual cases, affirms due process values and continues to provide some protection from arbitrary state power.

If the development of the rule of law, or what we call the long nineteenth century of criminal justice, continues, despite the apocalyptic premonitions of many criminologists, it may still be undergoing fundamental alterations. Rooted in the development of sovereign nation-states, the rule of law is being challenged by developments above and below this level. We saw how it is being extended through the recognition of cosmopolitan norms like the ECHR but it is being challenged by an increasingly prevalent practice of security operating in the European Union that affects migration and border control. At the level below the state, governments are trying to increase the participation of communities in the provision of their own security by promoting consultation and subsidising surveillance projects. In one respect, this communal involvement resiles from the rule of law which has been characterised by an effort to take justice away from communities. But on another level, by extending and deepening the level of 'protected consultation', it might actually dampen the possibility of vigilante justice.

So far, we have talked about how judicial adherence to the rule of law can secure rights against the machinations of the executive, whether it is exemplified through the wars on crime or terror. Dworkin himself, whose ideas we have enlisted to support this notion, has counselled that 'it would be a terrible mistake for those who worry about civil rights and liberties to pin too much hope on the judiciary in times of crisis' (quoted in Zedner 2005: 526). Despite this downbeat assessment, Zedner still advises judges to 'throw their weight around and in so doing, to tip the balance in favour of individual liberties' (2005: 529). Advancing this engine of judicial oversight requires the 'carriage of due process' (2005: 529) to preserve a space of liberty from executive encroachment. There is a danger of setting up some zero-sum game between individual and state, in which the advancement of autonomy for one represents a diminution in the independence of the other. But it may well be that the sources of domination for some people reside within civil society and that state intervention may well prove to be a redress. Adjusting procedures of due process that cut into the freedom of some may be a necessary condition for justifiably augmenting the autonomy of others. In cases involving alleged sexual offences, it may well be that procedures regarding the exclusion of certain kinds of evidence harbour unjustified stereotypes. Changing this procedure would probably elicit little dissent but it does show up the problems of counterposing due process with a model directed towards the control of crime or terror. The vital intervening mechanism that allows us to assess whether these should be in opposition or not is whether this move augments the autonomy of those most dominated or else further diminishes their freedom (Vaughan 2007).

Only by examining how the rule of law interacts with and is amended through these influences will we be able to understand whether the long nineteenth century of criminal justice is coming to a close or whether it is entering a new stage of development. Only by engaging in this kind of legal and historical analysis will we be able to prophesy whether, as

Angela Carter put it, the *fin* has come a little early this *siècle* as so many predictions of a criminology of catastrophe would have us believe (O'Malley 2003).

## Plan of the book

We undertake this argument as follows. In Chapter 2, we articulate our own understanding of the kinds of transformation that may be affecting contemporary justice systems through an encounter with some of the most resonant criminological accounts offered today. We examine the work of three notable theorists; John Lea, Pat O'Malley and John Pratt. While we learn from each of them, ultimately we argue that their vision can be reduced to either a neo-conservative account that governs through crime to maintain a basic level of social solidarity and/or a neo-liberal account that adapts to crime by treating the offender as a manageable problem. What gets expunged is any idea that change might occur as a people marshal norms to argue that the workings of a criminal justice system are discredited. Obviously, there is a very lively current debate which argues along the lines that the 'system needs to be rebalanced in favour of the victim'. This sets up a zero-sum relationship between rights and the rule of law but people may also argue for a more productive relationship between them as they call for the state to become less exclusionary and more respectful of rights in its administration of justice.

It is not a matter of choosing between one or the other but understanding that the development of criminal justice encompasses both. In Chapter 3, we outline how the rule of law developed through the establishment of a system of inculpatory justice that afforded various procedural protections to criminal suspects rather than presume them guilty until proven otherwise. The social relations operative in England and Wales at the time moderated the apparent harshness of this latter model of exculpatory justice. Divisiveness was much more apparent on John Bull's other island, Ireland, and the lack of reliance on local justice elicited a more forceful state presence. As urbanisation took hold in Britain, the incapacity of this system to protect the interests of the propertied class and regulate the urban poor diluted traditional English distaste for a system of state justice. A new model of justice emerged that detached itself from local roots and emphasised the formal equality of citizens and the protections that should accrue to them if accused of a crime, summed up by the 'equality of arms' principle that equalises relations between accused and state.

Ireland was an equally ambivalent convert to this new system of justice and retained an attachment to the use of emergency law even after it seceded from Britain in 1921. In Chapter 4, we show how the persistence of violence perpetrated by paramilitary groups entailed that law resided under the shadow of the gunman. The Irish state made continuous use of emergency measures that departed from the rule of law and diluted the level of protection granted to terrorist suspects. Ireland's use of these measures is of more general interest since it shows that a cross-over effect can occur as these anti-terrorist measures are normalised and used by police to combat 'ordinary crime'.

Maintaining our theme of the ambivalence of justice, the existence of emergency measures does not automatically lead to the criminal justice system being contaminated with a lack of respect for rights. In Chapter 5, we highlight how the Irish state did develop its own version of inculpatory justice and embedded the equality of arms framework in the incremental case-law fashion that Dicey foresaw. As rights that centred upon the trial developed, they exerted a significant check on the level of arbitrariness with which state agents could behave. We deploy a series of vignettes from recent case law to show that these protections still persist, are not illusory and do have significant effects in constricting state power. Two other objections have to be considered: these protections are stripped bare by the kind of populist alarm triggered by criminal or terrorist incidents and most police activity is not concerned with bringing suspects to trial but shoring up certain versions of social order. The equality of arms framework is obsolete in preventing the kinds of abuses of power that can arise out of these efforts. We consider these objections in the next two chapters.

In Chapter 6, we attend to the attempt by the state to augment its armoury in the 'fight against crime' and weaken the defences granted to criminal suspects. Much of the impetus, such as increased periods of detention without charge and dilution of the right to silence, is derived from tactics used against paramilitary groups, as was argued in Chapter 4. By legislating for these increased powers, the state legitimises a new intensity of coercion to be directed against those whose actions are deemed adverse to the state. This seems to accord with the classic Weberian definition of the state as embodying a legitimate monopoly on physical violence. But we document other developments in this chapter that depart from this standard. Increasingly, the Irish state is using civil orders to control rather than reorientate behaviour through some form of legitimate violence visited on the body of the offender through arrest or imprisonment. The unintended consequence is that crimes become demoralised and treated as regulatory problems. And the rise of regulatory crimes should make us question another prime feature of the Weberian state, namely its claims to monopoly. For the agencies investigating alleged regulatory crimes work autonomously of the Director of Public Prosecutions (DPP), ensuring that justice is disaggregated, spread out among different organisations working to different agendas. Obviously, this has always been true of the traditional criminal justice system of police-courts-corrections especially given the constitutionally recognised independence of the judiciary. But there was a conviction that the criminal justice system was and is answerable to the government, and recently the executive has tried to make the judiciary more compliant with its wishes through mandatory sentencing schemes. Assailing the judiciary in this way and depicting them as out of touch with the public mood addresses the remaining aspect of the Weberian state, namely legitimacy. However, the regulatory agencies possess a strong degree of independence from government (Shipan 2003), which must call into question their public legitimacy. And yet concerns about the legitimacy of the traditional criminal justice system in Ireland have been addressed in some areas by efforts to make it more inclusive. Restrictive rules about the status of certain kinds of evidence and witness have been overthrown, allowing hitherto suppressed voices to utter their testimony about crimes that had been tolerated behind veils of secrecy. To use O'Malley's (1999) phrase, the operation of justice is becoming more volatile and contradictory.

In Chapter 7, we trace these intense contradictions to the emergence of political authority above and below the state. During the long nineteenth century of criminal justice, the state assumed a monopoly over the means of violence within a nation by employing police, courts and prison officers. This arrogation of power is now under question from these alternative sources of political rule. State-legitimacy is deemed to be under threat from globalisation and a common alleged response is for states to emphasise security, to reassure their citizens that they are still capable of acting decisively in the interests of society. These interests are not so self-evident as many people believe and globalisation may help specify what they are rather than threaten them. An increasingly prevalent discourse of human rights, derived from transnational norms – what we term the Europeanisation of human rights – is drawn down to contest excessive securitisation on the part of the Irish state. We refer to efforts to make Irish policing more accountable, in line with Dicey's view that state agents should be made subject to the rule of law. Some reform took place in the 1980s but it was not until the cessation of paramilitary violence in Northern Ireland that the protection of human rights assumed a much greater prominence. Developments in Northern Ireland exerted a magnetic pull on policing in the Irish Republic, forcing change in line with international human rights standards. Developments at the sub-national level have also occurred with the establishment of the first formal consultative links between police and communities. It is quite possible that these two occurrences may jostle uncomfortably with each other, with the first promoting more circumspect policing and the second eliciting calls for intensified policing against local problems.

The transformations that criminal justice systems are undergoing do not amount to a complete rupture with the past since some vital continuities are maintained. Terrorism has caused some western democracies to dilute the rights afforded to suspects but these efforts have been hindered by judicial adherence to the rule of law. Even though the executive often has the power to alter the legislative content of the rule of law, the judicial *habitus* may be a reluctant convert and unwilling to transmute these rules into operative norms. And the state itself or its executive is not some kind of 'unmoved mover', immune from various influences outside its territorial borders. Nations have become more permeable since Dicey's time and states can no longer claim unqualified supremacy. The rule of law is not animated solely by parliament but supplemented by international norms and advanced by an advocacy coalition disturbed by potential state excesses or oversights. This campaign for rights is not reducible to security processes governed by the war on terror; rather it cuts across their course and skews their navigational systems. The world is, as the Northern Irish poet Louis Macniece put it, 'incorrigibly plural' and there is more of it than we can often think. We hope that this book goes some way towards representing the inevitable and inescapable plurality that irrupts within our lives and the legal systems that regulate them.

## Chapter 2

# Justice, rights and reciprocity

Let no one be in any doubt; the rules of the game are changing.
(Tony Blair, Press Conference, 5 August 2005)

### Introduction

Rather than impose our own argument forthwith, beginning, as Hegel said, like a shot from a pistol issuing forth from our inner revelation, we wish to proceed in a more dialectical fashion by considering some of the most important contemporary discussions on the subject of penal change. Having stated the absolute necessity of avoiding what one writer has called a sociology of the present tense that negates the conditional influence of the past (Archer 1995), we turn to one of the most sophisticated historical accounts of the development of the rule of law and processes of criminalisation within the modern period, John Lea's *Crime and Modernity* (2002). Lea's work has not been without critics, the most prominent being Pat O'Malley (2003), who accuses him of constructing a 'criminology of catastrophe', a nihilistic account that passes over contrary evidence that points to the persistence of the rehabilitative ideal and suffocates any hope of a more optimistic future. O'Malley stresses the need for a more politicised account but his chosen genealogical method makes it difficult to see how this can be constructed. The set of arguments derive from the civilising process propounded by Norbert Elias and stated with greatest clarity by John Pratt offers such an account by interpreting penal developments as wrought by changes in people's sensibilities. Although Pratt mainly uses Elias to argue for a 'decivilising' account that shares a good deal with Lea, it is possible to use Elias' ideas to argue for a more ambivalent, janus-faced account of contemporary control that is grounded in a politicised struggle as various actors strive to have their claims recognised by and acted upon by those in authority. While criminologists often only look at the underside of contemporary control, its negative aspects, we wish to affirm the positive aspects of recognition embedded within it.

## Crime and modernity

The following quote from Lea applies to much of modern criminology and law:

> A purely juridical perspective, concerned with the administration of the law, generally deals with a concept of the criminal offender as already in court, and spends little time thinking about the processes, and particularly the informal ones, whereby he or she arrived there. (Lea 2002: 13)

Lea's work is concerned with establishing the configuration of social relations that underlie crime control within the past and present. These relations can be broken down into four constituent parts: state, offender, victim and community. Each of these parts can be understood as related to the other three, comprising a square of crime. The customary mode of thinking about the relationship between state and offender is to reflect on the relative powerlessness of the latter. This weakness allows the state to maintain a respect for due process while maintaining a relatively effective system of crime control and allows the community to communicate with the criminal justice system without fear of reprisal. On the community's part, there must be a certain connection with the victim and detachment from the offender, both socially and emotionally, to enable the state to conduct an enforcement process.

This is a very abstract rendition of a historically grounded process which means that the format of these relationships changes as their social conditions do. For example, in pre-industrial times, communities had an ambiguous relationship with criminality, often relying upon it themselves to survive or thrive. The label of criminal was often reserved for those people who dwelt outside the haven of local communities. The state was only just beginning to assume a monopoly of legitimate violence and its sovereign figure was more concerned with protecting its own lineage rather than defending a given territory. The sovereign only acted against 'crimes' that were considered a threat to his or her interests. Dramatic public executions were the exception rather than the rule.

## From sovereignty to government

A major change occurred by way of what Lea calls a shift from sovereignty to government with the onset of industrialisation. Government is not characterised by a sporadic obedience from a loose collection of individuals who had to swear fealty to a monarch. It centres upon the preservation and reproduction of a society, recognised as a complex entity in its own right rather than a collection of groups. Government is concerned with diffusing habits of restraint and foresight among the whole population although this civilising mission was mainly concerned with adjusting the habits of the working class. Attention shifts from crime as a personalised dispute between two parties with few ramifications for the rest of society towards seeing crime as disruptive to the workings of society. The function of the police shifted from one of occasional protectors towards overseers of a stable society, a much more permanent and sustained presence.

The police were but one agency dedicated to this task and had a much broader conception of their job than crime detection. Rather their task was the preservation of order within society, monitoring public places to ensure that proper order was being observed. Crime became more marginal to the lives of this community as newly articulated mores dictated the proper place of women – the home – and children – the school. This form of ordering allowed the state to isolate criminals from their communities, as the various 'moral panics' of the nineteenth century show.

Sidelining criminals had important consequences for how they were dealt with once they came into contact with criminal justice systems. Prior to the growth of urban centres, the criminal law was couched and used in a very personalised way. People were warned against particular activities in distinct locations rather than being subject to a general injunction. Prosecutions were based around a confrontation between victim and accused and the outcome was often affected by the status of the parties involved. The growth of government meant that infractions of the criminal law were viewed in a more general way while the locus of crime was seen as pathological criminals existing on the periphery of society. Their relative weakness – and the change in sensibilities initiated by penal reformers that will be dealt with below – lay behind a series of changes in criminal procedure in the nineteenth and early twentieth centuries that gave greater protection to the accused. These new legal rights granted the accused some protection against arbitrary punishments but also signalled that he or she remained a citizen who retained some inviolable rights. This was part of a larger process of assimilation initiated by the state in the nineteenth century and continued well into the twentieth century.

Lea considers that the welfare state consolidated this process of assimilation well into the twentieth century, although certain sectors such as commercial enterprises and family affairs were not subjected to relations of crime control. Instead, these were defined as zones of autonomy, allowing what we now know as white-collar crime and domestic violence to thrive. Lea considers this marginalisation of crime control by the welfare state post World War Two as an interregnum between the moralising of the working class in the nineteenth century and the re-emergence of crime control since the 1970s.

### The fragmentation of modern crime control

The force for change lies in the changed relationship between capital and labour. Capital is no longer dependent upon a mass of the working and lower middle classes for its continued profitability. Thanks to globalisation, capital becomes more footloose and free, scouring the world for profitable havens of low taxes and poorly paid labour. The compromise that was the welfare state becomes redundant and this produces social fractures throughout societies. According to Lea, there is growing inequality, increasing insecurity and an increasing social divide between rich and poor. The opting out of a sense of common citizenship by the former is from a position of strength, but the growing exclusion of the latter develops from weakness.

These tendencies are exemplified in how life is lived in our cities. Urban centres are no longer seen as collective living spaces, shared and improved by all. Increasingly cities are viewed as sites of collective consumption to be enjoyed by those with the ability to do so. Those who do not have the necessary resources are excluded (Coleman and Sim 2005). The emphasis in social relations has shifted from integration to one of exclusion and management of risk that unexpected meetings between vastly different social groups might produce.

This new emphasis on risk management is managed through actuarial processes that plot the behaviour of groups according to the probability of its occurrence. Instead of seeking to change people through socialisation as in the era of government, the emphasis now is on minimising disruptive behaviour through strategies of exclusion. Rather than policing being part of a host of socialising agencies, it is now the sharp end of an authoritarian state concerned with minimising risk. Just as the criminal is no longer considered a weak marginal figure, so too does crime control assume a greater prominence in the strategies and outputs of government.

Since criminality is assumed to be more prevalent and resistant to socialisation, the state tools up in an effort to suppress such behaviour. Part of this tooling-up effort involves a downgrading of standards and burdens of proof. This is applied both to high and low policing, that is policing dedicated to protecting the state itself and policing oriented towards issues of internal security of the populace (Brodeur 1983). Earlier we spoke of the development of procedural protections afforded to criminals as their position, relative to the state, weakened. This is not the full story of policing since not all threats to states occupied such a lowly position. Political threats, or more pejoratively terrorism, have usually elicited a response that circumvented constitutional protections afforded to pedestrian suspects. High or political policing stands apart from the restrictions that govern low policing and has several distinct features.

It is distinguished by its capacity for extensive information gathering, reaching into the seemingly private depths of civil society. Its activities are not necessarily bound by antecedent legislation; the force of threat that it combats can often smooth the way for the granting of extraordinary powers to the police. Unregulated discretion can often lead to judgements about the pros and cons of not proceeding against ongoing criminal activity for the sake of future benefits. As Brodeur (1983: 514) comments, 'this type of policing is, therefore more deeply involved in crime management rather than crime repression'. This is best illustrated by a further feature of high policing, namely the use of informers and undercover agents. Enlisting informants by the police runs the risk that some crimes will be ignored for the sake of getting 'the bigger fish'. Protection of the community, as opposed to the interests of the state, is merely a side-constraint rather than an overarching objective.

High policing can deal with threats in two ways. One is through the intensification of criminal measures while downgrading due process requirements. Alleged members of paramilitary organisations in the Republic of Ireland, for example, can be tried in non-jury courts on the basis that juries might be intimidated. The decision to forfeit a jury trial is made by the Director for Public Prosecutions. No reasons are given and the practice cannot normally be reviewed. The checks typical of criminal procedures relating to 'low policing' are absent due to the perceived threat to the state.

The other way through which high policing deals with threats is via punitive civil sanctions, exemplified by the powers granted to police in England and Wales and Ireland enabling to them to seize suspected criminal assets. The tactics are increasingly based on civil standards of proof and a reversal of the presumption of innocence. Individuals can now be required to demonstrate that their assets are not derived from criminal activity on pain of confiscation. At the low end, people may be subject to restrictions on their behaviour such as a curfew or impeding their right to travel or association if it is thought likely that they will engage in criminal behaviour. This marks a fundamental reorientation of the criminal process. Hitherto, police investigations might begin on the basis of a hunch. Effort to accumulate evidence to substantiate this intuition and satisfy a criminal standard of proof would follow. Now, it seems that there has been 'a reduction of legal processes of proof to the dynamics of police investigation' (Lea 2004b: 87). Lea speculates that this amounts to a 're-medievalisation of criminal justice', which did not operate according to a dichotomy of innocent/guilty. Instead, guilty status was achieved on an incremental basis so that an inability to satisfy one's interrogators amounted to a degree of guilt and hence of punishment (2004b: 94). In effect, a presumption of guilt operated that was up to the defendant to refute. Verdicts were formed by judgements about the defendant's character and reputation, which revealed guilt or innocence. As Lacey (2001: 257) puts it, 'the mid-eighteenth century criminal process was geared to identifying, holding responsible and punishing those whom the local community regarded as incorrigible: those who lacked support among their peers on the basis of their previous conduct and reputation'.

For Lea, these new strategies are a response to the growing disengagement between communities and state as the information flow from the former either dries up or becomes more difficult to access. The state tries to compensate by undertaking more intrusive surveillance and by co-opting agents in civic society to act as reporting agents. People working within the banking, legal and accounting sectors are now obliged to report what they believe are suspicious transactions, acting as 'unpaid auxiliaries for law enforcement agencies' (Lea 2004b: 94).

Lea (2005) considers that the same kind of repressive processes are being extended against terrorism as exemplified in the UK Prevention of Terrorism Act. This legislation allows the Home Secretary to impose control orders that may involve house arrest and restrictions on movement and travel. House arrest requires a derogation from the European Convention of Human Rights, which a High Court judge may reject if the order's rationale is 'obviously flawed'. Lawyers with security clearance represent the proposed subjects of the order but do not have access to them. The Home Secretary can activate the latter restrictions without judicial scrutiny although they may be subject to later review. Lea contends that this *modus operandi* 'simply drags the judiciary into the vortex of collapsing due process' (2005).

The rationalisation for these moves might proceed as follows. Western states are engaged in an unprecedented conflict with groups that seek the destruction of these countries. In previous wars, the public agreed to a relaxation of due process but this struggle does not have a clear end in sight, and therefore requires more permanent legislation to counter the threat. The net result is 'international terrorism as one side of the coin, and illegal military activities and contempt for international law and institutions on the other' (Lea 2005). Again the picture is one of bleakness as the moves against terrorism are part of a wider assault against due process. The public have become inured to these adjustments in the criminal realm so they mount few objections to this increasing disregard for due process values.

#### Inevitable tooling-up?

Lea's work is a bold and innovative attempt to link developments in crime control with their social preconditions. This leads to a greater understanding of the processes of criminalisation, the means by which some actions come to be designated as crimes and subject to intrusive state intervention. Viewing these processes through a historicised version of the square of crime – the four sides relate to state, victim, offender and community – enables Lea to show how changes in one vector affect all relations. As communities have been beset by 'great thunderstorms' of economic recession, this has inhibited their capacity for crime control. Rising crime rates have encouraged more aggressive forms of policing which have stripped the criminal justice system of some of its legitimacy and so the flow of information about offending is constricted. Criminal justice organisations are compelled to seek alternative means of information-gathering and/or lower the standards by which such information is judged.

A possible disadvantage in taking such a resolutely sociological account of the relations of crime control is that the possible range of responses may be restricted. The relationship of labour and capital is thought to be so influential that it leaves little scope for either national variation or for political intervention to shape the force and thrust of these dynamic changes. It does not seem that the economic trajectories that Lea describes, based mainly on American and English evidence, necessarily fit with the experience of other countries. Furthermore, it seems curious that Lea does not mention how the British executive's search for extraordinary powers has been checked at various stages.

Control orders were introduced after the House of Lords objected and found that the indefinite detention of foreign nationals without trial was an unjustifiable incursion on subjects' human rights. In 2006, the High Court found that the process governing control orders was 'conspicuously unfair' and the 'thin veneer of legality' covering it could not conceal the manifest inequity (*Independent*, 13 April 2006). The Court of Appeal later ruled that control orders were incompatible with the right to a fair trial.

These continually contested outcomes point to one of the shortcomings in Lea's account, namely that the political response to the structural problems he outlines seems restricted. Lea is not inattentive to how politics can shape outcomes but often suggests that in both judicial and social spheres, developments will tack to the lowest common denominator, which entails the sidelining of more sensitive crimes such as sexual assault and racial violence (Lea 2002: 180). Expanding the role of communities in crime prevention is thought to 'exaggerate rather than ameliorate social fragmentation and division' (2002: 180). But this conclusion can only be reached by ignoring the way in which citizens can press for recognition of their plight.

In short, what is needed is a more politicised account of how relevant actors capitalise on the opportunities presented to them by large-scale structural realignments. What is crucial is not so much the existence of critical moments but the interpretation put on these events by actors. The crises identified by Lea are important because they have fuelled the belief that existing arrangements are unsustainable and needed to be reoriented. This escapes accusations of determinism while leaving space for a variety of political responses, and can be clearly identified with the work of Pat O'Malley.

## Volatility of arrangements

O'Malley's starting point is the 'bewildering array of developments occurring in penal policy and practice' (1999: 175). One can find evidence of punishments that restrict offenders' movement, that shame them, that offer incentives and that rehabilitate offenders. Although volatility has always been the hallmark of modern punishments, O'Malley believes that the inconsistency of the current era has few precedents in penal history. How can this best be explained?

One line of reasoning argues that criminal justice policies, coming to terms with high crime rates, are chronically split. There is a fundamental ambivalence between denouncing crime through punitive displays and diffusing responsibility for crime prevention throughout society. The logic of the former is one of denial and the latter is one of adaptation. This portrayal is plausible yet O'Malley wonders whether it convinces by focusing on the most extreme inconsistencies and ignoring a host of others. Moreover, trends in crime control may well be reflecting broader trends in governance as the state divests itself of many instruments of direct control, and then delegates provision of services and takes up an oversight role.

These practices derive from the political doctrine of neo-liberalism, which expresses scepticism about the efficiency of the state and the primacy of individual responsibility. Neo-liberalism encompasses many diverse penal developments such as decentred crime control and just deserts but it seems incapable of explaining the manifest inconsistency between many penal developments such as stigmatising and restorative justice. The explanatory value of neo-liberalism may well be a conjuring trick, as it conceals the different themes mobilised behind this over-arching doctrine.

O'Malley considers it a mistake to believe that current penal developments are animated by a single doctrine. Rather, the importance of neo-conservative thinking in contemporary political thought should be recognised. Although combined with neo-liberalism in support of a relatively unfettered economy, neo-conservatism partakes of a social authoritarian strand that emphasises order and discipline. The two converge on an allegiance to the market and distrust of the state but diverge on the importance of communal values and freedom of choice. This uneasy alliance explains the 'rather bi-polar pattern of development that is extending the diversity or range of sanctions' (1999: 189). Volatility of punishment is guaranteed in matters germane to the sovereignty of the state since both political doctrines have contradictory positions. The neo-conservative position emphasises an intrusive state with a Manichean moral vision of stark good and evil whereas neo-liberalism sees morality as a product of individual choice and collective endeavour as optional. Fusing these two positions combines the 'state bellicosity and devolution' (1999: 190) as well as a host of intermediate ones aligned with both innovation and nostalgia.

This uneasy combination is no longer the preserve of governments or political parties of the right. Increasingly, the political strategies of purported left-wing regimes are infused with such principles. Governments have disavowed social governance that was dependent on 'the cultural homogenisation of the population' (Lea 2002: 81), which, in turn, provided the sociological rationale for rehabilitation and reintegration. O'Malley believes that it is the changing paradigms of government rather than anything as dramatic or catastrophic as the 'emergence of post-modernity or … the limits of the sovereign state' (1999: 192) that have introduced such dizzying volatility into penal sanctions.

It is difficult to disagree with O'Malley's aspiration to provide a non-deterministic account of penal policies and politics. However, one can still wonder whether this method provides an adequate explanation of changes in terms of their origin, development and range. O'Malley believes that neo-liberal political rationalities were constructed in the face of the 'problems' of late modernity (2003: 188). There is no way of proving how 'real' these crises were but the crucial fact is that they were identified as real. This allows for a measure of political autonomy without downplaying major shifts in the social and political environment. The price to be paid, however, is that the nature of these large-scale structural changes is unclear. Are they connected with changes in the relationship between capital and labour, as Lea believes, or might they be related to the rise of the new social movements that had formerly been disregarded? If there is uncertainty regarding the drivers of change, it becomes much more difficult to speculate about which progressive developments are possible and which are implausible. This is not looking for predictions in the sense of universal covering laws but of seeking a compass for orientation, a necessary task for the kind of politics that O'Malley advocates.

A second issue is whether O'Malley's account offers up the resources for the more progressive politics he desires. Dividing responses between a neo-liberal and a neo-conservative outlook shares a striking affinity with David Garland's (1996, 2001) characterisation of the paradigms of contemporary criminologies as 'self' and 'other', a dualism that O'Malley thinks inadequate. The former paradigm views the criminal as a rational consumer, amenable to intervention and is typified by situational crime prevention; in the latter, the offender is portrayed as an irredeemable outcast. Neo-liberals work with a thin skein of morality, congregating together for only as long as it proves mutually effective (O'Malley 1999: 188). Neo-conservatism is said to be socially authoritarian, ranking communal needs over individual ones and reserving harsh justice for those who transgress. In the space between these two doctrines lies an 'amalgam of persisting welfare, disciplinary and regulatory sanctions' (O'Malley 1999: 189). It is not clear if these sanctions are left untouched by changing patterns of governance or have adapted where the two rationalities overlap, as is the case with the use of incarceration as a deterrent. It is not clear where initiatives, like restorative justice or mentoring, that try to forge emotional connections with offenders fit. These kinds of measures are deemed to exemplify new modes of governance, where the community has replaced society as the pivot point around which obligations turn. Groups within civil society are now the main referent for obligations (O'Malley 2004a: 75). Maybe neo-liberalism envelops this relatively thick notion of morality with a more individualistic, entrepreneurial one or is this burdening the explanatory capacity of this category to breaking point?

O'Malley believes it vital that some variant of neo-liberalism be introduced to moderate the baleful influence of neo-conservatism. The most malign consequences of this creed are produced in the phenomenon of actuarial justice that uses risk-analysis to disable 'a category of subjects who are politically and governmentally demonized and excluded' (O'Malley 2002: 211). Not surprisingly, this form of conservative neo-liberalism is most evident in the United States but O'Malley argues convincingly that this is the result of a political choice rather than the dispassionate selection of an optimal technique.

Since actuarial justice is causally contingent on the appropriate political conditions, its advance across the globe is not inevitable. The use of risk analysis is not predestined to be exclusionary; rather, this is one of the fates that politics of a particular stripe may place upon it. By contrast, one can imagine a drugs strategy, based around harm minimisation, which uses risk-analysis in a neutral fashion to help inform drug-users and afford them the choice to desist or not from their addiction. There is little trace of coercion or exclusion; instead, drug-users are enabled to choose a path into rehabilitation, resulting in a 'neo-liberal inclusionary justice' more typical of the Australian penal regime (2002: 216). What sets Australia apart and prevents it from succumbing to US-style actuarial justice is its social-democratic tradition, which O'Malley views as more typical of a country such as Canada.

Attention to the distinctive political cultures of particular nation-states helps to ward off the dystopian analyses of the so-called 'criminologies of catastrophe' (O'Malley 2003). Respite is gained through dissolving the clear binary categorisation of neo-liberalism and neo-conservatism that was outlined earlier. Clinging on to a conceptual schema for the sake of intellectual economy makes little sense if one is drifting without direction. But the notion of a social democratic version of neo-liberalism is almost invoked as a *deus ex machina* and raises some vital questions. How many variants of neo-liberalism are there? Is it the case that the categories of penal regimes could multiply as the distinctiveness of each national system is appreciated? For example, is there a corporatist version typical of mainland Europe, as Esping-Andersen (1990) argues in the case of welfare regimes? The purpose of O'Malley's original categorisation was to help understand the sheer diversity of penal sanctions in the present era. Yet if the number of explanatory categories multiplies according to the number of cases studied, the typology begins to lose its explanatory force and becomes mainly a taxonomy of national political cultures. The question of what inspired these cultures and how they have manifested themselves in particular penal regimes is not explored in depth.

O'Malley invokes 'social democracy' in order to avoid the appearance of 'neo-liberalism' driving events. Demonstrating how neo-liberalism always operates in a hybrid fashion according to the political context in which it is situated serves to emphasise that history doesn't follow a linear route. But laying so much emphasis on contingency makes it difficult to assess how stable or faltering political and hence penal arrangements are. Another politically inspired question is to ask how legitimate are these rationalities; how do they interface with the expectations of the public?

Answering such questions is surely central to the kind of politics that O'Malley seeks. For this task we need to enquire what has inspired and driven these political rationalities. One option would be akin to Lea's, seeing them as reflecting the social division of labour. Alternatively one could argue that any innovation in penal regimes is ultimately rooted in the sensibilities of the population at large. This is the option taken by those inspired by the work of Norbert Elias and his concept of the civilising process.

## The civilising process

The civilising process is characterised by a reduction in the use of overt physical violence and an increase in the intensity of psychological control. As people became more dependent upon one another for their personal welfare, their conduct became more disciplined and restrained. This interdependency depends on three closely related phenomena (Elias 1994).

The first is the emergence of states that began to enjoy a prerogative over the initiation of violence. Thanks to this, pacified social spaces emerge in which the threat of general violence declines and becomes more predictable. States assumed a 'survival function' as they operated to 'protect its members from being physically wiped out' (Elias 1978: 138). It is this 'survival function' that created 'interdependencies of a particular kind' (1978: 139), namely emotional bonds between the members of a distinct society. This pacified space helps to encourage a web of interdependency, as the division of labour becomes more specialised. The cascade effect continues down to the individual level as regulation is transformed from being based on control by others, since the overt use of violence is reduced, to one whereby the individual internalises self-restraint. This process was pioneered in court society where nobles could no longer rely on pugilistic prowess since this was the monopoly of the monarch. Instead, codes of conduct became stricter and members of the aristocracy were expected to demonstrate restraint. Elias suggests that this *habitus* of refinement and foresight crystallised outwards from the nucleus of the court.

This process of refinement and restraint is particularly marked by the seclusion of activities that were once uninhibited. Emotions become less spontaneous and rash behaviour less likely as conduct becomes more controlled. This emphasis on manners and etiquette becomes a new battleground for recognition replacing military process. For example, the middle-class penal reformers of the eighteenth and nineteenth centuries disparaged the perceived excesses of capital punishment. Their sensibility was 'status-affirming ... a way of differentiating the feeling bourgeois self not only from the unfeeling mob but also from an arrogant and exclusive aristocracy' (Gatrell 1994: 232). Through opposition to executions, the middle classes were able to demonstrate that they possessed the proper modicum of feelings and passions that they believed were appropriate to any well-bred person. The middle classes campaigned against the aristocratic ethic of restraint by arguing that a person's ethical sensibility was judged by their reaction to the plight of others. This reaction was, in turn, judged by the degree of compassion and pity that was evoked. Insensibility became a synonym for cruelty and signified one's lack of virtue.

As Lea commented, the late nineteenth and twentieth centuries witnessed a process of social inclusion that left its mark on penal reform. What Elias underlines is that this structural change only achieved its effects in the penal sphere thanks to a change in general sensibilities towards offending behaviour. Criminal justice prior to the eighteenth century was characterised by sporadic but forceful violence undertaken by communities rather than the state, and usually directed at people who were set apart from these communities. In the nineteenth century, criminal justice took on a more modern, impersonal hue, increasingly initiated by agents of the state who were detaching the administration of justice from communities. It was 'the chief boast and glory of Great Britain, that equal justice is administered to all' but the partiality of justice 'according to the geographical situation of the place where it is admitted' (Buxton 1818: 7) was seen as an embarrassment to be dislodged. Hence, the British state – and Ireland was a colony at the time – assumed a greater responsibility for regulating the populace as it laid claim to a monopoly on legitimate violence.

## A breakdown in civilisation?

John Pratt believes that the declining public involvement in our control, which is a hallmark of the civilising process, carries within it the potential for reversal. As the public participates less and less, and responsibility is divided among countless officials, the seeds of indifference grow and it becomes possible for abuses to be perpetrated. But this is only a potentiality; what activates it?

Pratt (2002) develops the idea that implicit within modernity is a fear of others, what he labels, following Bauman, 'heterophobia'. This is produced by occasions when people feel impotent before events that are attributed to the machinations of those who are radically different. It would seem that what has kick-started a punitive process is a lack of tolerance. What has brought this about? The first cause is the restructured role of the state that no longer assumes near total control of the dangers that threaten its population. The second influential factor is the fragmentation of previously secure interdependencies, usually oriented around class and relatively hierarchical communities. These two factors cause an upsurge of anxiety in people, as the risks seem to multiply, which is only exacerbated by the apparent impotence of the state. In turn, states try to shore up their legitimacy by producing ostentatious crime control measures to reassure a fretful public (Garland 1996; Pratt 2000), deliberately steering a populist course. Acceptance of public involvement in policing and punishment is the defining feature of this decivilising process (Pratt 2007).

Yet the civilising process still throws up features that inhibit punitiveness. As the state becomes more involved in efforts to control its population, the apparatus necessary to deal with this is increasingly managerial and bureaucratic in tone and substance. In addition, restorative justice has won support precisely because it seems to be an alternative to the conveyor-belt approach of the penal system, which merely processes rather than prevents criminal behaviour. In part, it has advanced from a perception that criminal justice organisations have retreated into a set of self-referential rituals that more often than not compound the original transgression. Procedures of restorative justice seek to halt a cycle of offending by vividly demonstrating the emotional consequences of offending behaviour.

So what looked like a straightforward trajectory of punitiveness is complicated by managerial and restorative turns. On balance, Pratt still believes that the 'impact of the new punitiveness is likely to outweigh other more liberal sensitivities' (2005: 269). It would seem that the civilising process is janus-faced (Vaughan 2000), pointing in different directions simultaneously. Once this is accepted, it is by no means the case that criminal justice systems are more repressive. To see why this is the case, it is worth re-examining the social trends that have given rise to the allegedly 'decivilising' turn.

## Moral decay or expansion?

Relying on an increasingly anxious and intolerant public as the main explanation puts Eliasean adherents in an awkward situation. One of the features of contemporary times is a greater acknowledgement and acceptance of difference than has hitherto been the case, a typical element of the onward march of the civilising process. As Pratt himself admits (2005: 263), the 'increasingly cosmopolitan and pluralistic nature of societies in the post-1970s period is likely to lead to an increase in tolerance of minority groups and differing personal arrangements regarding marriage, sexual preferences and so on'. Once the basic equality of formerly excluded groups is admitted (De Swaan 2001), it is likely that regulation will become more dependent on individual self-monitoring rather than external checks, what Cas Wouters (1999) calls informalisation. Reliance on formal protocols weakens as these are seen to be too rigid to adapt to the personal exigencies of everyone. Hence the upsurge of interest in conferencing and mentoring which seems to be better able to adapt to the demands of particular situations. Conferencing aims to use shame to 'civilise' offenders but also to ensure that victims do not overstep the mark.

Affirming equality has profound effects in terms of social control. The regulatory space is vastly expanded: that is, the number of actions that are denoted as detrimental to public welfare multiples. This is because organisations responsible for the affirmation of norms are compelled to recognise the claims of previously excluded groups. Often this occurs through the proscription of actions via the criminal or civil law. Wouters (1999: 422) notes that

> as previously superior groups and those who had risen socially became more obliged to take more and more account of each other, more and more ways of inflicting humiliation and injustice came to be perceived and branded as such. They were increasingly seen as intolerable displays of arrogance or self-aggrandizement and were sanctioned accordingly with stronger individual shame, collective repugnance and moral indignation.

The implication of this is that increased levels of control are not primarily explained by rising anxiety or insecurity brought about by globalisation. They may be an unintended product of a politics of recognition that seeks to check many of the harms publicised by groups looking for (and partly obtaining) a semblance of equal status. This would account for the rise in *ex-ante* regulation that is typical of an interventionist state (Moran 2003). And it can also account for the kind of *ex-post* regulation that so concerns criminologists. Matthews (2005: 179) illustrates this issue when he writes:

> If, for example, a particular type of activity such as domestic violence changes in public perceptions from being a 'private' matter to one deserving of formal legal sanctions, as long as the sanction directed toward offenders is widely seen as appropriate and not excessive, we cannot identify such a change as an example of punitiveness.

What are interpreted as symptoms of 'populist punitiveness' (Bottoms 1995) may be misread as some sort of atavistic, archaic tendency. Instead, they may be more accurately represented as part of an ongoing civilising offensive on the part of some groups to achieve more equal treatment for themselves. Underlying the idea of the civilising process is the notion of a reduction in power differentials between groups and an increase in the scope of mutual identification and hence a firmer guarantee of equality. The civilising process does not present a *fait accompli* where the state instantaneously secures a monopoly over all violence. Domestic violence is a good example of this. Although there may have been increased sensitivity to assaults within the home (Ruff 2001) over the centuries, the state still has not succeeded in extinguishing this kind of violence. In classic 'civilising process' fashion, the reduction in overt public violence may have distracted attention away from its persistence within domestic havens and so helped to contribute to its continuation. Diminution of violence within the home rests on campaigning groups publicising the issue, demonstrating the attendant inequalities, gainsaying state intervention and changing widely held beliefs around the issue. All of this is part of a civilising offensive on the part of a social movement rather than some kind of abstract civilising process. As long as this process is incomplete, it is unlikely that control can rest on informalisation as predicted by Wouters (1999). Before this stage, it is likely that the state will have to engage in relatively hierarchical forms of control to kick-start the civilising process into relatively uncharted territory.

## The reciprocity of rights and the rule of law

This process might best be conceived as part of the internal renegotiation of democracy as excluded groups struggle to expand what is seen as the proper borderline of politics, its internal periphery (Arditti 2003). What is involved is a debate about the nature and scope of citizenship: who is accorded recognition as a political citizen and what are the obligations arising between citizen and state? Citizenship is not some sort of treasure trove, a fixed set of resources that can be bequeathed to those who are seen to have a legitimate demand upon it. Its redefinition involves 'disagreement about the nature of justice inevitably spill[ing] over into debates concerning who is recognised as worthy of respect and how their beliefs are represented' (Bellamy 2001: 18). Consequently, citizenship is constitutive of constitutional politics rather being derivative of it. A more juridical notion of citizenship tends to see a constitution circumscribing, via the enunciation of rights, the extent to which political struggles can impinge upon people's liberty. It reifies current constitutional arrangements rather than seeing them as the outcome of a continuous political struggle and therefore subject to continuous revision and reinterpretation. Accepting that rights should both serve to protect us from inappropriate state intervention and that they can be legitimately circumscribed might leave us open to the charge of ambivalence about rights. This is true but merely reflects that rights have too often been interpreted in a manner that privileges individual autonomy over social interdependence and so avoid the question of how people might best live together (Loader and Walker 2007).

Redrawing rights involves adjustments to the subjects, scope, sphere and style of politics (Bellamy 2001): that is, determining who is deemed worthy of the protections of citizenship, the basis on which such inclusion occurs, the space in which such action occurs and the means by which inclusion is secured. Returning to the example of domestic violence, it has become more politically prominent because its occurrence demonstrates how citizenship rested on a public/private dichotomy, with the domestic sphere being one in which states did not customarily intervene. Domestic space was one in which more powerful agents could initiate violence without fear of reprisals from the state. As this failure of the state is highlighted, the scope and sphere of politics is then expanded to encompass a fuller definition of citizenship that makes matters within the home worthy of attention. And this intervention might be thought to be effective only if the style of politics changes through such instruments as mandatory arrest, barring orders and so on. From an Eliasean perspective, the state's survival function is extended to envelop the plight of women, resting on the presumption that there is no good reason why mutual respect and identification should not include women. The inverse assumption is that those who persist with violent behaviour towards women will be penalised where this was not the case before. It would seem that any subsequent undertakings by the state may not be best interpreted through a framework of punitiveness or authoritarian control, since:

> However strong the impression of moral decay may be, its explanatory power is limited, because at the same time, the development of more egalitarian relationships has exerted pressure towards a rise in the moral standard and a higher level of mutually expected self-restraints ... Accordingly, departures and transgressions are met with stricter social sanctions. (Wouters 1999: 420)

Contemporary strategies of social control have often been understood as designed to restore a faltering moral consensus against those who can be easily ostracised. For instance, Lea argues that authoritarian power of neo-liberal states represents a regression from government to sovereignty, as it dispenses with the inculcation of requisite social capacities and depends increasingly on sporadic order maintenance. Similarly, Pat O'Malley and others (Garland 2001; Feeley 2003) locate a neo-conservative tone in contemporary crime control strategies, hearkening back to an era when the social order was more settled and the roles into which people slotted more stable. And followers of Elias also cannot avoid this archaic reading when they suggest that punitiveness is part of some decivilising process, akin to what transpired in the Middle Ages. For example, Pratt uses the notion of heterophobia, which is remarkably similar to the kind of suspicion that Lea thinks was directed to outsiders suspected of crimes in pre-industrial times. Each of these interpretations cannot avoid the impression that there has been what Wouters calls a moral decay that precipitates a punitive turn.

By contrast, a modified Eliasean reading interprets contemporary developments in terms of expanding rather than contracting moral horizons. As the scope of citizenship increases to include aspects of people's lives that were formerly overlooked, the state is impelled to deploy its powers against those who persist in infringing on the newly recognised rights of citizens. There is a fundamental ambivalence at the heart of this process since endorsing the citizenship of some may involve curtailing the rights of others.

Citizenship is conditional in two senses. It is not extended to everyone but is bestowed upon those who have demonstrated their fashion to act in a certain capacity (Vaughan 2000; Brown 2005). This, in turn, creates a dual set of exclusions: certain agents do not enjoy a presumption of citizenship rights and those who do not exemplify and uphold those standards necessary for citizenship are debarred temporarily from full citizenship. Both sets of exclusions can only be effaced through conduct that shows that they can regulate themselves in accordance with expected standards.

Brown (2005) goes further than this and suggests that the new punitiveness displaces political subjects from the field of political citizenship whereas previously punishment was only concerned with attenuating this right, often through a period of enforced incarceration or supervision. Foucault labelled this an 'economy of suspended rights' (1991: 11). It might seem that our definition of 'temporarily debarring' corresponds to this latter definition and so might be outmoded. However, Brown (2005: 283) goes on to define the 'new punitiveness' in terms of the question: 'Does this penalty or measure tinker with the rights of political subjects, or does it radically transform the status of the individual with the state into one structured around obligation?'

Why should a greater sense of obligation arise? One of the consequences of the spread of interdependencies that Elias documents is greater sensitivity to a range of harms. Behaviour that would have been both unregulated and unsupervised becomes increasingly subject to norms, thanks to the increasing extent and density of ties between people. What was deemed commonplace now becomes a shameful activity in light of the opinion of other people. Emotional transformations like this help to explain the disdain into which capital punishment fell. A novel set of obligations is transmitted among sensitised populations and towards a regulatory agency, usually the state, obliging it to take action against newly shunned activities. As a population becomes more heterogeneous yet more extensively bound to one another in a web of interdependency, it is likely that the range of activities that are thought to be injurious will grow. Calls for the state to intervene to regulate situations, to make individuals conduct themselves with greater care and take account of others will grow.

On this basis, the most profound change has not been in transforming rights around the principle of obligation but around that of reciprocity. Traditionally, rights have been interpreted as providing a space of individual liberty and freedom from intrusion. Thus the rule of law developed, as Lea demonstrates, to protect individuals from the caprice and whims of the sovereign. But this only occurred because of the growing interdependence or reciprocity between sovereign and population. As government becomes less dominated by sovereign states, and involves sources such as social movements below the state and supra-national sources above it, the need for reciprocity becomes all the more evident as previously undocumented harms are highlighted. As reciprocity deepens, it is inevitable that individual autonomy for some will decline, producing a 'story of loss, lack and privilege as well as of gain, recognition and justice' (Woodiwiss 2005: 11). On this reading, the fact that traditional freedoms are being circumscribed as the rule of law is redrawn is not necessarily to be lamented. It may signal a decrease in domination for some whose plight had gone unnoticed.

The difficulty lies in deciding where freedom is being justly restricted and where this represents an arbitrary movement on the part of governing figures. This issue is posed most starkly with respect to dealing with novel forms of terrorism, although also arises in tackling crime. Terrorism seems to demand the most dramatic restrictions on rights that may cut into classical freedoms as defined by the rule of law. Public anxiety about these intrusions is normally sated by the reassurance that the measures are only temporary and that the legal situation will soon revert to normal. Terrorism since 9/11 seems to elicit a new response since 'this emergency has no foreseeable end and so is permanent', producing what Dyzenhaus calls 'the normalization of the exceptional' (2006a: 2) or what we previously labelled a 'perpetual state of emergency' (Kilcommins and Vaughan 2004).

Dyzenhaus argues that the principle of parliamentary supremacy in common law countries ultimately means that all national constitutions are 'exposed as suicide pacts by the challenge posed by the state of emergency' (2006a: 12) since the will of the people can overturn a constitutional order. Maintaining this line of argument is to portray the nation-state as a container of society, which is to remain with the anachronistic world-view of Schmitt (1985) who sees the executive of state as supremely sovereign. Instead, we live in a world that has borne a 'multiplication and proliferation of sovereignties' (Walker 2006: 80) that are by no means in concert with each other. To take one example, the fact that members of the European Union have subscribed to and incorporated the European Convention on Human Rights (ECHR) in some form or other undercuts the possibility that fundamental rights can be negated through a populist pact to rewrite a national constitution. Supra-national influences extend beyond this negative blocking influence to positively enjoin states to take action in spheres that would not traditionally be considered as criminal, such as those pertaining to competition, the environment and occupational health and safety. With the proliferation of government beyond the nation-state, actions that may have been tacitly approved of are increasingly being regulated as a result of edicts from the European Union.

These regulations are not enforced directly by the European Union but transmitted to what are known as non-majoritarian regulators (NMRs), unelected organisations that are formally separated from governments and enjoy regulatory powers through endorsement or formal delegation by public bodies (Coen and Thatcher 2005: 330). The importance of these NMRs is that they enjoy substantial prosecutorial powers but may operate differently from the organisations traditionally analysed by criminologists, beguiled by the 'myopia of [a] police-court-corrections' (Braithwaite 2000: 58) perspective. While the proliferation of these agencies points towards a 'splintered' (Cerny 1999) or 'disaggregated' state (Slaughter 2004) that cuts across any tendency for an authoritarian state to emerge, there is still a concern over the extent to which these agencies are subject to the rule of law. The concern is not that the exercise of power has a negative impact upon rights but that it is not normally reviewed leading to the prospect of it becoming arbitrary and thus inimical to the rule of law.

## Conclusion

As Tony Blair commented, the rules of the game are changing but it is still too early to say whether the long nineteenth century of criminal justice is ending, as states erode individual rights, or moving to a new stage of development, as supra-national norms add a further layer of protection. To answer this question, we need to reach back into history and show how the transition from sovereignty to government affected the process of criminalisation and made state rule more predictable. We seek to show that the move towards a criminal justice system bound by the rule of law has always been checked by a clamour for emergency powers that slipped free from restraints. Yet there has been no clear division between a system based on the rule of law and a lawless world (Sands 2005). Instead, the two have become intertwined as the Irish constitution has been amended to allow for emergency powers while the judiciary have still been able to review these powers. Beyond the courts, there exist a 'range of institutions tasked with the protection of human rights' (Harvey 2004: 306), often networked to similar organisations in other jurisdictions who trade information about best practice (Slaughter 2004).

David Garland has complained that critics of his work (Garland 2001) have overlooked one of his 'central insights – namely, the emerging tendency towards a break-up of the state's supposed monopoly of crime control' (2005: 170), that involves a 'system involving state and non-state partnerships' (2005: 167). It is within these newly emerging institutional relationships that there lies the possibility of 'non-punitive modes of managing crime ... and new conceptions of culpability, harm and victimization' (2005: 170). We share his impulse to document the formation of the monopoly of crime control through the establishment of a rule-bound system of inculpatory justice and its current reconfiguration.

## Chapter 3

# Reconstructing truth in the criminal law: Moving from an exculpatory to an inculpatory model of justice

### Introduction

The purpose of this chapter is to explain the emergence of the modern assumptions, commitments, and strategic priorities that have shaped the position of the accused in the justice system. In particular it seeks to demonstrate how the paradigm of prosecuting and investigating crime moved from an intensely local, unstructured and victim-precipitated arrangement – where it was incumbent on the accused to actively participate in the proceedings – to a structured, adversarial, state-monopolised event where the accused was largely silenced in the courtroom. Such a transformation acts as an important backdrop within which to query the confluence of approaches that currently shape and determine state and societal relations with the accused.

Engaging in such a wide-ranging historical analysis of how the accused has been depicted and represented over time is of course fraught with dangers. To begin with, criminologists and especially lawyers who attempt to understand criminal legal method through the prism of history often fall into the fallacy of creating linear lines of development between the past and the present. Such lines facilitate neat reassuring narratives of continuity but they make for poor, uncritical history (Garland 2002; Gordon 1984). In this chapter we will be mindful of the need to avoid naked presentism – still such a strong preserve of the discipline of law given the tradition of precedent and 'the never ending tracing back to original precursors' (Foucault 1972: 4; Hay 1984: 1–4) – in outlining the ways in which different justice frameworks have construed and represented the accused.

Secondly, lawyers of the formalist persuasion often engage with legal materials in a monist manner. They view such materials in blinkered but splendid isolation, excluding everything other than *a priori* juristic principles. Notwithstanding that the craft of law necessarily embodies operationally closed elements which helps it generate its own meanings, values and traditions (Thompson 1977: 258–62), legal rules are rarely if ever framed in such apolitical or asocial contexts. Instead they are set against cultural and social backgrounds that determine what is and what is not permissible (Kennedy 1982: 45–51).

Thirdly, tracing epistemic shifts in the ways in which the justice system has depicted and signified the accused necessarily involves broad, often sweeping, generalisations about changes in social life and in the criminal legal structure. Searching for patterns and trajectories of the *Gemeinschaft* and *Gesellchaft* variety can in many instances do violence to historically specific particulars and phenomena that do not fit with the selective frameworks and periodisations adopted. From our perspective, identifying irruptive points in the history of accused relations, and formulating ideal or working justice types, almost by definition exposes us (and the readers) to the danger of not paying sufficient attention to the engrained traditions, old routines and cultural and social peculiarities that are forced into the frameworks created, or worse still, excluded. Justice, like most other routine phenomena, has a fluid rhythm that does not easily or naturally lend itself to partition, compartmentalisation and capacious reasoning or inquiry. Formulating concrete systems of justice *qua* those accused of crime across 300 years of history and two jurisdictions necessarily results in some individuality and factuality being ignored or under-emphasised. There are still very good reasons for engaging in such an exercise as long as it is remembered that some local particulars might not unerringly conform with the generalised patterns produced. Our purpose in this chapter is to attempt to paint a very large landscape, capturing broad contours and the sharpest of contrasts, rather than a portrait that is consumed by detail and precision. Provided that we spare the paint when drawing the contours – by not over-engaging in a process of false-homogenisation that creates labels of convenience for what are in fact much more complex and contested issues – we believe that the exercise can prove valuable. In particular, it can help us to identify and consider different trends, tendencies and currents of reflection that broadly comprise patterns of action *vis-à-vis* those accused of crime at different historical points in time.

Moreover, it should be borne in mind that a concrete framework of justice does not simply emerge as a fully unified functioning entity with crisp lines of division between it and the model it replaces; nor does it break down into sharp discontinuous forms. The various strands that comprise a model develop at different paces and are embedded to different degrees. This ensures that the lines of demarcation between one model and another are often blurred, contested affairs. This point is often lost in the language of generalisation and discontinuity. This caution takes on an even more important resonance in this chapter given that the generalisations are formulated not in respect of one jurisdiction, but two – England and Wales, and Ireland. Though as a result of colonisation Ireland also operated the same model of justice as England and Wales, the contours of the Irish model were often a lot rougher, ensuring that the trajectories of development did not precisely mirror or imitate each other.[1] Nevertheless, bearing the cautions about generalisation and discontinuity in mind, we are happy to sacrifice depth for breadth in this chapter. Employing broad historical brush stokes can serve the very useful heuristic purpose of illuminating sharp contrasts on the canvas, notwithstanding that the contours might be less than precise in parts. Highlighting the broad historical changes in the assumptions and realities that governed accused relations under pre-modern exculpatory and modern inculpatory models of justice will help us focus on and amplify the dynamics and principles that shape and determine our current arrangements. For the purposes of this amplification, the chapter commences by tracing in broad outline the contours of the exculpatory model of justice as it existed in relation to the accused in the eighteenth century in Britain and Ireland. It then moves on to examine in more detail the operation of justice in Ireland, where a more 'uneasy governance' existed that tested the old hegemonic order to the limit and was a key determinant in its eventual change. It will be argued that even when a more settled rule of law framework had emerged in the nineteenth century, justice in Ireland, it seemed, continued to embody exceptional tendencies. The chapter then moves on to document the conditions of emergence of the modern inculpatory model of justice.

Condensing the Irish story between both models of justice sacrifices a proper chronology of the history in question. This lack of symmetry was, however, felt to be necessary so as to pay sufficient, though somewhat brief, attention to the exceptional tendencies inherent in justice in Ireland under both the old exculpatory order (where differences in the collective consciousness ensured that the tradition of liberty and consensus governance as witnessed in England was not replicated to the same degree) and the new inculpatory order (extraordinary measures, such as martial and coercive laws, operated outside the modern rule of law framework of justice). A proper diachronic sequence is thus traded in the chapter for a condensed analysis of 'Irish exceptionalism' (to borrow and amend Alexis de Tocqueville's phrase) as regards accused relations in the period between 1700 and 1922. Structuring the chapter in this way serves three important functions. First, it enables us to illuminate the impetus that Ireland provided in amending the localised and paternalistic order of justice. Secondly, and in contrast, it also helps us to bring in to sharp focus one important strand of continuity in the modern Irish order – the employment of special zones that operate outside the rubric of ordinary law. This theme will be developed in subsequent chapters. Finally, herding Irish exceptionalism into one chronologically disordered section of the narrative also enables us to keep our focus on the real goal of this chapter, which is to trace the general logics that governed accused relations during the period in question.

## The exculpatory model of justice

The peculiar geometry of eighteenth-century penal relations comprised a savage penal code ameliorated by a well-established machinery of concessions in the form of judge and jury discretion, and executive clemency. Hegemony was thus maintained both by the use of the theatre of execution – and the exemplary display of terror inherent therein – and the flexible employment of concessions. They could be granted for a whole variety of reasons. They included the following: the guilty party was relatively young or of otherwise good character; the guilty party was pregnant (known as 'the benefit of the belly') or could read a prescribed passage from the Bible (the 'benefit of clergy'); it acceded to the petitions of the victim or the local gentry; it propitiated the 'winds of public opinion'; or, the jury engaged in a form of 'pious perjury', ensuring that the accused did not hang for the offences committed (Rawlings 1999: 39–53; Kilcommins 1998). Such a 'lottery of justice' must be understood against a backdrop of historically specific social relations and social control. The great majority of petitions for mercy in the eighteenth century were written by the gentry and landed aristocracy on behalf of those accused of crime. Concessions ensured, to some extent, that a good many offenders left the courtroom indebted to their more 'noble' peers and convinced of the merciful nature of justice. In this way, the criminal justice system attempted to instil compliance through examples of brute terror – but not so many as to destroy the perception of justice or rupture the bonds of paternalism – but also in a much more subtle fashion through examples of mercy. Balancing these dyads was particularly important in an epoch where tight social control in the form of professional policing did not exist (Hay 1977).

Sufficient numbers of offenders were thus enmeshed in the 'punishment as spectacle' rituals which bore witness to the majesty of the law and the 'dissymmetry of power relations' between the sovereign and his citizens (Foucault 1991: 49). As Paley suggested, 'by this expedient few actually suffer death, while the dread and danger of it hang over the crimes of many' (1833: 161). At the same time, enough offenders escaped the clutches of this theatre of terror through the mercy that the system of justice offered. Such elasticity in the form of mercy was, according to Blackstone, designed to 'endear the sovereign to his subjects, and contribute more than anything to root in their hearts that filial affection, and personal loyalty, which are the sure establishment of a prince' (as quoted in Hay 1977: 48; Fletcher and Stevenson 1985: 1–40).

Eighteenth-century justice also emphasised at every turn the important role of communal participation. Crime was not generally perceived in terms of a transgression of nationally accepted law. The machinery of justice was by and large constructed around informal, communal networks that could not conceive of criminal behaviour in an abstract way. With no sense of abstract crime or harm, there could be little possibility of a system to prosecute such offences. In a social world that was localised in character, responsibility for order, in keeping with the consensus justice paradigm, was in large part entrusted upon ordinary citizens (Herrup 1989). Such a system, as Philips has pointed out, 'did not rest on the modern idea of catching and prosecuting all offenders, but rather on the idea of catching, prosecuting and punishing exemplarily, a sufficient number of offenders to deter others' (1980: 160–1). Few, moreover, wished law enforcement to be more formalised for feared of the centralised despotism that might result. With such sporadic and unpredictable enforcement, there emerged what Foucault called 'tolerated illegality': 'the non-application of the rule, the non-observance of the innumerable edicts or ordinances were a condition of the political functioning of society … illegality was so deeply rooted and so necessary to the life of each social stratum, that it had in a sense its own coherence and economy' (Foucault 1991: 82). These spaces of discretion and freedom were not some regrettable residue of an otherwise efficient system; in fact, they were essential to the maintenance of the system of social control as it operated in pre-industrial times.

The machinery of justice was thus by and large constructed around informal networks. It relied heavily, for example, on the provision of private and statutory rewards for information leading to the conviction of offenders (Langbein 1983). It utilised professional 'thieftakers' who, through intelligence networks, secured evidence of guilt against those accused of crime in return for the rewards available from the courts, as well as from victims who paid to have their stolen property returned (Paley 1989: 301–30). It also witnessed the emergence of private associations for the prosecution of felons, which organised at common expense posses to pursue offenders, patrols to supervise localities, and the prosecution in court of offences committed against members (Philips 1989; Shubert 1981). The justice system also created a hierarchy of pardons and immunity from prosecution for those who could be induced to turn against the criminal fraternity from which they operated. Pardons as an absolute right could be claimed by accomplices in return for evidence that would convict those who committed one of a number of specified offences. Pardons could also be claimed under royal proclamation made by the government in respect of specific offences (Radzinowicz 1956: 40–2). Accomplices also retained the hope that they might not be prosecuted, or at least receive a lighter sentence, if they made a full and fair confession and their evidence was used to convict other offenders. In such circumstances, accomplices were not entitled as of legal right to any better treatment. They gave their evidence *'in vinculis'* [in chains] and it depended on their behaviour whether or not they were entitled to an equitable claim (*R v Rudd* 1775 1 Leach 115 at 119).

In keeping with the local orientation of justice, the 'paradigm of prosecution' in the eighteenth century rested on victims of crime (Hay 1983: 167). They were the principal investigators of crime and the key decision-makers in the prosecution process (King 1984: 27). As Bentham (1830: 427) disapprovingly noted: 'The law gives to the party injured, or rather to every prosecutor, a partial power of pardon ... in giving him the choice of the kind of action he will commence ... The lot of the offender depends not on the gravity of his offence but on ... the injured party ... The judge is a puppet in the hands of any prosecutor.' Victims could elect not to invoke the law and let the criminal act go unpunished; they could engage in a personal settlement or private retribution; or, they could prosecute but shape the severity of any criminal charge (capital or non-capital) through their interpretation of the facts. It is, as Philips suggests, a very modern idea

> to think that every discovered offence should be followed automatically by prosecution; for centuries, the English system had worked on the principle that indictment before a court was the last resort to be tried; there were all sorts of alternative informal means which the potential prosecutor might try to use short of formal prosecution. (Philips 1980: 158)

Conflicts remained the property of the parties personally affected and this often involved recourse to informal dispute settlement (Christie 1977: 1–15). As King noted:

> formal prosecution was the exception; negotiation and informal sanction the norm. The major courts had no monopoly over punitive sanctions in the eighteenth century. Indeed, they usually had to content themselves with processing a few scraps and particularly tough morsels which those involved in informal sanctioning processes threw their way or spat out as indigestible, and as therefore requiring the tougher teeth of the criminal law. (2000: 22–3)[2]

If victims did proceed with a prosecution, it was their energy, for the most part, that carried the case through the various prosecution stages. Victims engaged in the fact-finding, gathered witnesses, prepared cases, presented evidence in court as examiners-in-chief, and bore the costs involved (Beattie 1986: 35).

Moreover local knowledge about the character of the accused was not confined to that narrow space between conviction and the imposition of sentence. Rather it occupied a more central role in the determination of the accused's guilt or innocence (Lacey 2001: 361–2; Green 1988: 281). In addition to playing a key role at trial, character witnesses were also very influential in support of an accused's plea for mercy post conviction. Jurors too were chosen from the locality and had a 'keen knowledge of the good and rotten apples in their barrel' (Friedman 1993: 27). As Sir Robert Peel admitted, 'it might be hard to say to a man, that his life should be valued at a particular rate, depending upon local or temporary expediency. But this was the very reasoning upon which the law was founded' (as quoted in McGowen 1983: 110–11). As King noted:

> The criminal justice system was … about accommodation. Accommodation with victims who wanted, and gained flexibility in deciding whether to prosecute, compound or forgive, in deciding what charge to bring, in deciding whether or not to turn up on the day of the trial; accommodation with the mitigating tendencies of semi-autonomous juries …; accommodation with the sentencing and pardoning priorities of the good mind. These compromises not only enabled a system that was heavily dependent on popular participation to work fairly effectively; they may also have done something to prevent the law from losing its broader ideological usefulness to the propertied elite. (King 2000: 371)

Indeed accommodation permeated social relations more generally. Community participation in the form of crowd protest and disorder, for example, was a tolerated constituent of eighteenth-century life. Group disturbances in relation to issues such as food prices, executions, press-gangs, wages and turnpikes was perceived by the authorities as part of a paternalist reciprocity model of local social relations (Thompson 1971; Lacquer 1989: 353–4).

The legal landscape was dominated by the intimate interaction of two features: a criminal offences calendar that was generously peppered with the use of the death sentence on the one hand, but which was moulded into a justice system that was highly elastic, personal and merciful. It was the combination of both terror and discretion that was critically important in legitimising the *status quo* (Hay 1977: 26). The substantive criminal law itself was amorphous in character. This is not surprising given the low level of reporting and recording of cases (Langbein 1983: 3; Cornish and de N. Clark 1989: 565). Nor was it legitimated, as it is today, on its detachment from the local and particular circumstances of the crime. Rather guilt was determined by a much looser conception of culpability, which was closely tethered to moral blameworthiness and to local knowledge of the character of the accused. The current preoccupation with structuring the criminal law in terms of voluntary conduct, responsibility, and excusing conditions – the 'analytic framework of *actus reus/mens rea*/defence' (Lacey 1998: 23; McAuley and McCutcheon 2000: 1–32) – was notably absent in the eighteenth century. As Lacey suggested about its earlier configuration:

> This model, operating in a world in which professional policing and prosecution and an elaborate law of evidence had yet to be developed, worked on the basis of lay evaluation of normative, character based – rather than subjective or psychological – evidence and assumptions about the individual defendant. (2001: 361)

Criminal trials in the eighteenth century were personal altercations, involving face-to-face confrontation between private prosecutors and accuseds (May 2003: 21). They were amateur, hasty and relatively unstructured affairs. As compared with more modern trial arrangements, the accused was compromised in many ways. To begin with, he or she could only give unsworn testimony. Defence witnesses could not be compelled to testify; when they did testify, it was received unsworn (Langbein 2003: 52; Beattie 1991). Those accused of crime were also denied access to depositions, to copies of indictments (except in trials for treason) and to the names of prosecution witnesses before the trial. Their peremptory right to challenge the composition of the jury was circumvented by not being able to see the jury list until their actual trials (Gatrell 1994: 536–7; Baker 1977: 36). More fundamentally, they were not, for the most part, entitled to have arguments made for them by counsel in felony trials. As Hawkins observed in *Pleas of the Crown* in 1721:

> every one of common understanding may as properly speak to a matter of fact as if he were the best lawyer … It requires no manner of skill to make a plain and honest defence … ; the simplicity, the innocence, the artless and ingenuous behaviour of one whose conscience acquits him, having something in it more moving and convincing than the highest eloquence of persons speaking in a cause not their own … Whereas on the other side, the very speech, gesture and countenance, and manner of defence of those who are guilty, when they speak for themselves, may often help to disclose the truth; which probably would not so well be discovered from the artificial defense of others speaking for them. (Quoted in Langbein 1983: 123)

Moreover, there was no explicit presumption of innocence. In 'accused speaks' trials, as they have been referred to, the onus was always on the accused to engage in self-exculpation (Langbein 1994: 1047; Allen 1931: 260). He or she was viewed as a vital 'testimonial resource' (Langbein 1999). Once the prosecution case concluded, the judge would turn to the accused and say something to the effect: 'you have heard the evidence: what do you have to say for yourself' (Beattie 1986: 349). The implication was clear. If those accused of crime were innocent, then they were going to have to demonstrate it through an active defence where their version of events could be heard and their demeanours observed (Cairns 1998: 49). Indeed the right of those accused to speak – rather than the right to silence – was viewed as being the fundamental safeguard in their defence of criminal allegations under this exculpatory model of justice (Langbein 1994).[3] The theory was that the prisoner should speak 'either to clear himself or to hang himself' (1994: 1053). In addition, few limitations existed over the evidence that could be adduced against an accused at trial and there was nothing in the way of a set of crystallised exclusionary rules of evidence.[4] The burden of proof too was not as sharply drawn as it is today.[5]

Though those accused of crime were much more limited in the civil liberty rights that they could rely upon in the eighteenth century, some elements of equilibrium did exist in courtroom relations. First, and as we have already seen, hegemony was in part maintained through judicial discretion and mercy in the form of executive clemency and 'pious perjury'. A good many accused left courtrooms having benefited from one of the various forms of mercy that the system of justice offered. Secondly, trial judges, to some extent, protected the interests of those accused of crimes at trials (Beattie 1991: 252). As Coke noted in the early seventeenth century: 'the court ought to be ... of counsel for the prisoner to see that nothing be urged against him contrary to law and right' (quoted in Langbein 1994: 1050). They would, for example, ensure that illegal procedures were not allowed to the detriment of those in the dock; they would strike out erroneous indictments; and they would on occasion cross-examine prosecution witnesses whom they suspected of giving false testimony. The aphorism that a judge was 'counsel for the prisoner' should not, however, be overstated. A judge's primary duty was to ensure the legality of the various events that occurred at trial. Though a judge may have kept a watchful eye on the accused's corner, he did not help him or her to select or build a defence (McGowen 1983: 105; Cairns 1998: 52).

Thirdly, a very strong formalistic practice existed in respect of the framing of indictments and search warrants. The slightest inexactitude could invalidate an indictment. In *Long's case* in 1605, for example, it was declared that 'indictments of felony which are counts and declarations for the King against the parties, ought to have certainty expressed in the record of the indictment' (1605 5 Co. rep. 120a at 120b–121a). Similar protection existed in respect of a citizen's dwelling. In *Semayne's case* in 1604, it was noted: 'The poorest man may in his cottage bid defiance to all the forces of the Crown. It may be frail – its roof may shake – the wind may blow through it – storm may enter – the rain may enter – but the King of England cannot enter – all his force dare not cross the threshold of the ruined tenement' (1604 5 Co. Rep. 91a).[6] Formalities of this nature in indictments in the seventeenth and eighteenth century were described by Sir William Holdsworth as 'this extraordinary and irrational set of rules that have grown up round the wording of indictments' (1908: 618–19).[7] This strict interpretation of procedural rules was crucial in maintaining hegemonic order. The perceived objectivity of justice fitted very neatly in the English collective consciousness with a reified awareness of its fundamental liberty rights as free-born citizens. As Hay noted: 'When the ruling class acquitted men on technicalities they helped instil a belief in the disembodied justice of law in the minds of all who watched. In short, its very inefficiency, its absurd formalism, was part of its strength as ideology' (1977: 33; Baker 1977: 45–7).

Fourthly, the fact that an accused's guilt or innocence in respect of a felony charge was determined 'by the country', men from the locality who constituted the jury, was seen as a further safeguard against the intrusions of arbitrary or despotic power. Trial by jury was a 'grand bulwark' of an accused's liberties. The merciful use of partial verdicts and 'pious perjury' heightened this sense of liberty. Blackstone, for example, noted that the trial by jury was a 'barrier … between the liberties of the people and the prerogative of the Crown' because 'the truth of each accusation … [must] be confirmed by the unanimous suffrage of twelve of his equals and neighbours, indifferently chosen and superior to all suspicions' (1765: 349–50). Juries in the eighteenth century also, unlike their contemporary counterparts, played a powerful role in the mitigation of sentences (Green 1988: 284). This was possible in an era when the *guilt determining functions* and the *sentencing functions* in criminal trials were woven into a relatively seamless design (Langbein 1994: 1064).

It can be said that the justice system that existed in Britain and Ireland in the period in question was exculpatory and localised in nature. When formal justice was invoked, which was the exception rather than the rule, it relied heavily on victim and popular participation. Formal resolution of grievance remained very much the property of individual victims or associations of victims who monopolised the investigative and prosecutorial functions. The criminal trial itself was a personal, largely unregulated altercation with the working assumption that the accused was, in the absence of exculpation, guilty. This ensured that the accused was at all times an active, participating trial actor, a vital 'testimonial resource' whose self-exculpatory narrative was closely scrutinised by the judge and local jury in determining culpability. The degree of culpability itself was heavily shaped by moral and local knowledge considerations. Moreover, few restrictions existed on what could be admitted in trial. Most evidentiary facts that had broad probative value as regards the offence committed were heard in open court and required defence rebuttal regardless of their prejudicial effect on the accused.

## The machinery of justice in Ireland

Though this cocktail of terror and mercy was also evident in Ireland, it was mixed somewhat differently. Indeed, if anything, Ireland tested this model to the limit and was an influential impetus in its change. This is not surprising given that the ideology of law did not transfer as smoothly, or permeate as deeply, between the ruling and poorer classes. Its foreign and repressive components ensured that the task of unmasking its 'false consciousness' was made a good deal easier. Ireland was a colonial society and deference to elite hegemony was not as forthcoming. The perceived tradition and heritage of the liberty of free-born citizens in England, which helped maintain the *status quo* between rulers and ruled, worked in the opposite direction in Ireland. The defeated, dispossessed, disenfranchised Catholic lives of many Irish acted as a point of solidarity around which they could protest against maintaining the *status quo* with the ruling elite. As a result, a more 'uneasy governance' – which oscillated more towards order being secured through repression rather than consensus – existed in Ireland in the eighteenth and early nineteenth century (Palmer 1988: 35–56; Boyle 1972: 125–6; Connolly 1988: Henry 1994; Carroll Burke 2000: 27–36). The neatly conceived, if perhaps overly romanticised, hegemonic order in England (Brewer and Styles 1981), premised in part on bonds of paternalism and an objective system of justice, was not replicated on the same level. Though disorder also existed in England and was to some extent tolerated, the nature of illegality in Ireland was perceived by the administration as being more collective, permanent and threatening. Differences in the *collective consciousness* of both societies was captured by one English traveller in 1830:

> An Englishman cannot fail to remark the different behaviour of the two countries in one particular. We were never saluted with a bow or courtesy from any of them, from the beginning to the end of our journey, conduct quite unnatural, and only to be accounted for by the relation in which they stand to the native gentry. (Quoted in Palmer 1988: 52)

Furthermore, and though Ireland similarly employed the private prosecution procedure of England in the eighteenth century, it was not anything as successful. No doubt many criminals in England escaped the clutches of the law through intimidation of victims during the period. The scale of intimidation, however, was far more widespread and organised in Ireland and was tied in to the political situation that endured. This ensured that the victim's task was, in many instances, at worst 'perilous and at best extremely difficult' (McEldowney 1989: 430; 1980: 21). This was especially so if the criminal acts were perceived to be 'political'. Agrarian and sectarian disturbances were pervasive and persistent in the latter half of the eighteenth century. Systematic campaigns of violence and intimidation against landlordism, sectarianism and the Crown were orchestrated by secret societies which emerged during the period such as the Whiteboys, the Oakboys, the Rapparees, the Rightboys and the Defenders (Dickinson 1997; Whelan 1996; Smyth 1992). Indeed, in order to maintain order in the eighteenth and early nineteenth centuries, the authorities often had to resort to special coercive measures such as restrictions of movement of citizens, on the possession of firearms, on assembly, and on publications. *Habeas corpus* and, as we shall see, jury trials too had to be suspended on occasions.

The communal participation that formed such an integral constituent of social control in England was, not surprisingly, also less in evidence in Ireland. Gladstone captured the difficulties succinctly when he suggested to an audience in Wigan in the mid nineteenth century: 'On this side of the channel, public authority administered the law in sympathy with the people. On the other side, it does not, law wears in Irish eyes a foreign garb' (quoted in McEldowney 1989: 430). Testifying before a parliamentary committee in 1852, an Irish magistrate similarly commented:

> There is that sort of feeling against the law: it is exactly contrary to the feeling which prevails in England, [where] every man is in favour of the law, and aids it in almost every way. It appears that in Ireland crime is generally, somehow or other, the crime of the community, whereas in England it is the crime of an individual. (Quoted in Palmer 1988: 47)

There was, for example, a marked reluctance to join associations for the prosecutions of felons. An Irish magistrate in 1815 informed Sir Robert Peel of the problem in the following terms: 'I applied to many farmers of approved loyalty and endeavoured to persuade them to enter into associations – the universal answer was, "we dare not, ... we should certainly be put to death if we associated as you advise us" (quoted in Hay and Snyder 1989: 32). Thus the divisive nature of social relations in Ireland and the resulting 'crime, agrarian outrage and near revolution made government by ordinary processes [i.e. by locally based gentry] almost impossible' (Broeker 1970: 22).

In addition, the more turbulent nature of Irish society ensured that there was more juror intimidation. There was greater jury sympathy for those accused of crime too, which tended, in the eyes of the authorities at least, to take a more perverted form than that practised by their English counterparts. One judge, according to legal folklore, is said to have dismissed an accused with the following words: 'You have been acquitted by a Limerick jury, and you may now leave the dock without any other stain upon your character' (Jackson *et al.* 1999: 205). Dicey saw this as a reason for curtailing the right to a jury trial in Ireland: 'But the trial by an Irish jury means it is urged in the case of every man accused either of political or of agrarian offences all but certain acquittal. The reason in short why coercion measures are necessary is that Irish juries will not as matters now stand return verdict for the Crown' (quoted in McEldowney 1980: 29). Varying tactics had to be employed to control jury trials. They included: the extension of the jurisdiction of summary courts; the transfer of trials to non-local venues; the use of 'special jurors'; the reduction of charges to convince those accused to plead guilty; the extensive use of the Crown's right to stand by without showing cause (McEldowney 1979: 275); and, on some occasions, the suspension of jury trials altogether (Jackson *et al.* 1999: 205–6). Though many of these practices were also employed in England, it appears that much tighter control of Irish juries was required. As Peel noted:

> In Ireland, as in England trial by jury and all its concomitants are indispensable. You cannot get a conviction for murder, for sedition, for seditious libel, for treason, excepting through a jury. Now trial by jury is an institution utterly unfitted to a country where the majority are prejudiced against the law. The effect must ultimately be to paralyse the government and to ensure impunity. (Quoted in McEldowney 1980: 23–4)

Even in the nineteenth and early part of the twentieth century, when, as we shall see later in the chapter, a more settled liberal democratic polity had emerged, the Irish, it seemed, 'remained banded against all order, law and government' (quoted in Townshend 1983: 49; Laird 2005: 15–42). Spurred on by a variety of 'dimensions of difference' and a psychology of dispossession and colonisation, agrarian violence and militant nationalism was never very far from the foreground of social and political relations.[8] Rebellions in 1798, 1803 (by the United Irishmen under Robert Emmet), 1848 (by the Young Irelanders), 1867 (the Fenian Rising organised by the Irish Republican Brotherhood), 1916 (the Easter Rising) and the early 1920s (the War of Independence) ensured that severe responses in the form of martial and 'coercive' laws continuously abrogated the ordinary legal system. Hillyard estimates, for example, that 105 'coercion' laws were introduced in Ireland in the nineteenth century.[9] Martial law, which had not been invoked in England since the mid seventeenth century, was introduced in Ireland after the rebellions in 1798, 1803 and 1916, and again in December 1920 during the War of Independence (Townshend 1982).

A vast array of political offences were incorporated onto the statute books, including treason, administering or taking illegal oaths, the murder or conspiracy to murder upholders of authority, and attempts to seduce soldiers form their allegiance (McDowell 1979: 519–93). Powers introduced included: the ability to proclaim 'states of disturbance' in counties; the introduction of curfews; restrictions on movement and the possession of firearms; the suppression of organisations, meetings and publications; internment; the suspension of *habeas corpus*; wide powers of police search; alterations of trial procedures; the trial of persons by courts martial; and the introduction of military inquiries into violent deaths rather than coroners' inquests (Lyons 1982: 417; Boyce 2005; Vaughan 1976: 726–73). When martial law, for example, was declared on Easter Monday, 1916 in Dublin, and was extended the following day to the rest of the country, 3,509 persons were arrested and taken into custody. Of these, 1,497 were released after investigation; 171 persons were tried by court martial and all but one were convicted with 15 being executed; and the remainder were sent to England and interned (Lyons 1982: 375–6).

Ireland was already guilty of testing to the limits the old paternalistic and localised model of justice in the eighteenth and early nineteenth centuries. In jumping ahead of ourselves chronologically, one can say that the exercise was repeated in respect of the new rule of law model of justice that replaced it. The persistent employment of extraordinary and special provisions – operating outside the strictures of normal law – to preserve social order, particularly in the early twentieth century, stretched and strained the veracity of the ethical and political sensibilities associated with a liberal democratic vision of the use of non-arbitrary executive power as expressed through the rule of law.

## Altering the mechanics of exculpatory justice

From the late eighteenth century onwards, however, the assumptions, commitments and priorities that sustained the equilibrium between patrician and plebeian were beginning to break down. With the rise of a 'middling sort', notions of deference, discretion, dependency and paternalism increasingly gave way to an emphasis on values such as equality, certainty and proportionality. This reorientation in commitments was greatly aided by profound elite concerns with phenomena such as population increase, rapid economic change, urbanisation and, as we have seen, developments in Ireland. The dawning of industrial capitalism, in particular, witnessed the introduction of a new economic order which centralised production, 'commodified' the labourer, and emphasised *task-oriented* toil over *time-oriented* toil (Thompson 1967: 60). In such an environment, the inefficiencies of parochial value determinants of the old criminal law system, where order was conceived of in local terms, came under attack (Stone 1987: 248; Thompson 1981). Criminal law had to become more systematic, logical and regular. It had to be premised on a rationally calculating criminal – juridical man – who knew in advance the certain penal consequences that would follow if he threatened the new forms of wealth and property that were produced during the period (Norrie 2001: 20). This meant that many of the previously 'tolerated illegalities', such as workers picking up the residues of their labour, were now seen as prejudicial to the interests of property-owners and were proscribed by law. As Lea noted: 'What is criminal is no longer the sanctity of property of this or that landowner but property in general; no longer violence against this or that person but violence in general' (2002: 37). A new technique of criminal and penal semiotics was required which discarded the inefficient use of discretionary violence and relied instead on a 'play of representations, and signs circulating discreetly but necessarily and evidently in the minds of all' (Foucault 1991: 101).

The growth of cities was also one of the significant consequences of the industrial revolution. In 1750, for example, there were two cities in Britain and Ireland with more than 50,000 inhabitants – London and Edinburgh; in 1801 there were eight and by 1851 there were 29, including nine with a population exceeding 100,000 (Hobsbawm 1968: 67). The harsh conditions of dislocation generated by the concentration of transient populations in centres such as London, Birmingham, Glasgow, Liverpool and Leeds also quickly challenged the prevailing paternalistic and parochial social control apparatus. The Gordon Riots of 1780, the impact of the French Revolution, the spread of radicalism and Jacobin ideas, the level of disturbance in Ireland, and the violent industrial discord associated with the Luddite movement all, in varying degrees, confronted the settled polity and resulted in increased calls – predominantly from the newly emergent industrial bourgeoisie – for a system of justice that was more certain than that espoused under the prevailing hegemonic order (Thompson 1963: 484). For example, with the dawning of industrial capitalism, plebeians were no longer permitted to utilise collective violence as a means of equalising power relations. As a consequence of the changing social, political and economic order, the old equipoise could no longer be sustained. A new set of social relations evinced itself in which the propertied classes were increasingly indisposed to mediate with the moral economy of the crowd and the threat of perennial rioting that it posed. In its place a new governing consensus was emerging which demanded that disorder and illegality would not be tolerated in a growing industrialised and rationalised society (Storch 1980; Brewer 1980).

Cesare Beccaria's text in 1764, *On Crimes and Punishment*, was also very influential in drawing attention to the arbitrariness and ineffectiveness of a justice system that relied heavily on discretionary gross exemplarity.

Criminal justice, according to Beccaria, had to become a more rational instrument of government. Adopting a Hobbesian view of the social contract,[10] he argued that the rule of law was the framework under which free and independent citizens united to form a society. Each individual negotiated away some of his or her liberty rights to secure peace and safety under the protection of the sovereign. The individual, however, gave up no more liberty 'than suffices to induce others to defend it'. Obedience to authority was, through this analytic social contractarian construct, grounded in the proper exercise of authority. The sum of all these sacrificed portions of liberty legitimated the sovereign right to punish – 'all that exceeds it is abuse and not justice' (1995: 120–1).[11] To secure effective order, punishment had to be certain, calibrated in accordance with the offence committed, and designed to prevent the commission of crime. The certainty of punishment, according to Beccaria, 'will always make a stronger impression than the fear of another which is more terrible but combined with the hope of impunity: even the least evils, when they are certain, always terrify men's minds' (1995: 130). In concluding his treatise, which he originally published anonymously, he also suggested: 'In order for punishment not to be, in every instance, an act of violence of one or of many against a private citizen, it must be essentially public, prompt, necessary the least possible in the given circumstances, proportionate to the crimes, dictated by the laws.'

This notion of the social contract, where individuals cede part of their freedom to a sovereign in return for security and freedom, is one of the cornerstones of the modern liberalist agenda.[12] It is premised on a rule of law framework which restrains the arbitrary or coercive exercise of executive authority, where a strong state must have respect for and indeed in some instances yield to a weak enemy. Though each citizen acceded some freedom to the sovereign in the interests of self-preservation, and the protection of liberty rights and human entitlements, the *quid pro quo* nature of the arrangement[13] ensured, through a rhetoric and logic of liberal legalism, that the sovereign guaranteed to respect the liberty, equality and freedom of each citizen. The sum of power ceded could not be employed arbitrarily to usurp freedom or liberty. Thus the old hierarchical order of patronage was increasingly being undermined by a classical liberalist and utilitarian belief in the free individual who possessed 'negative' rights which could be construed as freedoms *from* government (Bellamy 1992; Gray 1986; Berlin 1969). The ascriptive status of individuals under the old hierarchical model of authority, where individuality was to some extent subsumed into a person's attachment to a particular location, grouping, and placement within that grouping, was overtaken by a new horizontal vision that emphasised rationalism, liberalism, egalitarianism and freedom (Shapiro 1986: 80-150). The primacy of the individual and his or her self-determining and self-realising capabilities was now taking centre stage. In contrast to the fixed identities fashioned by pre-modern status relationships, modern progressive societies were viewed as oscillating more towards relations that recognised the importance of individualism and individual autonomy. Anchored to a Cartesian subject, the self-determining tendencies of *contract* now replaced *status* as one of the organising principles of society (Maine 1927: 100; Kilcommins 2004). Lea refers to this process of 'criminalising abstraction' – 'abstracting an accused's criminality from the complex of other characteristics which make him what he is' – as one of the foundation stones of modern criminal law and criminal justice (2002: 1–3).

There were also more specific concerns about the justice system. Though the idea of a centralised police force was seen as anathema to English sensibilities on liberty in the eighteenth and early nineteenth centuries, it was also apparent that the old system of law enforcement, which was heavily reliant on rewards, thieftaking and accomplice driven prosecutions, was not working in a more urbanised and industrial setting. Too much had been conceded to localism and heterogeneity resulting in a 'badly regulated distribution of power' (Foucault 1991: 79). The system of private prosecutions and prosecutors was also increasingly called into question. In many instances the actions of victims were seen as vengeful, capricious and open to intimidation and blackmail, 'resulting in the shameful perversion of the criminal trial for private ends' (quoted in Rock 2004: 338). The enactment of the Dublin Police Act in 1786, which was rejected the year previously in London, also helped to focus the political elite's attention on new methods of law enforcement (Palmer 2003; Boyle 1972). Once centralist authority in Dublin Castle had won out over personal liberty, and was seen to work, it provided subtle energy for reform of policing in England.[14] This, as Lea suggests, helped mark a transition from *sovereignty* to *government*, 'from a world in which crime was simply a wrong, a personal interaction between individuals or individuals and their superiors, to one in which crime was disruption, in which an offence against the criminal law was a disruption of the public peace and of the effective working of society' (Lea 2004a: 6).

Finally, the justice system was also influenced by the increased lawyerisation of the criminal trial process in the late eighteenth and early nineteenth centuries. This helped reconfigure courtroom relations along more adversarial lines that tipped the scales of justice in the direction of the accused (Landsman 1990: 539). The gradual influx of criminal lawyers altered the dynamic of proceedings in a number of ways:[15] it subjected the evidence adduced against an accused to much closer scrutiny; it shifted the burden of proof to the prosecution; it helped expand and develop the rules of evidence (the rule of hearsay, for example,); it ensured that the accused knew in advance the precise charges laid against him or her thereby allowing a better defence to be prepared; and, it permitted a more thorough cross-examination of all prosecution witnesses including thieftakers, accomplices and reward seekers after 'blood money' (Beattie 1991).

### The inculpatory model of justice

In these circumstances the personal knowledge and benevolence of the exculpatory model of justice seemed too arbitrary and discretionary. The goal was to 'rout the personal from the courtroom' (McGowen 1983: 116) through establishing a new administrative machinery for investigating, prosecuting, trying and sentencing for criminal wrongdoing. Gradually the trial shifted from an intense local 'kind of morality play' (Green 1988: 363) to a more structured affair that relied on ideals such as proportionality, equality and uniformity, where the focus was on the actions rather than the character of the accused. Thus over the course of the nineteenth century the criminal trial jettisoned its amateur, semi-personal and unstructured tendencies. As Wiener (1990: 66) suggested:

> removing the personal element from the workings of the law would, it was hoped, lower the emotional intensity of the subject's relationship to the law. In the place of the metaphors of the family, which encouraged both unpredictability and excessive release of the passions by plaintiffs and accused, the law and its courts were to be imbued with the character of a market, a meeting place of self-contained, self-disciplining individuals rationally pursuing their own interests under the impersonal arbitration and discipline of the unvarying rules of law. Passionate contest was to be placed in the professional hands of lawyers, for whom passion was an instrument of calculation, and confined by the rules of law, presenting no danger to society. Out of their contest, as out of a noisy but rule-governed marketplace or stock exchange, justice would emerge.

The trial thus evolved from an 'expressive theatre' that sought *the discovery of truth* via an 'accused speaks' forum to a more reflective, categorised process[16] that sought *the determination of justice* through testing the prosecution case (Langbein 1994: 1048). For Wiener, this was part of a broader trend: 'during the first half of the nineteenth century criminal justice was pressed to move from a series of expressive semipersonal confrontations ... to a more restrained, rule governed, predictable, depersonalised process' (Wiener 1990: 65).

The logic of adversarialism that unfolded had a number of important consequences. First, the evidential case presented against the accused began to be defined by more explicitly formulated evidentiary rules of law in the late eighteenth and early nineteenth centuries. The *beyond reasonable doubt* standard of proof, for example, crystallised into a legal formula and it became recognised as a 'maxim of ... law that ten guilty men should escape rather than one innocent man should suffer' (*R v Hobson* (1823) 1 Lew CC 261).[17] As Foucault suggested, the system of proof under the old inquisitorial model was giving way to a new logic, supposedly premised on science and common reason, that demanded that the 'truth of the crime will be accepted only when it is completely proven' (Foucault 1991: 97). Facilitated by the lawyerisation of the trial process, exclusionary rules of evidence were also formulated as rules of law. These rules increasingly acted as filtering devices that examined prosecution evidence through the lens of its possible prejudicial effect on the accused. They included: the inadmissibility of hearsay evidence; greater scrutiny over the voluntariness and fairness of confessions; the introduction of corroboration warnings in respect of accomplice testimony; more rigorous examination of the competence of prosecution witnesses; and the exclusion of bad character evidence to raise a presumption of guilt against an accused (Beattie 1986: 363–77; Langbein 2003: 180–251; King 2000: 225–8). As a result, the criminal trial process gradually became a search for *justice*, not *truth*.

Secondly, and in line with this, there was also a dramatic reconfiguration in courtroom relations. Where previously the accused, judge and jury had played pivotal roles in the pursuit of truth, now it was the lawyers that monopolised the gatekeeping function that determined what constituted truth (McGowen 1983). As a result the focus came increasingly to bear on the prosecution case and 'away from the objective that had preoccupied the old altercation trial which was to see how the defendant responded to the prosecution case' (Langbein 2003: 271). The accused was thus freed from the burden of self-exculpation and was no longer an informational resource for the prosecution. In addition to silencing the accused, the reconfiguration in relations also significantly reduced the role of the judge in adducing fact evidence. Under this new inculpatory model of justice the trial judge did not actively examine and cross-examine witnesses, or engage in the protective benevolence of the accused's interests. The judge's function now became much more impartial and less active – to secure justice through enabling the adversarial contest to take place (Langbein 1994: 1071; 2003: 312). Juries also became more tightly controlled. Their role, as self-informing, 'semi-autonomous institutions' (Green 1988: 310) engaged in mitigation of sanctions could not be sustained under a *Zeitgeist* that recoiled from personalism, localism, discretionary accommodations, and anti-rule of law practices. Though jury mitigation of sanctions would continue, it would be on a greatly reduced basis.

Next, the state also very gradually began to monopolise the prosecutorial function as the view emerged that the security of society could not be left at the whim of individual victims. Sir Robert Peel, for example, had argued in 1826:

> if we were legislating *de novo*, without reference to previous customs and formed habits, I for one should not hesitate to relieve private individuals from the charge of prosecution in the case of criminal offences justly called by writers upon law – public wrongs. I would have a public prosecutor acting in each case upon principal, and not on the heated and vindictive feelings of the individual sufferer, on which we mainly rely at present for the due execution of justice … and I would by the appointment of a public prosecutor guard against malicious or frivolous prosecutions on the one hand, and on the other, I would ensure prosecution in cases in which justice might require it. (Quoted in May 2003: 194)

The 'formed habits' referred to by Peel, particularly the fear of centralised despotism, remained steadfastly apparent in nineteenth century England. Nonetheless, centrally organised schemes of prosecution were also operating on an *extempore* basis in the first half of the century in parts of Durham and Northumberland (Rock 2004). Scotland, India and Ireland had also made the task of prosecution an executive function. In Ireland, for example, crown solicitors were appointed to prosecute criminal cases in each of the circuits in 1801 and by the mid nineteenth century sessional crown solicitors were appointed in each of the counties (Delaney 1979: 43–4; McEldowney 1989: 435–6; Bridgeman 2003).[18] In England, a statute passed in 1879 created the Office of the Director of Public Prosecutions, thus facilitating the gradual emasculation of the victim's previously pivotal role in initiating and carrying on criminal proceedings (Hay 1983; Langbein 1973). By now, the duties of investigation, prosecution, sentencing and punishment – all of which had previously been premised to a large degree on popular participation – had become more privatised, focused and discrete state-accused events.

Violence and justice were now to a greater extent monopolised by the central authorities. The era of victim justice as 'accommodation' and theatre was at an end. Conflicts were no longer viewed as the property of the parties most directly affected. Previously strong stakeholder interests such as victims and the local community were gradually colonised in the course of the nineteenth century by a state apparatus that acted *for* rather than *with* the public. In monopolising the investigative and prosecutorial functions, the state obviously imbalanced the equilibrium in power relations. Though constituted as a rational being, the accused in such circumstances was now seen as vulnerable in that he or she was pitted against the unlimited resources of the state. In this context, it is not surprising that a whole corpus of exclusionary rules and fairness of procedure rights emerged to ensure that the accused was afforded the best possible defence against unfair prosecution and punishment. Since, and to paraphrase Stephen, the state was so much stronger than the individual citizen, and was capable of inflicting so very much more harm on the individual than the individual could inflict upon society, it could afford 'to be generous' (1883: 354).[19] The local *victim* justice system thus increasingly yielded to a Leviathan *criminal* justice system that was governed by a new set of commitments, priorities and policy choices.[20]

Criminal law also underwent reform to become a more rigid and impartial set of prescriptions that purportedly bound all members in the same manner (Norrie 2001: 21). Increasingly its focus moved away from the notion of 'manifest criminality' based on the disposition of the accused to a more formalised conception of criminal liability. Hierarchy, status and patronage had no place under this rule of law vista which advocated certainty, coherence and systematic application. The initial anchoring point of this more rationalised approach to criminal law was the 'reasonable man', a responsible, rational, self-disciplining subject who, it was thought, was capable of being deterred by a properly proscribed system of criminal laws and a tariff of enforced sanctions (Lacey 1998; Farmer 1996: 66).[21] This more codified approach to law also impacted on the image of the human subject who increasingly came to be constituted as a rational, autonomous and self-governing being. As Wiener (1990: 54–5) noted:

> The ideal of the responsible individual came to stand ever more at the center of the law. Its administration was overhauled to better embody the assumption that the members of the general public were to be considered more rational and responsible than they had been hitherto ... A crucial supposition underlying early Victorian law reform was that the most urgent need was to make people self-

> governing and that the best way to do so was to hold them, sternly and unblinkingly, responsible for the consequences of their actions.

Thus in the course of the early to mid nineteenth century the accused was gradually constructed as an abstract juridical subject who was free and equal, and capable of logically determining what was in his or her best interests.

This drift towards the creation of an asocial subject also had important consequences in terms of the penal disposal of convicted offenders. In keeping with the ideology of individualism, rationality and self-governance, judicial sentencing in the nineteenth century increasingly embodied a policy of deterrence and retribution, the former 'to deny the utility of crime, the latter to reconstitute the social contract after breach' (Garland 1981). The discourse of individualism and moralisation held that criminal acts – like actions in any other realm where the ideology of economic liberalism could permeate – were the outcome of rational choice, calculation and volition. Such an archetype of sentencing, as noted, is premised on presumed rationality: 'thus conceived, criminal law becomes a wholly abstract construction, taking cognisance only of the crime, while ignoring the criminal … Crime becomes a legal abstraction, after the manner of a geometrical construction or an algebraic formula' (Saleilles 1968: 43).[22] In effect, the system of sentencing created focused on the materiality of the crime 'where the subjective criminality of the agent was determined by the objective criminality of the deed', and where the system of disposal for the judiciary rested on 'crystallised' and mechanical punishments (1968: 43).[23] Garland (1985: 18) neatly encapsulated the asocial juridical framework that emerged in the nineteenth century when he suggested:

> The offender is defined as a legal subject, a citizen inscribed with rights and duties, entitled to equal treatment before the law. The State which punishes does so by contractual right in accordance with the terms of a political agreement. Its power to punish has its source in the offender's action – it is the agreed consequences of a contractual breach. The State has here no intrinsic or superior right. It meets the citizen on terms of equality and must not encroach upon his or her rights, person or liberty except in circumstances which are rigorously and politically determined in advance – *nulla poena sine lege*. In this penal vision we meet the ideology of the minimal legal state, the liberal dream, guardian of the free market and the social contract.

Thus in the course of the nineteenth century, the criminal complex was gradually redrawn as a new statist administrative machinery emerged for investigating, prosecuting and punishing crime.[24] The penal field increasingly dissociated itself from the local, personal and arbitrary confrontations that governed criminal relations in the eighteenth century and became a more depersonalised, rule-governed affair with the state at the centre. Private disputes and vendettas were gradually monopolised by the state apparatus and rerouted into the courtroom. A society in which 'the law operates more and more as the norm' (Foucault 1979: 144) slowly emerged – reflecting the 'public interest' and the 'will of the people' – in which the temptation to commit crime would no longer be countered by a sovereign will to command and a display of terror (McGowen 1986: 313–17). When this process was completed, 'sovereign power was transformed into a public power' (Garland 2001: 30). Within such a society, executive arbitrariness and discretionary power abuses were constrained, egalitarianism advocated, and procedural justice increasingly promoted in addition to substantive justice. In distilling the criminal process into a more privatised state-accused event, an 'equality of arms' framework was created as part of a broader rule of law value system. This addressed the problem of the previously 'bad economy of power' which 'vested too much ... on the side of the prosecution ... while the accused opposed it virtually unarmed' (Foucault 1991: 79). Redistributing this economy of power meant an expansion in the exclusionary rules of evidence that could be employed by the defence against the prosecution case, clearer and greater obligations imposed on the state to prove its case against the accused, better opportunities afforded to the defence to prepare its case and test the prosecution case, and the removal of any obligation of self-exculpation on the accused. Even when the case was proved against the accused, he or she was subjected to a new power to punish in which 'an economy of continuity and permanence ... replace[d] that of expenditure and excess' (Foucault 1991: 87).

In order to complete the modern picture, there is one further strand that must be traced – the need to individuate justice. Sentencing in the late nineteenth and early twentieth centuries gradually extricated itself from the assumptions and commitments underpinning mid nineteenth century sentencing practices (individualism, the rationality of offenders and a focus on the proximal conditions of crime) to become a more 'knowledgeable form of regulation' (with an emphasis on individualisation, the distal conditions of crime, and the creation of a plethora of 'non-equivalent' penal disposals).[25] Alongside the 'generous' – and mostly already won – procedural safeguards provided to the accused at investigation and trial stages, a person guilty of a crime became entitled at conviction stage to have his or her individual mitigating circumstances factored into any decision about penal disposal. Justice, it was reckoned, could not be satisfied by 'any penalty which … [had] been exactly fixed beforehand'; punishment, from now on, had to 'be fitted to the criminal rather than to the crime' (Boies 1901: 114). The all-powerful state had again decided to be generous and noble with its weak enemies as it gradually recoiled from the *laissez faire* individualism and the postulate of free-will which had been key policy ingredients of sentencing and the social contract for much of the nineteenth century.

The more collectivist notions took hold in the late nineteenth and early twentieth centuries, the more policy-making deviated from the status to contract trajectory posited for much of the nineteenth century. Tarde, for example, inverted the status to contract metaphor when he suggested that 'in proportion as society becomes civilised, should responsibility become individualised' (1912: 148). Law was being socialised and this had important consequences for the modern sentencing model of justice. Increasingly the notion that 'man was a free moral agent with power to choose what he would do and a responsibility coincident with that power' seemed illusionary, not least because of developments in science and criminology (Pound 1912–13). Saleilles referred to this new archetype of sentencing in the following terms: 'punishment is to be determined not by the moral gravity of the crime, not by the injury done, but by the nature of the criminal' (Saleilles 1968: 8–9).[26] What had changed was that relations between the offence and the offender became more equalised as a result of the specialised and professionalised knowledge that began to be constructed around the latter.

It is, of course, important not to overemphasise the extent to which this 'special savoir' (Pasquino 1991) was constructed around the criminal. In some respects, it simply constituted *talk* rather than any *real action*. For example, the infrastructure that underpinned the 1960s 'Great Society' and 'Welfare State' projects in the US and UK respectively – and even in these jurisdictions practice and discourse did not always correlate (Zedner 2002) – did not materialise in post World War Two Ireland. In many respects values such as classical legalism, intuition, pragmatism and expediency – values that point in the opposite direction to the 'whole set of assessing, diagnostic, prognostic, normative judgments' (Foucault 1991: 29) that were meant according to discourse to be directing sentencing and punishment – remain starkly apparent in Ireland even up to the present day.

## Conclusion

The purpose of this chapter has been to highlight the characteristics and strategy choices that gave a distinctive shape to the modern system of justice. By contrasting the modern inculpatory model of justice with the exculpatory model that preceded it (and even allowing for the ways in which Ireland tested both models), it has enabled us to identify the various elements that comprised the two justice networks. It should be clear that substantial differences exist between them. The accused, situated within the boundaries of a modern framework of justice, could expect to face a powerful state apparatus seeking to enforce the law on behalf of 'the people'. Criminal wrongdoing was thus increasingly reconstituted as a public matter to be resolved through one legitimate forum – the criminal court. Localism and heterogeneity, elements cherished under the old order, were actively jettisoned under this modern arrangement.

The state increasingly became the only show in town for dealing with crime. It could draw upon a centralised police force and a public prosecutor's office, which would gather and present evidence in the public interest. As a consequence, in part, of this process of state monopolisation of policing and prosecutorial functions, a discourse and practice of liberal legalism emerged (emphasising the universality, liberty and sameness of the individual person) to rebalance power relations in the justice arena. For the accused, this meant that the justice network was restructured to incorporate a clearer and more substantive body of due process rights that would guarantee him or her, as far as practicable, not only substantive justice but also procedural justice. In particular, this ensured that the dynamic of the courtroom altered so that the trial gaze reoriented itself to focus almost exclusively on the prosecution case. Even when convicted of the crime, the offender was still protected from the state – exercising the will of the people – through the entitlement of having a proportionate punishment imposed, one that accorded both with the crime committed and his or her individual circumstances.

## Chapter 4

# Law in the shadow of the gunman

### Introduction

In the last chapter we outlined how the modern inculpatory model of justice incorporated more safeguards and principled protections for the accused in his adversarial contest against a powerful state apparatus. In the next chapter we will demonstrate how this model was built upon in Ireland throughout the twentieth century. In this chapter, however, we want to develop one of the threads alluded to in the previous chapter, that of the employment of emergency laws to combat the threat posed by Irish insurgency. The use of emergency laws in Ireland did not dissipate upon Irish independence. Instead two parallel systems of justice emerged, one committed to the rule *of* law (which we will examine more fully in the next chapter), the other to the rule *by* law. In this chapter we wish to detail the rule *by* law part of the narrative – something which has gathered significant international import in recent years – to provide a proper symmetry to the history of the accused/state relations in Ireland but also to demonstrate the impact that a long history of emergency laws can have on the ordinary criminal process.

From its inception in 1921, the legitimacy of the Irish state was disputed by republicans who took up arms over its affiliations with Britain. To ensure the survival of the Irish state, policing gave way to outright militaristic repression, as extra-judicial executions and internment figured prominently. Such an environment militated against what Brodeur termed low or normal policing but the curious feature of Ireland is that once the threat of physical-force republicanism receded after World War Two, there was hardly enough crime to stimulate low policing as the Irish police force acted largely as agents of general social order. It was only in the 1960s, as crime increased, that something like low policing emerged or what Packer called a model of crime control. When the conflict in Northern Ireland escalated in the 1970s and spilt over into the Republic of Ireland, with kidnappings and bank robberies, the Irish police, empowered by emergency legislation, produced convictions on the basis of confessions obtained in Garda custody.

Emergency law has become increasingly become part of the habitual legal armoury of the state, creating a dual system of justice. As recorded crime attained new levels in the 1980s, there was an increasing confluence between the 'ordinary' criminal justice system and extraordinary law. Analysing how the Irish state has made use of these extraordinary measures and incorporated them into its legal system provides vivid examples of how anti-terrorism measures flourish far beyond their original function and become a normal response to crime.

### Holding the centre of a new state

Many states are born out of conflict but the origins of the Irish state were rooted in a colonial conflict with Britain, followed almost immediately after by a civil war. Many Irish believed that problems of order within Ireland were rooted in the relationship with Britain and that peace would descend once Ireland detached itself from its colonial master. The Irish Republican writer Erskine Childers claimed that criminality was a product of an oppressive political regime. A more legitimate regime, based on the will of the people, would produce an almost crime-free society.

> Ireland is an almost crimeless country in the ordinary sense. Judge after judge has been receiving white gloves for a white assize, while courts-martial fill the gaols with state created criminals guilty, or suspected of being guilty of offences, many grotesquely trivial and all directly attributable to the absence of the first condition of an orderly society, a government chosen by the people. A very few, a marvellously few, serious crimes occur; for the whole system is an invitation, an incitement to crime. (Quoted in Ferriter 2004: 194)

On 21 January 1919, following a general election in Ireland in December 1918, members of Sinn Féin (Ourselves Alone) established Dáil Eireann – the equivalent to the House of Representatives or House of Commons – as (in their eyes) the first legitimate Irish parliament. The British government initially adopted a wait-and-see attitude to this development. However, skirmishes with the forces of the Crown as part of a campaign of guerrilla warfare against British rule made this policy obsolete. Although the British government tried to portray the Dáil and the associated campaign for independence as a product of extremists, their reaction actually pushed many moderate members of the Irish public into the hands of these supposed outliers. The notorious Black and Tans, a supplemental force to the relatively passive police force of the Crown, the Royal Irish Constabulary (RIC), engaged in savage reprisals against the civilian population and ensured enmity against Britain. The illegality of this counter-insurgency belied the image of a liberal government combating extremists.

A truce and treaty between Britain and Ireland were achieved in 1921 although the elusive ideal of a republic remained beyond the grasp of the Irish revolutionaries. The Irish negotiators accepted dominion status for Ireland, which entailed swearing fealty to the Crown. The treaty won through in the Dáil by a narrow majority. However, many embittered republicans refused to recognise the legitimacy of this decision. Childer's 'government chosen by the people' was showing signs of internal division. Civil war slowly unleashed itself in Ireland, between those who accepted the treaty and those who held out for a republic, free from British ties. The government of Ireland (or what was termed the Free State by republicans) responded to growing internal unrest by adopting a series of draconian measures or emergency powers and tacit assent to executions. William Cosgrove, president of the Dáil in 1922 that introduced the Constitution of the Irish Free State, was clear that the will of the nation might demand the extermination of minority rights: 'I am not going to hesitate and if the country is to live and we have to exterminate 10,000 republicans, the 3 millions of our people are bigger than this 10,000' (quoted in Ferriter 2004: 263).

Some of the killings were carried out by an armed plain-clothes police force known as the Criminal Investigation Department (CID). The function of this unit was to suppress the more militant republicans who opposed the pro-treaty government, a task that was to extend as far as assassination rather than attending to the 'niceties of arrest, charge, and trial or detention of suspects' (O'Halpin, 1999: 14). It is estimated that perhaps as many as 150 republicans were murdered in custody or while evading capture (Campbell 1994: 162).

This counter-terror campaign was facilitated by the adoption of the Army Emergency Powers Resolution. This established military courts with powers to pass a death sentence on non-military personnel and instigate indefinite detention without trial. After a pro-treaty political representative was assassinated in December 1922, four captured republicans were killed as an official act of reprisal. Kevin O'Higgins, Minister for Home Affairs, exhorted that 'there should be executions in every county. The psychological effect of an execution in Dublin is very slight in Wexford, Galway or Waterford [areas some distance from the capital] … I believe that local executions would tend considerably to shorten the struggle' (quoted in O'Halpin 1999: 32). Approximately 150 people were arrested every week in the first half of 1923, for the purposes of gathering intelligence and internment. Accusations of ill-treatment by both the army and CID were rife with sustained beatings apparently commonplace (Campbell 1994: 184–5).

However unpopular with militant republicans, emergency measures did no lasting political damage to the government and the republican forces accepted an amnesty offered in May 1923. By August 1923, the first piece of temporary emergency legislation was introduced to replace martial law. The Public Safety Act 1923 allowed for arrest, detention and internment without trial, the death penalty for certain offences, flogging for others, and the seizure of suspected stolen money. When it expired, it was succeeded by two other similar pieces of legislation.[1]

While the inchoate government had successfully stifled opposing forces, its victory raised some awkward and unanswered questions. How sustained was Ireland's commitment to liberal democratic values given that when faced with a crisis, it resorted to emergency powers that cut across any notion of the rule of law? The military courts and committees[2] made little pretence of due process, with the head of the army often specifying the appropriate sentence *in advance* of a trial (Campbell 1994: 199). Convictions were sustained in 85 per cent of cases in which a finding was reached and the death sentence was imposed in 29 per cent of all cases tried. Occasionally, the military courts might operate a suspended sentence of execution to encourage other republicans to desist. The attorney general of the day admitted that this course of action was 'foreign to all ideas of fair play and humanity' (1994: 212).

In the early years of the Free State, the judiciary proved amenable in facilitating the state's campaign of counter-terror. In the case of *Johnstone v O'Sullivan* (1923), the applicants sought a writ of *habeas corpus* and a forestalling of their trial in a military court. One judge confessed that 'if courts were authorised to interfere with the acts which any such government thinks it right to take during a war, it would make it impossible for it to carry out that which is its permanent duty', that is the restoration of order (quoted in Campbell 1994: 252). This acquiescence was displayed again when the constitutionality of the Public Safety Act 1924 was challenged by an internee on the basis that he had been detained without trial whereas he maintained that he should have been tried 'in due course of law' as the Free State Constitution (article 6) specified. However, the judiciary interpreted this phrase as simply meaning whatever the Oireachtas had legislated. One judge recognised that a permanent law permitting internment would violate the Constitution but the measure in question was 'a temporary law made in abnormal times and for a temporary purpose' (quoted in Hogan and Whyte 2003: 1536). However, circumstances would dictate that internal security deviated from the rule of law quite frequently.

The patent incapacity of CID to tackle any of the problems associated with low policing motivated the government to build up an unarmed police force known as the Civic Guard in March 1922. There was early criticism that this force was but a simulacrum of the RIC and internal dissension about a perceived reliance on ex-RIC personnel. In 1923, the name of the Civic Guard was changed to An Garda Síochána (guardians of the peace). During the parliamentary debate introducing this new body, a Labour deputy, Cathal O'Shannon, presciently remarked that:

> The strength of arguments may be in favour of that particular kind, that is a strongly centralised police force, at this moment, and until such time as things in Ireland become somewhat normal, but undoubtedly, if we were in normal time there would be a great strength of feeling in favour of a different and, perhaps, more localised police force. (Dáil Debates, 31 July 1923, vol. 4, col. 1694)

Probably because of their unarmed status, the Gardaí naturally gravitated towards dealing with 'low crime', leaving the armed forces to deal with insurrection. In this way, they were spared the ignominy associated with military executions. As peace tenatively developed in Ireland, the government was faced with the dilemma of investing responsibility for state security and domestic intelligence in a permanent body. Defenders of CID argued that it should be charged with collation of intelligence on most sections of society and the deployment of a number of informants. This proposal was scuttled by O'Higgins, who wished to establish the primacy of the conventional police – and who believed that only 25 out of the 86 CID personnel were of a 'good type' (Campbell 1994: 185) – and by the Minister for Defence, Richard Mulcahy, who resented the implied incursion into military matters. CID was dissolved in November 1923, with some of its members becoming part of what would be known as the Special Branch section of An Garda Síochána dedicated to dealing with 'crime special' or crime with a political connotation that threatened the overall security of the state. In 1925, the Dublin Metropolitan Police was amalgamated with An Garda Síochána, as O'Higgins rejected any notion of an advisory committee drawn from the local authorities since 'police problems cannot be shared between the police officer and a body of thirteen laymen – thirteen civilians – elected haphazard by a half-dozen local authorities' (Dáil Debates, 3 February 1925, vol. 10, col. 51). The leader of the Labour party characterised this as an 'adhesion to the idea of a centralised force responsible only to the Minister, who in turn is responsible to a body – the Dáil – representing the whole country, and collectively a body without any definite local responsibility' (col. 53).

This idea of policing as a monopoly of the central state, not to be shared even with local government, persisted until the beginning of the twenty-first century. The ever-present prospect of unrest prodded political representatives into accepting a centralised police force. Continuing social ferment could only be dealt with by a greater armed presence. The question was who would be deployed. It was agreed that the role of the detective branch should be expanded to about 200 armed men, divided into parties of ten or twelve and posted to various divisions throughout the country.

The distinction between high and low policing was enshrined within the detective division with a section dealing with crime ordinary and with crime special. From the mid 1920s on there was continuous spate of violence between the Gardaí and the IRA. Disconcertingly for the Gardaí, they began to lose the popular goodwill that had built up in the few years after their formation as they became associated with forceful repression.

> Criticisms in the Dáil and Senate became more frequent, newspaper eulogies of the Garda Síochána became a thing of the past, and local bodies and representatives became increasingly concerned at what the considered to be the employment of the police in the wrong manner and in the wrong problems. (Brady 1974: 148)

The murder of Kevin O'Higgins by republicans in July 1927 marginalised militant republicanism by forcing its political wing, Fianna Fáil (Soldiers of Destiny), to recognise the legitimacy of the Dáil and take their place in opposition. The Public Safety Act 1927 was passed allowing *habeas corpus* to be suspended in certain circumstances. In 1928, the IRA responded by resorting to a campaign of intimidation against the justice system and in 1929 shot two jurors who had convicted an IRA member. The commissioner of An Garda Síochána continuously pressed the government for the introduction of emergency legislation, especially since republicans were suing the Gardaí in the civil courts for harassment and false imprisonment. In October 1931, an amendment (article 2A) was inserted into the Constitution. The purpose of this legislation was to free the executive from 'legal red-tape' (Ó Longaigh 2006: 114) by suspending jury trials in favour of tribunals manned by army officers. The Department of Justice emphasised that the tribunal 'should have the power to accept ... *anything* in the nature of evidence and demand of the accused that he shall admit, deny or explain the police allegations against him' (2006: 115, emphasis in original). Refusal to give evidence would constitute sufficient evidence against the defendant and the tribunal could alter procedure as it saw fit. A judge, who upheld the legality of article 2A upon challenge by an appellant, commented that 'its provisions pass far beyond anything having the semblance of legal procedure and the judicial mind is staggered at the very complete departure from legal methods in use in these courts' (quoted in Hogan and Walker 1989: 177). It worked to the extent that the 1932 general election was held in relative peace with the ironic result for the Gardaí that Eamon De Valera's – who had opposed the 1921 treaty with Britain – Fianna Fáil party came to power.

One of De Valera's first acts was to suspend the operation of article 2A, leaving the Gardaí to rely on normal powers against the IRA. The opposition accused the nascent government of failing to maintain the supremacy of the state by indulging the IRA. The Minister for Defence retorted that 'ever since the government has assumed office a number of nervous people wanted us to crack a lot of heads, as was the policy of the late government when people who were a danger to them got their skulls opened' (quoted in Brady 1974: 172). Following a second election victory in 1933, Fianna Fáil dismissed the Garda commissoner, Eoin O'Duffy, because, in the words of De Valera, 'we want a chief of police of whom no section of the community can say that that man is deliberately and politically opposed to us' (1974: 179). A group that became known as the Blueshirts emerged to act as a counter-weight to the IRA given that the Gardaí felt hamstrung in defending the right of opposition political parties to unhindered public speaking. The Gardaí felt an affinity with the Blueshirts, not surprisingly since O'Duffy headed the group, and were reluctant to move against them. They were equally reluctant to move against the IRA for fear that the machinery of government was too favourably disposed to them.

During 1933, confrontations between the Blueshirts and the IRA were an almost nightly occurrence in some parts of the country, with anti-Communist rallies making an occasional showing. In August 1933, in fear of a Blueshirt takeover and a perceived lack of loyalty on the part of the Gardaí, article 2A of the Constitution was invoked again in order to make the Blueshirts a proscribed organisation. As a measure of the distrust between government and police, 200 new recruits were hastily drafted into the police force – their training consisted of a ten-minute lecture and the acquisition of a revolver. All of these recruits were drawn from the ranks of Fianna Fáil supporters and became known as the Broy Harriers.[3] Many Gardaí interpreted this as an attempt to emasculate the force, a suspicion that was heightened by the flagrant appearance of republican groups throughout the country who attempted to disrupt the campaigns of De Valera's opponents. The Gardaí took a tougher line against the IRA, but often through physical force rather than relying on typical powers of arrest and prosecution.

The Gardaí were also pitted against the Blueshirts due to a dispute over rates between the government and the large farming sector from which the Blueshirts drew much support. The outcome was the Gardaí were increasingly armed, and delegated to seize livestock and property from farms; in effect they became an 'unthinking instrument of government security policy' (Brady 1974: 223). Orders often came directly from the Department of Justice to the Broy Harriers, circumventing the normal chain of police command. And the Harriers, given the lack of training and rudimentary knowledge of the law, were not disposed to resort to lawful means of apprehension.

The Blueshirts dissipated under the misdirection of O'Duffy, and the government's attention turned to the IRA. While the organisation itself was not proscribed immediately, the government attempted to suppress the activities of its members. In March 1935, 40 IRA men were rounded up and given terms of imprisonment by the military tribunals established through article 2A. In June 1936, after two killings perpetrated by 'physical-force' republicans that shocked many, the IRA was declared an illegal organisation under article 2A. The head of the Department of Justice admitted that Article 2A was 'grotesque … It must go … [but] so long as we have the idea of a "normal" written constitution, with all sorts of snags and pit-falls for the executive, we [the government] must have something, somewhere along the lines of Article 2A' (quoted in Ó Longaigh 2006: 158).

A new Constitution came into force, following its approval by a referendum, in July 1937. As compared with its 1922 predecessor, it provided for a much more entrenched system of judicial review, redefined the range of *habeas corpus* safeguards, and gave greater protection to a range of personal rights. Nonetheless, the history of paramilitarism in Ireland ensured that provision was also made for the security menace still posed to the state. The establishment of special non-jury courts (under article 38.3), whose powers, composition, jurisdiction and procedures were to be established by legislation, and provisions in respect of treason (under article 39) all signpost the contingencies that were still being made to protect state security from subversive activity (Hillyard 1987). More broadly, article 28.3.3 also gave constitutional immunity to any law that was 'expressed to be for the preservation of public safety of the state in time of war or armed rebellion'. Once a declaration of emergency was made by both Houses of the Oireachtas, constitutional rights and safeguards could be abridged.

With the prospect of war looming in 1939, De Valera was determined to adhere to a strict definition of neutrality and to stifle any IRA campaign that could have scuppered that aspiration. A state of emergency was declared and in June 1939, the Offences against the State Act 1939 was passed. The 1939 Act forms the principal pillar in Ireland's permanent quest to protect state security. The first four parts of the Act are permanently in force. For example, part II deals *inter alia* with offences against the state such as the usurpation of the functions of government, obstruction of government, obstruction of the President, unauthorised military exercises, and the possession of treasonable and seditious documents. Part III contends with membership of unlawful organisations. On the other hand, part V, which makes provision for the establishment of the Special Criminal Court and the power of the government to schedule offences, only comes into operation when the government makes the appropriate proclamation that the ordinary courts are inadequate to secure the effective administration of justice and the preservation of public peace and order. In making such proclamations under part V, the government does not have to explain to the Dáil why such draconian measures are deemed necessary. The necessary proclamations under part V of the 1939 Act have been made for the periods 1939–1946, 1961 to 1962, and 1972 to date. The current proclamation can be annulled only by a resolution of the Dáil or when the government issues a proclamation declaring that part V is no longer in force (Kilcommins and Vaughan 2004).

This legislation had two significant consequences. Section 30 of the Act permits Gardaí to arrest a person suspected of having committed or about to commit what became known as scheduled offences, that is, unsuitable to be tried before an ordinary court of law (see Walsh 2002: 973). Any suspect arrested can be detained for 24 hours and a further 24 if a chief superintendent desires. Part V of the 1939 Act permits the government to declare ordinary courts 'inadequate to secure the administration of justice' and establish a special criminal (non-jury) court before which scheduled offences can automatically be tried. The Emergency Powers Act amended the Constitution so that there were no constitutional obstacles to how the government might act 'for the purpose of securing the public safety and the preservation of the State in time of war or armed rebellion' (article 28.3.3). A piece of amending legislation was passed in 1940 that allowed for the internment of Irish citizens and established a military tribunal to try scheduled offences summarily with the only available sanction being execution – which was unavailable to the special criminal court – and with no right of appeal. The case of George Plant is perhaps the most extreme example of the effects of this legislation. Plant, along with another individual, was accused of killing an informer. However, their trial collapsed amid accusations that two key prosecution witnesses had been beaten by Special Branch into giving incriminating statements. The government issued an emergency order enabling disavowed statements to be used as evidence and subsequently Plant was arrested and tried before the military court. He was found guilty on the basis of the disputed confessions and executed (Bowyer Bell 1989: 209). After the war, Minister for Justice, Gerard Boland stated that he had no objection to the military tribunal being described as a 'terror court' since it was a court 'set up to meet terror in a drastic and summary manner in order to save the nation from the perils which threatened it at the time' (Dáil Debates, 29 May 1946, vol. 101, col. 1116).

The power of internment meant that the actual sentence of imprisonment handed out to IRA members was immaterial. Most of the crimes were related to a refusal to answer questions yet internment lasted 'as long as the government felt an emergency existed' (Bowyer Bell 1989: 209). By May 1941, the numbers interned or convicted by the Special Criminal Court had reached a figure of approximately 550, equivalent to the total prison population convicted of 'ordinary crimes' (Dáil Debates, 28 May 1941, vol. 83, col. 1273–76). One of the few weapons left to interned republicans was the power of the hunger strike, yet the government felt emboldened enough to ignore republican demands even after two men had starved themselves to death. Conditions for the internees within the Curragh military camp were bleak, and when prisoners protested they were starved and beaten. Portlaoise prison was even worse, since the IRA were treated as ordinary criminals, a fate they tried to resist. Their resistance earned them isolated confinement where

> sitting month after month, year after year, in the bleak solitary cells, they were taken out once a week for a bath, and for the rest of the week lived the life of an animal trapped in a burrow. Even in solitary confinement, there was no privacy. The lights were turned on day and night at erratic intervals for security checks. There were no books, no contact with each other, no opportunity to talk with anyone. (Bowyer Bell 1989: 181)

By the end of the war, the IRA campaign had exhausted itself and political crime had virtually vanished. Yet the republican presence within Ireland had profound effects on policing and the rule of law. It meant that policing was continually directed against threats to the security of the state, forcing policing to take on an almost paramilitary role itself. This inhibited the capacity of the police force to undertake what has been termed ordinary or low policing or at least in a form that engaged and won over many people within communities. The administration of justice was also substantially affected due to the continuous adoption of emergency legislation that circumvented the rule of law due to the exigencies of the domestic situation. These deviations (hasty shootings, suspension of *habeas corpus*, trial before a non-jury court overseen by military personnel, proscription of organisations, mass internment, direct political control of police operations) are reminiscent of more modern policies in the current age of terrorism. The reasons for this similarity are not hard to find since they are rooted in an analysis that demands that state rule supersede the law for survival purposes. Exceptional circumstances, such as attacks on the integrity of the state, throw down a challenge to the capacity of rule-bound procedures of normal law to contain them. Only a sovereign figure can rescue the rule-bound state from defeat by invoking emergency powers, edicts that have the force of law but are no longer constrained by law (Schmitt 1985; Kilcommins and Vaughan 2004). Those suspected of launching attacks against the state are stripped of constitutional rights and occupy a legal shadow zone of military courts and internment without trial. Without legal status, these people are utterly dependent on the will of the sovereign. As De Valera commented in 1940, 'the very notion of the state is futile if it not be conceded that there exists within the state one single and sovereign power having the supreme right effectively to co-ordinate all wills in the pursuit of the common end' (quoted in Ferriter 2004: 365). The sovereign figure can decide whether the state of emergency or exception becomes the governing norm. Despite the end of World War Two, the government declared it 'not in the public interest, to take the irrevocable step of declaring the emergency formally at an end' (Dáil Debates, 22 January 1947, vol. 104, col. 2). The retention of the 'emergency amendment' to the Constitution (aricle 28.3) raises the question about how great was the commitment to a more 'normal' rule-bound system of justice in the decades following 1945.

## Rule-bound justice

After World War Two, Ireland enjoyed an extraordinarily low rate of 'ordinary crime', often hovering around 12,000 indictable crimes a year. In 1950, the Minister for Justice observed that since 'this country is very free from crime', it should give itself a 'pat on the back for being a law abiding people' (quoted in Kilcommins *et al.* 2004: 62). This state of affairs led Brady to describe the period 1945–56 as a policeman's paradise; it was the 'quietest period in the history of the force since its foundation in 1922' (1974: 239). In fact, the relative infrequency of crime may have prevented the development of low policing in the sense envisaged by Brodeur. Instead, police attention was devoted to non-criminal matters, including duties connected with unemployment assistance and travel permits. The matter of Gardaí dealing with stray cattle was often raised in the Dáil (Dáil Debates, 9 June 1949, vol. 116, col. 445). In addition, the Gardaí returned to one of their original missions of being 'Irish in Thought and Action' through the display of sporting prowess in Gaelic games (Brady, 1974: 117–19). As one political representative commented:

> From a cultural and athletic point of view, they [the Gardaí] have been a great boon to different parts of the country. Counties that were never heard of in Gaelic Athletic Association circles [the organisation responsible for fostering the indigenous sports of Ireland, chiefly Gaelic football and hurling] have sprung to the fore very largely as a result of the presence in these places of Guards who were good hurlers and footballers, and who could train teams. That is something well worth remembering. (Mr G. Boland, Dáil Debates, 7 July 1950, vol. 122, col. 1123).

It is undoubtedly the case that after World War Two, the Gardaí became an immense source of political pride and were regularly commended in the Dáil as comparing favourably with the best police forces in the world (Dáil Debates, 7 July 1950, vol. 122, col. 1150). What we do not know is how extensively the general populace shared this perception. Brady suggests that the Irish police were esteemed above the RIC because:

> the Guards could settle a troublesome situation with a few thumps on the appropriate skulls and a certain element of physical violence thus came to be an accepted part of the relationship between police and people. It was one of the vital differences between the RIC and the Guards. The RIC rarely withdrew a prosecution if they had one, for their system of ranks and their administration saw to it that due process was always followed on the English model. This had ensured that the RIC was an efficient police force but hardly a popular one. (1974: 116)

If there was rough-and-ready justice dispensed that avoided the intricacies of prosecution – which would partly explain the low crime rate – this came to be both challenged and championed by the rise in crime rates from the 1960s on and the onset of what became known as 'The Troubles' in Northern Ireland in the 1970s. In 1957 the IRA reignited their campaign north of the border and Eamon De Valera's government acted swiftly, interning over 200 republicans in the Curragh by 1958. In 1961 the Irish government re-established the military tribunals and by the end of December 25 men had been sentenced. What we have called low policing also began to manifest itself from 1958 on, as deputies made their concerns known over increases in the crime rate of the order of 10 per cent and 18 per cent the following year. The Minister for Justice, Oscar Traynor, lamented in 1959 that this was 'part of a world-wide crime wave' but denied that there was 'something radically wrong … with the Garda machine' (Dáil Debates, 9 April 1959, vol. 174, col. 230). Despite this denial, there was continuing pressure in the 1960s to modernise, as the force admitted women and shed a number of non-crime related duties and began to be more mobile through motor patrols, much to the disgust of some Gardaí (Kilcommins *et al.* 2004).

While the Gardaí struggled to adapt to increased crime levels, they also had to cope with the effects of political disputes in Northern Ireland that ushered in a republican paramilitary struggle against the British state. In May 1972, following three years of unrest in Northern Ireland, the Irish government invoked Part V of the Offences against the State Act. It declared that a state of unrest existed in the country that the ordinary courts were unable to rectify. Departures from ordinary processes of justice were legitimated and the Special Criminal Court was reconstituted. It remains in force, until such time as the government proclaims that it no longer holds sway.

Further power accrued to the state following the murder of the British ambassador in July 1976 when the Oireachtas proclaimed a state of emergency and passed the Emergency Powers Act 1976. This legislation allowed seven days' detention after arrest for a scheduled offence. Section 30 of the Offences against the State Act already allowed for detention for up to 48 hours and the Gardaí frequently resorted to this measure, especially since the phenomenon of detention short of arrest came under increasing judicial scrutiny in the late 1970s. The evidence reviewed so far would seem to suggest that in the 1970s, criminal justice operated according to the dualism that plagues all criminal justice systems, namely the tension between crime control and due process. The fact that neither one nor the other predominated is hardly striking. Yet what is perhaps peculiar is the fact that in some senses there operated a dual system of justice, dealing with ordinary crime and crime that invoked a sense of emergency. The obvious danger is that the measures deployed to deal with the latter, to wash away the sense of crisis, can be incorporated into the ordinary system of law, as we shall see later.

The sense of a crisis reoccurred after the largest terrorist killing on the island of Ireland after a splinter group from the IRA (the Real IRA) exploded a bomb in Omagh, Northern Ireland on 15 August 1998, killing 29 people. Both the Irish and British governments introduced emergency legislation. The Irish contribution built on existing legislation, namely the Offences against the State Act 1939, by the enactment of the Offences against the State (Amendment) Act 1998.

This legislation increases the period of detention permitted by the 1939 Act to a maximum of 72 hours and allows the court to draw inferences when a suspect is questioned about membership of an unlawful organisation. Commenting on similar British legislation introduced at the same time, Lord Donaldson said that the provisions constituted a 'charter for internment dressed up to look like the result of criminal justice' (quoted in Farrell 1998: 3). The legislation also created an offence of directing an unlawful organisation, carrying a sentence of life imprisonment. In 2003 Michael McKevitt, the alleged leader of the Real IRA, was convicted for membership of an unlawful organisation and directing terrorism. His prosecution rested largely on the testimony of a senior Garda officer and an agent run and paid by both the FBI and MI5.

The continued relevance of Ireland's domestic terrorist legislation can be gauged by the fact that when it came to adopting the European Union framework decision on combatting terrorism, the relevant legislation (Criminal Justice [Terrorist Offences] Act 2005) simply provided that the EU definition of a terrorist group be dealt with by way of the Offences against the State Act 1939 and the 1998 Amendment Act. Furthermore, other countries seem to be emulating some of the principal features of this legislation. For example, the *modus operandi* of the McKevitt case resonates with the more recent US Supreme Court judgment in the case of *Hamdi v. Rumsfeld* (542 U.S. 2004) where the plaintiff was challenging his status as an enemy combatant and the consequence that the executive could indefinitely detain him. Speaking for the plurality of the court, Justice O'Connor argued that although the plaintiff was entitled to some due process that would allow him to contest the government designation, this had to be tailored so that the executive would not be unduly burdened.

> Hearsay, for example, may need to be accepted as the most reliable available evidence from the Government in such a proceeding.

> Likewise, the Constitution would not be offended by a presumption in favor of the Government's evidence, so long as that presumption remained a rebuttable one and fair opportunity for rebuttal were provided. Thus, once the Government puts forth credible evidence that the habeas petitioner meets the enemy-combatant criteria, the onus could shift to the petitioner to rebut that evidence with more persuasive evidence that he falls outside the criteria. (p. 27)

Obviously, this represents a partial reversion to the standards of exculpatory justice recounted in Chapter 2, about which only Justice Souter expressed reservations. Perhaps this is because, as Lea (2005) has speculated, the way has been cleared by the dilution of rights afforded to those suspected of criminal offences. In Ireland, this can be best illustrated by showing how extraordinary law has been normalised to deal with typical criminal offences as public alarm grew.

## Crime-fighting and extraordinary law

The 1980s was the decade in which recorded crime peaked, with a fivefold increase in indictable crime between 1966 and in 1983 (National Crime Council 2001), with burglaries and larcenies making up a majority of the offences. One commentator was moved to remark that 'crime is to the 1980s what emigration was to the 1950s: a mark of the nation's failings' (Rottman 1986). To redress these failings, the agents of the Irish state made increasing use of legislation and practices that were originally intended for use against terrorist activity designed to subvert the state in the following five areas.

### *1 Gardaí holding and information gathering tactics*

Up to 1979, the Gardaí had on occasion utilised the tactic of 'holding suspects for questioning' for ordinary offences. This ploy acted as a 'useful' information gathering technique and it meant that the suspects did not need to be promptly produced before the courts as they were not *de jure* under arrest. In that year, however, the Supreme Court held that this practice constituted a *de facto* arrest and represented an unlawful invasion of constitutional rights. In *People (DPP) v O'Loughlin*, O'Higgins, CJ explained: '"Holding for questioning" and "taking into custody" and "detaining" are merely different ways of describing the act of depriving a man of his liberty. To do so without lawful authority is an open defiance of article 40.4.1° of the Constitution.'[4] Following the decision, the Gardaí, for a number of years, began to resort to the stratagem of arresting persons suspected of committing serious crime under section 30 of the Offences against the State Act 1939 (which then permitted a maximum period of detention of up to 48 hours),[5] an extraordinary piece of legislation designed, as detailed above, primarily to combat subversive activities and political violence. According to Hogan and Walker, the number of persons so arrested increased dramatically between 1979 (1,431 persons) and 1984 (2,216), the year in which the Criminal Justice Act authorised a maximum period of detention of 12 hours for ordinary offences punishable by a term of imprisonment of five years or more.[6] Indeed the same authors suggest that most persons wanted for serious crime – subversive in nature or otherwise – during this period were arrested and detained under section 30 of the 1939 Act.

Moreover, and as the UN Human Rights Committee and the Committee to Review the Offences against the State Acts recently pointed out, the manner in which section 30 was employed was also a cause for concern, particularly as it related to the disparity between persons arrested and those subsequently charged. In 1981, for example, 2,303 people were arrested but only 323 were charged with an offence. In 1982 the figures were 2,308 arrested (256 charged); in 1983, 2,334 (363 charged); in 1984, 2,216 (374 charged); in 1985, 1,834 (366 charged); and in 1986, 2,387 (484 charged) (*Report of the Committee to Review the Offences against the State Acts*, 2001: para. 7.14).[7] The Committee admitted that this legislation was 'routinely applied in cases of what came to be described as "ordinary crime"' (para. 7.12). According to one author, its commonplace use introduced a new word, 'sectioned', to Dublin inner city, as in 'Where's Johnny? He's been sectioned [arrested under section 30]' (Lyder 2005: 75).

The ability of the Gardaí to switch, virtually unimpeded, from ordinary to extraordinary detention procedures – bearing in mind the extensiveness of the latter – in respect of suspects accused of ordinary, though serious, offences demonstrates, to some extent, the ambivalence that has existed in Ireland about individual liberty safeguards. This is particularly so when one considers that the extraordinary provisions that legitimate such extensive detention periods without charge were initially designed only 'with actions and conduct calculated to undermine the security of the State' in mind.[8]

### 2 Extra-ordinary measures and non-paramilitary activity

This overspill from the paramilitary into the ordinary realm is also evident in the Supreme Court's sanctioning of the wider use of the extraordinary powers of arrest and detention permitted under section 30 of the Offences against the State Act 1939. Section 36 of the Offences against the State Act 1939 empowers the government to declare offences to be scheduled whenever it is satisfied that the ordinary courts are inadequate to secure the effective administration of justice.[9] As noted, a suspect arrested under section 30 may be detained for an initial period of 24 hours followed by a further 24 hours provided a certain direction is given. A further 24-hour period of detention without charge is now provided for under the Offences against the State (Amendment) Act 1998. Section 30 itself is very broad and permits a Garda to arrest anyone suspected of 'having committed, or being about to commit, or being or having been concerned in the commission of an offence', or 'having information in relation to the commission or intended commission' of any offence under the 1939 Act or a scheduled offence. There is no specific requirement that the Garda must show some reasonable basis for his or her suspicion. The section, in effect, has the potential to be a 'power of preventative detention'.[10]

The seepage from the extraordinary to the ordinary criminal justice realm as regards section 30 is evident in Irish case law. In the case of *DPP v Quilligan*,[11] for example, the defendants were suspected of breaking into the home of two elderly brothers; as a result both brothers had been injured, one fatally, and damage had been done to their property. The offences committed were not political or subversive in nature. At the time of the offences, malicious damage to property was a scheduled offence. Both defendants, accordingly, were arrested and detained under section 30 on suspicion of malicious damage which had been caused to a door and some furniture at the home of the victims. While so detained, both defendants made incriminating statements regarding the more serious, though non-scheduled, offence of murder. The trial judge, however, held that the considerations which prompted the introduction of the 1939 Act related to crimes of a subversive nature that threatened the security of the state. As no subversive elements attached to the crimes in issue, the arrest and detention of the defendants was held to be illegal, and a direction was given to the jury to record a verdict of not guilty in favour of each of the defendants.

This ruling was reversed on appeal to the Supreme Court. It held that as the arrest and detention by the Gardaí had been genuinely directed towards the investigation of the scheduled offence of malicious damage, the fact that they had come to be more attentive to the more serious though not scheduled offence of murder – which was *closely linked* with the scheduled offence of malicious damage – did not render illegal the arrest and detention process. In effect, the Supreme Court sanctioned the use of the minor holding charge (malicious damage to property) to permit questioning under section 30 in respect of the more serious, though non-scheduled, murder charge. All that was required was a link between the two offences and that the Gardaí, in good faith, suspected the accused of having committed the minor charge. In *People (DPP) v Howley*,[12] a non-subversive case involving a scheduled offence of cattle maiming and a non-scheduled offence of murder, the Supreme Court further enhanced Garda powers by holding that the link between the scheduled, minor offence and non-scheduled serious offence was not necessary, and that the predominant motive for the arrest did not need to be the minor, scheduled offence. All that was demanded was that the arrest be made in good faith, and brought about in circumstances where an actual Garda suspicion existed for the scheduled, albeit minor offence. Such decisions smack of Nelsonian blindness in that they sanction the detention of suspects under section 30 without the need for a connection to be made to the causal framework in which the scheduled offences were committed. Employing section 30 to arrest persons for offences not connected with paramilitary activity has facilitated the creation of an entirely capricious and discordant system of detention without charge, quite out of keeping with the spirit of the constitutional guarantee of personal liberty as provided for under article 40.4.1 of the Irish Constitution.

For example, under the law as it currently exists in Ireland, a person suspected of raping someone can only be detained without charge for a maximum period of 24 hours, as provided for under section 4 of the Criminal Justice Act 1984, as amended. If the same person was suspected of rape, and at the time the offence was committed of having possession of an unloaded gun (which was unconnected with the offence of rape), he could be detained for a maximum period of 72 hours under the Offences against the State Act 1939, as amended, given that the possession of a firearm is a scheduled offence. If, as the Irish Council for Civil Liberties has pointed out, section 30 had been confined to paramilitary-related offences, 'there would at least be a logical explanation for the discrepancy in detention periods'.[13]

From a historical standpoint, permitting offences with no subversive connotations to fall within the rubric of extraordinary legislation because, *stricto sensu*, they are scheduled appears to be at enmity with the reasoning behind the enactment of the Offences against the State Act 1939 – which was to safeguard the interests of the state against subversive elements. More practically, permitting terrorist legislation to be applied in such an insouciant manner represents a significant seepage from the extraordinary to the ordinary criminal justice realm. The creation of such a powerful investigative tool for the Gardaí in ordinary criminal procedure – detention without charge for a maximum period of 72 hours – also constitutes a significant encroachment upon the civil liberty rights of suspects. As Professor Dermot Walsh noted in his dissenting views appended to the *Report of the Committee to Review the Offences against the State Acts, 1939–1998*:

> In a society based on respect for human rights and civil liberties, a reasonable balance must be maintained between the individual's fundamental right to liberty and the police need to use arrest and detention for the effective investigation and detection of crime. Since section 30 constitutes a gross departure from the norms governing police powers of arrest and detention, it follows that its retention needs to be justified by very convincing arguments … [S]ection 30 constitutes an excessive and unwarranted intrusion on the individual's fundamental right to liberty in a 'normal' society based on respect for human rights … A more reasonable balance needs to be struck between the requirements of effective criminal investigation and the individual's fundamental right to liberty.

Some commentators, however, believe that we should not be surprised by the failure of judges to protect rights in times of emergency or when dealing with extraordinary measures. As Dyzenhaus (2006b: 12–14) noted:

> while judges are usually regarded as the guardians of the rule of law, in emergencies they have a dismal record when it comes to upholding law's rule. They tend to defer submissively to executive judgment. Even if their jurisdiction to review executive decisions is not expressly ousted or excluded by the statute or regulations that authorise detention, they are prone to impose on themselves a standard of review that requires that only official decisions that can be shown to be utterly irrational should be invalidated … [Very often] they will … give the executive the stamp of approval of legality as long as they can assert that it is they who wield the stamp.

Irish judicial interpretations of the use of section 30 lend credence to such concerns.

### *3 The retention of the non-jury Special Criminal Court for non-paramilitary activities*

Further evidence of this normalisation process can be gleaned from the continued retention of the non-jury Special Criminal Court, the reintroduction of which was justified on the basis that juries were likely to be intimidated by paramilitaries. It continues to be employed today despite little in the way of a risk assessment as to whether or not there is a possibility of continued paramilitary intimidation.[14] Moreover, the Special Criminal Court is increasingly being employed to try cases that have no paramilitary connections. Offences without subversive connections that have been tried in the Special Criminal Court include the supply of cannabis, arson at a public house, theft of computer parts, kidnapping, the murder of the journalist Veronica Guerin, receiving a stolen caravan and its contents, the unlawful taking of a motor car, and the theft of cigarettes and £150 from a shop.[15] Perhaps even more alarmingly, the decision to have such offences tried before the non-jury Special Criminal Court are not subject to any checks or safeguards. Under sections 46 and 47 of the Offences against the State Act 1939, the DPP has the power to have *any* case heard in the Special Criminal Court where he is of the opinion that the ordinary courts are inadequate to secure the effective administration of justice. Significantly, the decision of the DPP to have a case tried in the Special Criminal Court is not susceptible to judicial review in the absence of evidence of *mala fides* or of being influenced by an improper motive or an improper policy. Even despite its breach of the International Covenant on Civil and Political Right, and the fact that it was established under an anti-terrorist framework that is no longer applicable,[16] the arrangement continues to be justified on the basis of its usefulness to the state in combating organised crime – a form of crime that has, without much debate, assumed the 'folk devil' security-threatening status previously only associated in Ireland with political violence (Fennell 2003: 23).[17] Indeed, far from being disbanded on the basis of the notable downturn in paramilitary activity, the Irish government has recently announced that a second such court will be established to expedite trials (see Criminal Justice (Terrorist Offences) Act 2005). The establishment of this second court will, according to a government press release, 'serve to demonstrate the State's resolve to seriously deal with any activity which is a threat to the State and its people' (Department of Justice, 22 December 2004). The emboldening claim that one has a right to a jury trial in Ireland, as provided for under article 38.5 of the Constitution of 1937, seems much more fragile in the light of such developments. A permanent state of exception as regards the constitutional right to a jury trial seems a fundamental 'contradiction in terms' (Dyzenhaus 2006b: 19). As Fennell (2003: 28) suggests:

> the existence of an 'emergency' or extraordinary regime outside constitutional parameters in the context of the Special Criminal Court has … facilitated the existence of differential, exceptional or 'non-constitutional' treatment for certain offenders. Moreover … the phenomenon would appear to be ongoing as the demonisation of drugs and organised crime may ensure a future currency for this exceptional provision, and its persistence even in light of elimination or resolution of its originating *raison d'être*. This dissonance at the heart of the Irish criminal justice system in terms of departure from overt constitutional values is not insignificant in assessing its adherence to principle.

### *4 Seizing criminal assets without requiring a criminal conviction*

The Proceeds of Crime Bill was mooted in Ireland in the mid 1990s to combat the dangers posed to society by drug-related crime. The current Act was initially proposed as a private member's Bill, one week after the assassination of journalist Veronica Guerin (Meade 2000). The Act's cardinal feature permits the Criminal Assets Bureau to secure interim and interlocutory orders against a person's property, provided that it can demonstrate that the specified property – which has a value in excess of €13,000 – constitutes, directly or indirectly, the proceeds of crime. If the interlocutory order survives in force for a period of seven years,[18] an application for disposal can then be made. This extinguishes all rights in the property that the respondent party may have had.

The primary impetus for this model was derived, once again, from the terrorist domain where the Offences against the State (Amendment) Act 1985 empowered the Minister for Justice to certify that money held in banks that was the property of an unlawful organisation should be forfeited and vested in the Minister.[19] This certification by the Minister was not dependent on the initiation of criminal proceedings. The Act contained further provisions entitling a person who claimed to be the owner of the money to apply to the High Court for an order directing the return of the money if he or she could demonstrate that it was not the proceeds from the operations of an unlawful organisation. In introducing the Bill in 1985, the then Minister for Justice stated as follows:

> The necessity for this Bill arises from a specific situation that has arisen and which has such serious implications for the maintenance of public order in this country that the Government have no option but to move with speed and decisiveness to deal with it. Information has been conveyed to me by the Garda authorities

> that a large sum of money which is the proceeds of criminal activity by the IRA – specifically extortion under threat of kidnap and murder – has found its way into a bank in this country and is being held to the use of and for the purposes of the IRA ... This necessitated urgent action by the Government to prevent the money becoming available to the IRA to fund their campaign of murder and destruction. (Seánad Eireann, 19 February 1985, vol. 107, col. 316)

The 1985 Bill had a lifespan of three months and was only designed to combat the threat posed by the one terrorist incident cited by the minister in introducing the Bill. The powers conferred under the legislation were only ever invoked in respect of that one specific case. Indeed, the minister introducing the Bill recognised the draconian nature of the powers conferred but justified it having regard to the 'evils of the IRA':

> Before I conclude I want to say that the Government have not lightly brought forward this Bill and would not have done so were it not convinced that the Bill is essential and that there is no other way of dealing with the problem that now faces us. I do not deny that it is a strong measure and that the power it confers on the Minister is one that ought never to be used lightly. I can and do now give a firm assurance that I will not use it lightly but it may be more to the point if I say that I do not think that it can ever be used lightly ... (Seánad Eireann, 19 February 1985, vol. 107, col. 322)

Arising out of this one incident, the provisions of the 1985 legislation were held up to judicial scrutiny in the case of *Clancy v Ireland*,[20] where Barrington J, in a brief judgment, held that the abridgement of property rights provided for under the Act was a permissible delimitation of property rights having regard to the common good, and was not in breach of fair procedures. This 1985 terrorist legislation, and the decision to uphold it in *Clancy*, provided a constitutional template, albeit in the extraordinary realm, for the confiscation of assets in the absence of a criminal conviction. With only a slight skip and a jump, and the odd wink or two, the same template could be exploited in the ordinary realm having regard to proceeds of crime legislation. This is precisely what happened. For example, when introducing the Proceeds of Crime Bill to the Dáil, its initiator, John O'Donoghue, could suggest as follows (Dáil Eireann, 2 July 1996, vol. 467, col. 2409):

> The suggestion that this Bill is in some unspecified way unconstitutional is equally unsustainable. A clear and direct precedent exists for legislation of this type. The Offences Against the State (Amendment) Act, 1985, permits the freezing of assets of illegal organizations. The constitutionality of that Act was tested in the High Court in the case of *Clancy v Ireland* ... Similarly a direct precedent exists for the acceptance of the court of opinion evidence from a Garda Superintendent.[21] The Offences Against the State (Amendment) Act, 1972, provides in section 3(2) that the belief of a member of the Garda Siochana, not below the rank of chief superintendent is sufficient evidence on which to grant a conviction for membership of an unlawful organization.[22]

Such reasoning provides further evidence of the obfuscation of the clear lines that should exist between extraordinary and ordinary provisions. It is a sign of the dissonance that can exist in relation to constitutional values, and raises concerns about the extent to which the system irradiates with due process ideals. In seeking to constitutionally legitimate an ordinary Bill by reference to extraordinary provisions, John O'Donoghue swept over a breadth of history that acknowledges that statutes such as the Offences against the State (Amendment) Act 1985 are premised on emergency powers designed to combat the threat posed by subversives intent on overthrowing the state. The constitutionality of such extraordinary provisions is supposedly closely tethered to the notion that they are a proportionate, albeit draconian, response to the emergency threat posed. In particular, the *Clancy* decision must be seen against the legislative background of the Offences against the State Act 1939, which was enacted to combat the threat posed by unlawful organisations, such as the IRA, which engage in 'activity of a treasonable nature', advocate 'the procuring by force' of 'an alteration of the Constitution', or raise or maintain 'a military or armed force in contravention of the Constitution'.[23] Indeed, the possibility of an overspill from the extraordinary to the ordinary realm, as regards the Offences against the State Amendment Act 1985, was remarked upon by Senator Brendan Ryan. Commenting on the Offences against the State (Amendment) Bill 1985, as it passed through the Seánad (the Irish parliamentary equivalent of the House of Lords), he suggested:

> Every power that I am aware of that has been given under emergency legislation ... has been abused and extended beyond its initial intent and purpose. While it is not for me to weep over those who have millions of pounds on deposit in banks if the Minister for

> Justice or the Government choose to make life difficult for them, nevertheless I wonder about the possibilities that will be read into such a provision in years to come because the evidence in the past is that what may well be necessary to deal with a specific task can become very convenient to deal with a vast range of tasks. (Seánad Eireann, 19 February 1985, vol. 107, cols 328–9)

The enactment of the Proceeds of Crime Act 1996, as will be discussed more fully later in the book, has proved his point only too well.

#### *5 The acceptance of supergrass testimony in the ordinary criminal justice system*

On a slightly more remote footing – though evidence of the normalisation process and the result-oriented logic of the system more generally – is the introduction of a witness protection programme, set up following the murder of Veronica Guerin, to assist the Gardaí in the fight against organised crime. The type of witnesses protected by the programme are not simply run-of-the-mill self-confessed accomplices, but fall into a definitional category more in keeping with 'supergrass' testimony, a term made infamous following a series of paramilitary trials in the Diplock Courts in Northern Ireland in the 1980s (Greer 1986). The damning information that such witnesses have provided has been utilised by the state to apprehend and prosecute a series of high-profile individuals operating in the world of organised crime. In return for such information the witnesses, who themselves had also repeatedly partaken in criminal activities, were given the opportunity of an improved lifestyle. Aside from the possibility of jeopardising the entire criminal procedure process by admitting evidence that is highly susceptible to fabrication and exaggeration, and often incapable of being properly verified, the practice of utilising such witnesses has also increased the likelihood of Garda corruption, particularly in relation to information gathering. Current ambivalence about such testimony and the 'fluidity' in the operation of the programme[24] is even more surprising when one considers that only 20 years ago Irish politicians and the general public condemned with gusto the adoption of similar 'extraordinary' supergrass practices in Northern Ireland (Kilcommins and Vaughan 2004: 68–71). In the space of two decades, however, arguments about the right to a fair trial, the protection of the innocent, transparent management and basic human rights have been displaced by the need for a more efficient 'truth seeking' criminal justice system both for alleged criminals in the case of the murder of Veronica Guerin and alleged terrorists in the case of the trial of Michael McKevitt.

## 'National emergencies' and 'crime crises'

More generally, it can be said that those involved in serious crime currently in Ireland have quickly been elevated to the status of a security threat equivalent to that of the paramilitaries in the not-too-distant past. The intense outrage produced by such crimes, coupled with demands for the state to reassert its power through the criminal justice system, has resulted in a 'national emergency' that demands that ever clearer lines be drawn between a fearful public and 'monstrous' criminals. Increasingly, the state has been tempted to turn to its long history of extraordinary provisions to combat the threat posed by ordinary, 'folk devil' criminals. In many respects the benchmark provided by these extraordinary provisions has facilitated in some respects the fast-tracking of a crime control model of justice as it relates to issues such as an emphasis on efficiency, security, public protection and the devaluation of accuseds' rights. This benchmarking obscures the trade-off that takes place between enhanced public protection, on the one hand, and the commitment to due process values on the other. More importantly, it also takes place in an empirical vacuum about the actual threats posed by certain 'folk devils', the suitability of extraordinary provisions in the circumstances, or the impact on due process values in general.

For example, and has been noted elsewhere (Kilcommins and Vaughan 2004: 74–5), a glance at the Irish parliamentary reports, newspapers and judgments over the years demonstrates the 'metaphoric pathways' being created between terrorism and ordinary crime:

- '[D]rugs have replaced terrorism as the number one threat to the security of the State' (Dáil Debates, 6 February 1996, vol. 641, col. 284, *per* Mr Haughey).
- 'Just as President Clinton proclaimed in his visit to Belfast that the children of this generation in Northern Ireland have a right to be born and raised in an environment free from terrorist violence, so too do the children of this generation throughout Ireland have the right to be born and raised in an environment free from criminal violence and abuse' (Seánad Debates, 31 January 1996, vol. 146, col. 88, *per* Mr O' Kennedy).
- 'Whether we like it or not there is a state of emergency. It is no use saying otherwise. This has happened because … [civil libertarians] … who are always trotted out whenever there is a situation like that created by the dreadful murder of the journalist, Veronica Guerin, have been saying for a long time that criminals are entitled to their civil rights. These murderers and criminals do not recognise other people's civil rights. Why

should we recognise theirs? We should open up the Curragh [a former military camp] and intern them. People who are caught selling drugs, purchasing drugs, or selling them to get their own free deals should be taken out of circulation' (Dáil Debates, 4 July 1996, vol. 488, cols 554–5).

- '... I mentioned the threat the IRA posed, and continues to pose, to this State. I have also begun to wonder whether there is the same realisation of the threat posed to our society by the criminal underworld ... I was informed of a community meeting held in Dublin recently at which the drugs problem was discussed, when there was a discreet Special Branch presence outside the building endeavouring to ascertain whether there was any IRA presence ... I wonder whether all criminals nationwide are watched as closely. We must encourage rather than discourage such surveillance' (Dáil Debates, 3 July 1996, vol. 468, col. 373).
- The collapse of a murder trial in November 2003 lead to calls for more 'anti-terrorist type laws'.[25]
- In *Gilligan v Criminal Assets Bureau* the presiding judge concluded that there existed 'an entirely new type of professional criminal who ... renders himself virtually immune to the ordinary procedures of criminal investigation and prosecution' and that this necessitated the use of the 'lower probative requirements of the civil law ... not to achieve penal sanctions but to effectively deprive such persons of such illicit financial fruits of their labours'. The judge argued that the kind of crime to be targeted, drug-trafficking, was 'probably perceived by ordinary members of the community as more threatening and more likely to effect [sic] the everyday lives of themselves and their children [than terrorism]'.[26]
- Following a gangland killing in December 2006, politicians claimed that the 'country was in a virtual state of national emergency'; and calls were made for the Gardaí and the army to come together to round up the drug barons and murderers who it was claimed were 'reducing Dublin to a bloodbath'.[27]

The somewhat unique position of Ireland as regards its extraordinary legal powers raises interesting questions about the pursuit of the rule of law in a liberal democracy. Special zones were set up in which normal laws did not apply. As a result of public and political pressure, this zone expanded to incorporate more and more normal crime. There was not one supreme moment of sovereignty in which laws were suspended; rather the normalisation of the exception was achieved through a steady accretion of views that go largely unchallenged. The upshot is that a partial post-constitutional coma has occurred in which it is unclear whether the 'Law is King' or the 'King is Law'.

Such a phenomenon calls to mind the work of Carl Schmitt – one of the chief academic supporters of executive absolutism in Nazi Germany – and his infamous statement: 'sovereign is he who decides upon the exception' (Schmitt 1985: 5). He suggested that normal legal orders were entirely ineffective in combating dire crises. The technical complexities upon which they are premised – created through liberal constitutionalism – paralyses their capacity to make effective and vital 'friend/foe' distinctions. Schmitt believed that the defining question of politics was the distinction between friend and enemy, reminiscent of President Bush's observation that 'You are either with us or against us in the fight against terror'. In such a period, 'all legitimate and normative illusions with which men like to deceive themselves regarding political realities in periods of untroubled security vanish' (McCormick 1997a: 252) and the sovereign has a free hand to protect the community. The Hobbesian spectre of unchecked animosity motivates people to vest the state with the ultimate power of decision-making: to decide whether there exists a state of emergency and to decide what must be done to eliminate it. For Schmitt, the political sphere – with the mutually hostile relationship of friend and foe intrinsic to it – transcends and supersedes the legal sphere with its presumption to universalism. Political life cannot be bound by legal norms as it is the former that makes the latter possible. It is for the sovereign to decide whether the community is being threatened. This can only be done by recourse to a decision, motivated by an actual historical event, rather than a timeless legal norm. Law is subservient to politics and may need to be suspended so that politics can survive.

Schmitt suggests that throughout history states developed techniques that ignored standing constitutions and the strictures of formalised legal orders in times of emergencies. Liberal constitutionalism, according to him, has always largely neglected the functional necessity of such a phenomenon. In order to counteract extraordinary conditions such as invasion, insurrection, plague or famine, for example, states often in the past introduced emergency provisions that operated outside the parameters of normal legal relations. For Schmitt, these exceptional emergency provisions could be divided into two categories – *commissarial* and *sovereign*. The commissarial model was premised on a functional rationality that only permitted reliance on emergency measures when it was absolutely expedient to do so. The sole purpose of such measures was to facilitate the reimposition of the normal legal order. Once the specified crisis was averted, the emergency provisions were deemed superfluous and the *status quo ante* was restored. Procedural rules were in place that ensured a strict separation between the institution declaring the emergency and the one employing the extraordinary and exceptional powers under such conditions. Moreover, the operation of such powers was tightly circumscribed in terms of their duration and the objectives to be achieved. This approach to extraordinary powers champions the rule of law and constitutional order. Derogations in the form of extraordinary measures are strictly limited so as to maintain order, as far as practicable, within a rule of law/constitutional order framework (Dyzenhaus 1999: 39–98; McCormick 1997b).

The historical gold standard as regards emergency power that fell under a commissarial rubric is the classical Roman institution of dictatorship. In times of severe crisis, the Roman Senate would declare an emergency. Consuls were then requested by the Senate to appoint a dictator. Almost unlimited power was granted to the dictator to eliminate the emergency. However, in exercising such power, the dictator was strictly bound by *a priori* time and task-related limits, and the imperative to restore the regular legal order. A dictatorship, accordingly, that did not have the purpose of making itself superfluous under this model was considered 'random despotism'.

The sovereign model, on the other hand, the one favoured by Schmitt, takes the rule of law and constitutional order to be lifeless, and more oriented towards *discussions* rather than *decisions.* Antithetical to liberal values and human rights, it seeks to move towards a more absolute form of sovereignty in which the entire order between the sovereign and the emergency powers is made more seamless. The focus of this model is on permitting the state to react without legal restriction by creating a permanent condition of emergency that is not checked by duration or task. It specifically endorses the state's continuous right – through unchecked decisionism – to respond to unforeseen and unexpected occurrences in as efficient a manner as possible, free from the hindrance of excessive legal prescription. In such a political environment, the institutional distinctions between the decision to declare an emergency and the exercise of that power are collapsed (Scheureman 1993).

Though Ireland falls a long way short of the entirely post-constitutional order as depicted by Schmitt under this model, the continued maintenance of broad extraordinary decision-making powers that lift the subject out of the ordinary legally constituted order, as detailed above, and the lack of safeguards as regards their existence and employment, has meant, in part, that a conflation has occurred between the normal and extraordinary legal orders. The blind continuance of the Special Criminal Court, for example, calls into question the extent to which its presence is designed to preserve the constitutional order – by combating the specified threat and facilitating the restoration of the *status quo ante* – or to usurp it through abrogating the right to a jury trial.

Moreover, and though many of us may find Schmitt's naked endorsement of authoritarianism objectionable, his work can help us engage more with the mechanisms by which emergency or extraordinary situations are identified in Ireland, the separation that exists between the initiation of such powers and their exercise, the purpose of such powers (are they currently being employed to preserve or suspend the Constitution?), the checks on their operation, and the manner in which such powers are relinquished. It can also act as a stepping stone through which we can become more aware of the fragility of the rule *of* law and how it can be distinguished from rule *by* law, 'where the [latter] is taken to mean the use of law as a brute instrument to achieve the ends of those with political power while the [former] means the constraints which normative conceptions of the rule of law place on the instrumental use of law' (Dyzenhaus 2006b: 10). Many of the extraordinary measures employed in Ireland demonstrate rule *by* law tendencies. As Dyzenhaus notes:

> [The Rule of] Law … is not an autonomous constraint on actions but a constraint which those with political power will accept or not depending on their relative strength. If accepting the constraint is the only way elites can maintain the power they will, otherwise not. Not only is the choice to abide by the rule of law a matter of political incentives, the same is true of the choice to use rule by law to achieve one's ends. It follows that the weaker one's relative position, the closer one will find oneself to the normative, rule of law end of the continuum that stretches between rule by law and rule of law. One who is in a very powerful position will submit to ruling at various points away from the rule by law end of that continuum only when it is expedient to do so. (2006b: 10)

A recent ruling from the US Supreme Court, in the case of *Hamdan v Rumsfeld* (548 US 2006), shows the executive attempting to claim unfettered discretion in developing countermeasures against 'unlawful enemy combatants'. The Supreme Court contended that the military commissions established by the Bush government were illegal since they violated military law and the Geneva Convention. In the view of the majority of judges, while circumstances may have demanded an urgent response, they did not justify 'the wholesale jettisoning of procedural protections' and demanded that the Executive 'comply with the Rule of Law that prevails in this jurisdiction' (548 US 2006, 61, 72). The judges explicitly cited article 3 of the Geneva Convention, which states that sentences cannot be passed but by a 'regularly constituted court affording all the judicial guarantees which are recognized as indispensable by civilized peoples'. Of course, the court also insisted that it was simply maintaining that Congress had not given executive a 'blank check'. The Bush government could and did regularise proceedings by having the relevant legislation, the Military Commissions Act 2006, passed to enable the military commissions to function. This episode shows how a constitutional order can force the executive to trim its sails during the odyssey for emergency powers; that it also shows the vulnerability of rights only demonstrates the problems of maintaining liberties within a democratic order in which the wishes of the majority hold sway. However, the invocation of rights deriving from an international context shows how the perils of this particular sovereignty trap may be weakened if not broken. The next three chapters take up each of these three issues in turn.

## Chapter 5

# Entrenching the 'equality of arms' framework in the ordinary criminal justice system in Ireland

### Introduction

Following independence in 1922, and notwithstanding the shadow cast by the gunman, the political inclination in Ireland was to maintain the inherited social, economic and legal structures subsisting on the demise of the colonial state.[1] This meant that the 'ordinary' adversarial criminal trial – involving 'a contest morphology' that included oral presentation of evidence, cross-examination by counsel, relative 'judicial passivity' during the guilt-determining phase of the trial, and informational sources secured by both the prosecution and defence – became deeply ingrained throughout the twentieth century as the appropriate means of resolving criminal disputes (Damaska 1986: 88). It also meant that the ideological hegemony of liberalism, extolling the 'classical' negative need for citizens to be protected *from* the state but also the more positive need of citizens to be provided with an opportunity for self-realisation, gradually permeated most social, cultural and institutional strata. In the ordinary criminal realm, this ensured that standards of normative legitimacy – including the jury as a 'paradigmatic concept' and prophylactic procedural and evidential rules – were woven into the core of the ordinary pre-trial and trial process (Damaska 1975b).

More importantly, these common law and statutory standards also increasingly became fused with constitutional jurisprudence and more recently, and as we will see in greater detail in Chapter 7, with human rights jurisprudence.[2] Active judicial review, especially since the 1960s, has permitted the development of a great corpus of jurisprudence – constructing a 'meta-Constitution' – on the constitutional role in protecting the rights of the accused and on restricting state power.[3] In consequence, the ordinary criminal process has irradiated with assumptions and values that have emphasised the 'primacy of the individual', the subjection of state power to controls that have prevented it from 'operating with maximal efficiency', and a commitment to 'quality control that necessarily cut[s] down on quantitative output'.[4]

This chapter has two purposes. First, it seeks to demonstrate the ways in which the inculpatory model of justice continued to be assembled and reinforced in Ireland in the twentieth century. Indeed, with the expansion in safeguards for the accused, along with more entrenched protection through various constitutional and human rights provisions, the framework created came to be more properly described as a *due process* model of justice. This model was designed to offset the massive disparity in resources available to the state as ranged against the accused, and to protect the latter from abuses of power. Secondly, the chapter also seeks to demonstrate how these due process values and assumptions continue to resonate and compete for priority in the pre-trial, trial and sentencing compartments of the criminal process. The canopy of safeguards that has been created for those accused of crime has largely been marginalised and excluded in control talk – which only illuminates the dark side of the criminal complex – but it remains a formidable epistemic and practical force in Ireland. It is embedded in legal and judicial craft, if not in the public consciousness more generally, and tenaciously continues to shape conceptions and experiences of justice. Talk of its death, as was noted in another context, is greatly exaggerated.

In examining the embedded nature of these values in Ireland in this chapter, it will be necessary to travel to the swampy textual lowlands of common law, statutes, and various constitutional and human rights provisions, and judicial fidelity to same, so as to examine a broad sample of the anti-authoritarian safeguards that have been codified for those accused of crime. This will necessarily involve exposing the non-law reader to the tyranny of formalism and black letter detail in this section, which follows, unlike in previous chapters, a conceptual rather than a chronological form. Though broad and sometimes crudely descriptive, the analysis in this chapter is persevered with in the hope that it can serve the useful purpose of demonstrating the continued presence of due process values and commitments in Ireland.

In mapping out these safeguards there is, of course, the danger of over-idealising liberal constitutionalism and legalism, and of over emphasising the capacity of rights to act as a check on state power. It is undoubtedly true that many of the rights and safeguards discussed in this chapter are often contingent upon interpretation,[5] are inherently limiting, and do not always 'proactively direct the law making process' (Hunt 1998: 326). Too much reverence may also conceal the fact that 'juridical liberties' often sit side by side with – but in dissonant isolation from – more subtle mechanisms of domination and control, and indeed help mask them (Foucault 1991: 223).[6] Liberal rights and safeguards also have the capacity, as communitarians argue, to 'atomise' the legal subject at the expense of any responsibilities that he or she might have to the community (Hudson 2003: 78–108). It is not the intention of this chapter to over-idealise or eulogise about the safeguards that have been created for those accused of crime. The liberal ideology of legalism and constitutionalism is not without its problems. Nor is its hegemonic position as secure as it once was. This will become apparent later in the book when we discuss, among other things, the extent to which a more repressive 'logics of action' is taking hold through the persistent 'tooling-up' of the state in the fight against crime.

For now, however, the point being made is that the liberal ideology of legalism and constitutionalism has delivered, and continues to deliver, significant protections to those accused of crime that set some limits to the power of the state and the 'tyranny of the majority'. It has a power and a reach that remains significant and real. Its embedded nature offers more than token resistance to newly emerging, more control-oriented, orthodoxies. To dismiss it, or to afford it epiphenomenal status only (as 'law in books' or 'paper rules'), is to neglect its capacity to check power and to offer sustained and dogged opposition to the creation of a 'culture of control' society.[7] Its continued presence ensures that there is unlikely to be any sudden irruptive point in the trajectory of the Irish criminal justice system that moves us decisively in the direction of absolutist control. Any broad reconfiguration is more likely to be of the staccato kind, involving relatively rapid reversals in some areas, while encountering sustained resistance on others that will require much in the way of confrontation and negotiation.

## Pre-trial rights of the accused

The initial stages of the Irish criminal process are mainly anchored around the extensive array of powers of control and surveillance afforded to the Gardaí to investigate crime, apprehend suspects and gather evidence necessary to build a case and secure a conviction at trial. In this phase, the concept of *égalité des armes* is maintained by strict safeguards that apply to the exercise of such powers. To begin with, an accused person in Ireland has an unenumerated constitutional right to privacy and cannot be stopped from raising a question of the admissibility of evidence obtained in breach of that right, even if the breach reveals the accused's illegal purpose.[8] Furthermore, the liberty of the individual is guaranteed under article 40.4.1° of the Constitution.[9] This ensures that a person's movements can only be restrained on foot of specific common law or statutory powers. Such powers cannot be employed for any wrongful motive.[10] If an individual voluntarily assists the Gardaí with their investigations in a station, once he becomes suspected of the offence in question he should be arrested or informed of his right to leave the station at any time.[11] Summary arrest powers are also only exercisable on the basis that reasonable grounds exist for their employment. A person arrested must be informed of the factual basis for his arrest and the legal authority under which it is exercised.[12] If a person is arrested under the authority of an arrest warrant, he should be informed of this by the arresting Garda and the warrant should be shown to the person as soon as is practicable.[13] Upon an arrest, the arrestee must be conveyed to a Garda station as soon as reasonably possible,[14] or before a District Court judge so that he can be charged with the offence.[15]

Though members of the Gardaí have considerable powers to stop and question a citizen, there is generally no legal obligation on the person stopped to answer any questions posed.[16] Furthermore, Garda powers to stop and search can only be exercised if a suspicion exists that an offence has been or will be committed. If a Garda wishes to search a citizen under a relevant power, then the citizen should be informed that a search will take place, the basis for so doing,[17] and the legal power under which it is authorised.[18] If incriminating evidence is found upon a person following a lawful search, the Garda must arrest, caution and take the person into custody before questioning him further.[19] Without a warrant or permission, a Garda cannot enter the private dwelling of a suspect.[20] Even if the Gardaí have a warrant to enter a private dwelling such a power will be strictly interpreted by the judiciary.[21] Moreover, most search warrants are only issued by District Court judges or Peace Commissioners after receiving information under oath from a member of the Gardaí. Such a warrant can only be issued by a District Court judge sitting within the districts where the relevant premises are situated.[22] Furthermore, warrants can only be granted if the issuing authority is independently satisfied that reasonable grounds exist for the suspicion that a warrant is required.[23] This is to ensure that the issuance of such warrants by an independent authority is not merely a rubber-stamping exercise. Serious errors on a warrant – which go to the authority to issue the warrant in question – will render it invalid and any evidence obtained on foot of such a warrant will generally be inadmissible (Walsh 2002: 357–432).

In limited circumstances, the Gardaí can also detain an arrested person in custody without charge for the purpose of facilitating further inquiries.[24] Because the rights of an arrestee only become operational on his arrival in custody, it follows that there is an obligation on the Gardaí to bring him into custody as soon as is reasonably possible after his arrest.[25] The Member in Charge of the Garda station must also be independently satisfied that reasonable grounds exist for detaining the arrestee so as to properly investigate the offence.[26] If during his detention it becomes clear that there are no longer reasonable grounds for holding the arrestee in respect of the offence he was suspected of committing, he must normally be released immediately. Furthermore, should the arrestee be detained longer than the statutory maximum permitted period, he will be deemed to be in unlawful custody and the fruits of any evidence garnered during this period, such as a confession or an identification as a result of an identification parade, will be deemed inadmissible. Strict rules also apply about rearresting suspects who have been detained without charge and then subsequently released without charge.[27] Normally a suspect can only be rearrested for the purpose of being charged with the offence, or for further questioning because new information has come to light since the person's release and it has been authorised by a judge (Walsh 2002: 201–9).

Given that detention without charge constitutes a substantial encroachment on a person's liberty, extensive safeguards have emerged to protect suspects in Garda custody. These safeguards are designed to balance power relations in the Garda interview room and to ensure, as far as possible, the quality, integrity and legitimacy of the evidence emanating from such a detention. The safeguards attempt, therefore, to regulate Garda activity in the relatively hidden arena of the interview room, thus attempting to strike a proper balance between the community's right to investigate crime and the detainee's right to be fairly treated and not subjected to oppressive tactics.[28] The Criminal Justice (Treatment of Persons in Custody in Garda Síochána Stations) Regulations of 1987, for example, are applicable to all detained suspects in Garda custody. They relate, among other things, to the maintenance of a custody record for each person detained; the provision of meals, rest breaks and toilet breaks to an arrestee; the prohibition of ill-treatment of any kind; the provision of medical treatment; the provision of information on the offence for which the detainee has been arrested and his entitlement of access to a solicitor; the detainee's right to have another person informed of his detention; restrictions on the number of Gardaí who can interview a detainee at any one time; and provisions for the electronic recording of interviews in Garda stations.[29]

If the Gardaí breach any of these provisions, then a trial judge has a discretion to exclude any evidence obtained as a result of the detainee's detention.[30] The detainee will also benefit from the Judges' Rules, a body of nine rules originally formulated by the English judiciary in respect of interrogation practices.[31] These rules act as an important guide for a Garda when taking a statement from a detainee. A failure by a Garda to observe the rules may result in a trial judge exercising her discretion to exclude a confession made by a suspect.[32] In addition, bodily samples, such as blood or urine, can only be taken if there are reasonable grounds for suspecting the person has been involved in the commission of certain offences.[33] Consent is also required for more intimate samples such as blood or pubic hair, though a refusal of a suspect to give consent can be treated as corroboration of any evidence in relation to which the refusal is material. The sample may also need to be taken by a registered medical practitioner.

A person suspected of a crime also has a general right not to answer questions during Garda investigations and interrogations.[34] This is now constitutionally protected under article 38 of the Constitution[35] and under article 6 of the European Convention on Human Rights.[36] An accused must also be administered a caution to the effect that he is not obliged to answer any questions, but whatever he does say during questioning and interrogation may be taken down and used in evidence.[37] As a general rule, adverse inferences cannot be drawn as a result of an accused exercising his right to silence at the pre-trial stage.[38] There are numerous rationales for this right not to incriminate oneself, which, as we shall see in the next section, also includes the right not to give evidence at trial.[39] First, it is argued that the right not to incriminate oneself is premised on personal autonomy, on 'respecting the will of an accused to remain silent'.[40] It is also grounded in the right to privacy, a 'reflection of the common view that one person should so far as possible be entitled to tell another person to mind his own business'.[41] Thirdly, it is suggested that it is a corollary of the right to freedom of expression contained in article 40.6.1 of the Constitution.[42] Fourthly, it has been suggested that the right prevents the state from overly relying on the accused as a testimonial resource, thereby protecting the innocent. This rationale was adopted in the US case of *Escobedo v Illinois*[43] where Goldberg J, quoting Wigmore, stated as follows:

> Any system of administration which permits the prosecution to trust habitually to compulsory self-disclosure as a source of proof must itself suffer morally thereby. The inclination develops to rely mainly upon such evidence, and to be satisfied with an incomplete investigation of other sources. The exercise of the power to extract

answers begets a forgetfulness of the just limitations of that power. The simple and peaceful process of questioning breeds a readiness to resort to bullying and to physical force and torture. If there is a right to answer, there soon seems to be a right to the expected answer, – that is, to confession of guilt. Thus the legitimate use grows into the unjust abuse; ultimately, the innocent are jeopardised by the encroachments of a bad system.

Finally, some authorities suggest that the right not to incriminate oneself is closely aligned with the presumption of innocence,[44] and with the maintenance of a 'fair state-individual balance' which demands 'that the government seeking to punish an individual produce the evidence against him by its own independent labours, rather than by the cruel, simple expedient of compelling it from his own mouth'.[45]

Access to a solicitor while detained in Garda custody is also seen as a means of equalising relations between the accused and the state in the pre-trial process. The right is safeguarded by article 6(3)(c) of the European Convention on Human Rights.[46] It had previously been held in Ireland that an accused had a common law right of reasonable access to a solicitor while detained in such custody.[47] This right was deemed to be constitutional in origin in 1990.[48] A detainee also has the correlative entitlement to be informed of this right of access. If a detainee requests a solicitor while in custody, the Gardaí must make *bona fide* efforts to contact a nominated one.[49] If they choose a solicitor for the detainee where they know, or ought to know, that there will be a considerable delay in securing her attendance at the station, this will amount to a breach of the detainee's right to reasonable access.[50] Furthermore, once the solicitor arrives in the station, the detainee has a right, if requested, to immediate access with him or her. As part of this right of immediate access, the detainee must be permitted to communicate in private with the solicitor.[51]

Should any of these provisions be violated, the detainee will be deemed to be unlawfully detained and the fruits of any interrogation will be excluded so long as the breach of the constitutional right continues, unless it can be demonstrated that extraordinary excusing circumstances existed (McFadden 2002: 390; Butler 1993: 173). Furthermore, once a decision is made to charge a detainee with an offence, he must be brought before a court as soon as reasonably possible so as to determine whether he should remain in custody or be released on bail.[52] Any objections to bail on the grounds that the accused will evade justice – by not appearing for trial, intimidating witnesses or jurors, or tampering with evidence – or commit further offences while on bail must be supported by the evidence. Such objections 'cannot simply be made *in vacuo*, but when made must be supported by sufficient evidence to enable the court to arrive at a conclusion of probability' that bail should be refused.[53] Furthermore, the objections made to bail must be open to cross-examination by the accused.

The asymmetry that exists between the accused and the state is also observable in the different pre-trial disclosure obligations imposed on both parties. To begin with, the Supreme Court has declared that it is the duty of the Gardaí, 'arising from their unique investigative role, to seek out and preserve all evidence having a bearing or potential bearing on the issue of innocence or guilt'.[54] It is also well established that the prosecution must comprehensively disclose to the defence all the evidence that it has gathered in a case, including unused evidence that it will not adduce at trial 'and material evidence that would be helpful to the defendant'.[55] The accused, for the most part, is under no similar obligation to disclose information to the prosecution prior to trial given that it would infringe the privilege against self-incrimination (Mullan 2000: 174).[56] As Geoghegan J noted: 'Only the prosecution must show its hand. Subject to some modern statutory exceptions in relation to alibi evidence the defence is entitled to spring surprises and above all is perfectly entitled, pending the trial, to give no indication as to what issues might be raised.'[57]

## The trial rights of the accused

At the focal point of the criminal process, the adversarial trial, a number of procedural safeguards also exist for the accused (provided he has not pleaded guilty) in the contest that takes place between the prosecution and the defence. The 'diagnostic' procedural demand for accurate fact and verdict findings is circumscribed by the concomitant needs – now woven into the normative framework of the criminal process – to protect individual freedoms, check abuses of power and preserve basic fairness in state-accused relations (Ashworth and Redmayne 2005: 23–6). One of the primary building blocks designed to recognise the 'principled asymmetry' of government–citizen interactions in the criminal arena is the presumption of innocence (Roberts and Zuckerman 2004: 19). It demands that the state bear the burden of adducing sufficient evidence of all the elements of the offence charged against the accused, and that the guilt of the accused must be established beyond reasonable doubt. In practice this means that the accused does not have to account for his conduct or actions. He does not bear the onus of proving the circumstances that may reduce the charge against him or lead to an acquittal. All that is required is that the trier of fact is left with a reasonable doubt on some essential matter after the prosecution has been 'put to proof'. The normative legitimacy of this principle is rooted in the notion that a wrongful conviction is a deep injustice and a fundamental moral harm (Dworkin 1981). The procedural protection afforded by the presumption is designed to recognise that conviction constitutes public censure and, invariably, leads to a punishment. Innocent individuals need to be protected from this otherwise legitimate violence.

It is also a recognition of the huge disparity in resources between the state and the defendant and of the fragility of fact-finding at criminal trials (Ashworth 2006).[58] Thus in steering between the Scylla of acquitting the guilty and the Charybdis of convicting the innocent, the logic underpinning the presumption falls squarely within the latter camp. By allocating the 'risk of misdecision' to the state, the presumption acts as a foundational principle that affords the innocent (and sometimes the guilty) accused every possible chance to be acquitted (Ashworth 2006). It is an acknowledgement, in a democratic society that embraces the transcending value of the freedom and good name of every individual, that the social disutility of convicting an innocent citizen far exceeds the disutility of acquitting someone who is guilty (Ashworth 2006).

The English case of *Woolmington v DPP*[59] is generally regarded as the *locus classicus* in the field. In that case, Viscount Sankey LC, after embarking on a lengthy analysis of old legal authorities,[60] famously noted:

> Throughout the web of the English Criminal Law one golden thread is always to be seen, that it is the duty of the prosecution to prove the prisoner's guilt ... If, at the end of and on the whole of the case, there is a reasonable doubt, created by the evidence given by either the prosecution or the prisoner … the prosecution has not made out the case and the prisoner is entitled to an acquittal. No matter what the charge or where the trial, the principle that the prosecution must prove the guilt of the prisoner is part of the common law of England and no attempt to whittle it down can be entertained.

This common law position has been confirmed in a number of Irish cases.[61] More recently, it has also been elevated to constitutional status. In *O'Leary v The Attorney General*,[62] Costello J noted:

> It seems to me that it has been for so long a fundamental postulate of every criminal trial in this country that the accused was

> presumed to be innocent of the offence with which he was charged, that a criminal trial held otherwise than in accordance with this presumption would, prima facie, be one which was not held in due course of law … I have little difficulty … in construing the Constitution as conferring on every accused in every criminal trial a constitutionally protected right to the presumption of innocence.[63]

The accused also benefits from the presumption that knowledge of the wrongfulness of the criminal act (*mens rea*) is an essential ingredient in any determination of guilt. This presumption has been described as a 'silken thread in the fabric of the legal system ensuring a just process'.[64] The issue of the requirement of *mens rea* arose for consideration recently in Ireland in the case of *CC v Ireland and Others*.[65] Section 1(1) of the Criminal Law (Amendment) Act 1935 provided that any person who had carnal knowledge of girl under the age of 15 would be guilty of a serious offence, punishable by up to life imprisonment.[66] The accused, a 19 year old, was charged with four offences contrary to section 1(1) of the Criminal Law (Amendment) Act 1935. He admitted having consensual intercourse with a girl named in the charges but said that she had told him that she was 16 years of age when in fact she was only 14. The offence under section 1(1) of the 1935 Act, however, afforded no defence once the *actus reus* (the actual act) was established.

This derogation from the requirement of *mens rea* was traditionally justified under the utilitarian rationale that the legislation was designed to 'protect young girls, not alone against lustful men, but against themselves'.[67] Though such a provision had the potential to cause injustice in individual cases, it served the greater good because its '*in terrorem*' effect would prevent men from having sexual intercourse with young girls in circumstances where they did not know for certain that they were above the relevant age. Citing Canadian authorities, counsel for the accused in the case argued that the foundation of our criminal justice system did not rest on utilitarianism but on the precept that a 'man cannot be adjudged guilty and subjected to punishment unless the commission of the crime was voluntarily directed by a willing mind'.[68] The Supreme Court agreed, stating that the provision expressly criminalised the mentally blameless. This was intolerable under any 'civilized system of justice'. Hardiman J noted:

> It appears to us that to criminalize in a serious way a person who is mentally innocent is indeed to 'inflict a grave injury on that person's dignity and sense of worth' and to treat him as 'little more than a means to an end' … It appears to us that this, in turn,

> constitutes a failure by the State in its laws to respect, defend and vindicate the rights of liberty and to good name of the person so treated, contrary to the State's obligations under Article 40 of the Constitution.[69]

Accordingly, section 1(1) of the Criminal Law (Amendment) Act 1935 was declared to be inconsistent with the provisions of the Constitution. Following the decision, the legislature was forced to rush through the Criminal Law (Sexual Offences) Act 2006, which continues to make it an offence to engage in a sexual act with a child but now provides a defence for the accused if he can prove that he honestly believed that the child was over the relevant age.[70]

The Irish state also attempts to mitigate the imbalance in the equality of arms between the prosecution and the defence by paying for the legal representation of an impecunious accused. The provision of legal aid so as to afford the accused the opportunity to meet the prosecution case against him is seen as a requisite to the very existence of a fair trial. The Criminal Justice (Legal Aid) Act 1962 makes provision for free legal aid where it appears to the court that the accused's means are insufficient and that the charges are so serious, or the circumstances so exceptional, as to warrant legal representation paid for out of the public purse.[71] This right to legal representation, which was already safeguarded under article 6(3)(c) of the European Convention on Human Rights,[72] was accorded constitutional status in 1976 in the *State (Healy) v Donoghue* where O'Higgins CJ noted: 'Facing, as he does, the power of the State which is his accuser, the person charged may be unable to defend himself adequately because of ignorance, lack of education, youth or other incapacity. In such circumstances his plight may require, if justice is to be done, that he should have legal assistance.'[73] Moreover, the Irish Court of Criminal Appeal has accepted that a person's right to a criminal trial 'in due course of law' can be vitiated by the defective manner in which a legal representative conducts the defence.[74]

More generally, the principle contained in article 38 of the Constitution that no person shall be tried on a criminal charge save in 'due course of law' makes it mandatory that 'every criminal trial shall be conducted in accordance with concepts of justice, that the procedures applied shall be fair, and that the person accused will be afforded every opportunity to defend himself. If this were not so, the dignity of the individual would be ignored and the State would have failed to vindicate his personal rights'.[75] An accused facing criminal charges is possessed of a canopy of liberty rights under this broad constitutional provision. He cannot, for example, be tried retrospectively for infringements of the law which were not so at the date of their commission,[76] for an offence the ingredients of which are vague or indefinite,[77] or twice for the same offence.[78] Nor can he be punished unless he has been convicted of an offence recognised by law as a crime.[79] He also has the right to have the natural justice principle *nemo iudex in causa sua* applied to criminal proceedings,[80] to know what the charges are against him,[81] to have a proper opportunity to make a defence,[82] to have the trial proceed with reasonable expedition,[83] to ensure that any pre-trial publicity is not such as to create a serious risk of an unfair trial,[84] and to have his case heard in a properly constituted court.[85] Under Article 34.1 an accused person is also entitled, for the most part, to have justice administered in public.[86]

The accused also normally has a right to a jury trial in any case involving a 'non-minor' offence by virtue of article 38.5 of the Constitution.[87] In the Irish Supreme Court in the early 1980s, Henchy J stated:

> I am satisfied that the indissoluble attachment to trial by jury ... was one of the prime reasons why the Constitution of 1937 (like that of 1922) mandated trial with a jury as the normal mode of trying major offences. The bitter Irish race-memory of politically appointed and Executive-oriented judges, of the suspension of jury trial in times of popular revolt, of the substitution ... of summary trial or detention without trial, of cat-and-mouse releases from such detention, of packed juries and sometimes corrupt judges and prosecutors, had long implanted in the consciousness of the people and, therefore, in the minds of their political representatives, the conviction that the best way of preventing an individual from suffering a wrong conviction for an offence was to allow him to 'put himself upon his country,' that is to say, to allow him to be tried for that offence by a fair, impartial and representative jury, sitting in a court presided over by an impartial and independent judge appointed under the Constitution, who would see that all the requirements for a fair and proper jury trial would be observed ...[88]

A jury is ordinarily comprised of 12 persons from a pool broadly representing the community, but remains properly constituted provided it does not fall below 10 members. It is permitted to provide a majority verdict provided 10 members agree.[89] Under the Juries Act 1976, a person is eligible for jury service if he or she is over 18 and is less than 70, is entered on the Dáil register of electors, and is not ineligible[90] or disqualified.[91] A judge must warn the jury panel during the selection process that a panellist cannot sit on the jury if he is ineligible, disqualified, knows the parties involved, or would bring a partial or biased mind to the proceedings.[92] The accused, along with the prosecution, can challenge up to seven on the panel without having to show cause. Once challenged, the panellist is not entitled to sit on the jury. In addition, the accused, along with the prosecution, can also challenge any other panellist but must show cause.[93]

This constitutional right to a jury trial has been described in Ireland as a 'most important safeguard for the individual, a protection alike against the zeal of an enthusiastic executive or the rigidity of an ultra-conservative judiciary'.[94] Though a trial judge is always permitted to direct a jury to return a not guilty verdict, the converse is never true; a trial judge can never direct a jury to return a guilty verdict.[95] This issue arose for consideration recently in the Court of Criminal Appeal.[96] The accused, Padraig Nally, a 60-year-old man who lived alone in an isolated farmhouse, was charged with the murder of John Ward, a member of the travelling community. Nally – who had become extremely anxious about the possibility of being burgled and harmed by intruders – discovered Ward pushing open the back door of his house. He grabbed a single barrel shotgun and in the ensuing struggle Ward was shot once and beaten repeatedly across the head and upper body with a stick. As Ward limped away to the front gate of Nally's house, Nally reloaded the gun and shot him again, this time fatally. He then threw Ward's body into an adjoining field.

At trial, Nally pleaded self-defence. At the end of the evidence, however, counsel for the prosecution invited the trial judge to only permit the defence of self-defence to go to the jury in truncated form. Allowing a partial defence of self-defence to go to the jury would, it was argued, force the jury to find the accused guilty but would enable it to determine whether the killing should be reduced from murder to manslaughter. To permit, on the other hand, the full defence to go to the jury – thereby giving rise to the possibility of an acquittal – would be perverse having regard to the facts of the case. The trial judge, pressurised, as he later admitted, by the socially divisive nature of the case, agreed with this reasoning and instructed the jury that the full defence could not apply. By unanimous verdict, the jury found Nally not guilty of murder but guilty of manslaughter. On appeal, it was held that the trial judge's direction usurped the jury's ultimate power to return a verdict of guilty or innocent. The conviction was quashed and a retrial was ordered.[97] Even though a trial judge might believe that there is insufficient evidence to acquit the accused on the facts of a case, he or she has no power to pre-empt the jury's verdict by directing the members to return a guilty verdict. There exists therefore a power for a jury to be wrong in acquitting an accused. This was succinctly summed up in *People (DPP) v O'Shea* in 1982 (emphasis added):[98]

> The jury alone have the right to decide that the accused is guilty. Both judges and legislators have accepted that while a jury properly instructed by the trial judge have no *right* to bring in a verdict for the accused which is against the evidence, yet they have a *power* to do so; *and that the risks inherent in any efforts at controlling the exercise of that power would not be warranted.* The use of the power to err in favour of the accused is left to the consciences of the jurors. In any event, what may seem to judges to be a perverse verdict of acquittal may represent the layman's rejection of a particular law as being unacceptable. So it is that such verdicts have often led to reform of the criminal law.

An accused person is also protected by the fact that he cannot be called as a witness in his trial except upon his own application.[99] Nor can any adverse inference be drawn from his failure to give evidence in his own defence at the trial.[100] Indeed, in such circumstances, the jury must be expressly advised by the trial judge that the accused is not required to give evidence (McGrath 2005: 648–52). In addition, and as a general rule, the spouse of an accused is not a compellable witness for the prosecution. The modern rationale for this evidentiary rule is to promote marital harmony and preserve the institution of marriage.[101] Furthermore, and even though a spouse is compellable at the instance of the accused, any failure by such a spouse to give evidence on behalf of an accused cannot be the subject of any comment by the prosecution.

Given the right of an accused person to a fair trial under article 38.1 of the Constitution, a trial judge always has a general discretion to exclude prosecution evidence in circumstances where it has a propensity to cause unfair mischief to the accused.[102] Such evidence is excluded because its possible probative value is outweighed by its prejudicial effect on the accused – its capacity, for example, to be unreliable or to mislead a jury (Fennell 2003: 69). If such information was wrongly received in evidence at trial, it would be necessary to discharge the jury; a failure to discharge the jury may result in a conviction being quashed on appeal (McGrath 2005: 13). The recent case of *DPP v Wayne O'Donoghue* may serve as an illustration of this exclusionary rule of evidence. The case, which attracted massive media and public interest in Ireland, commenced on 29 November 2005 in the Central Criminal Court sitting in Cork. The accused, a 21-year-old man, was charged with the murder of his friend and neighbour, Robert Holohan, an 11-year-old boy. O'Donoghue was acquitted of the murder, but pleaded guilty to his manslaughter. He received a four-year prison sentence.

After the trial and conviction of O'Donoghue, it came to light that semen was found on the hand of the victim. The mother of the victim, in the course of a victim impact statement, stated: 'Our doctors have told us to get on with our lives but how can we, knowing that there was semen found on my son's body' (*Irish Times*, 25 January 2006: 1). It appears that a sample of this semen was taken by the state pathologist at a post-mortem of the victim and was sent for analysis to the Forensic Science Service laboratory in Yorkshire, England. Using a DNA testing technique called low copy number (LCN) – which enables matches to be found from very few sample cells – a forensic expert tested the swab taken from the victim's palm and compared it with a DNA sample taken from the accused. This expert concluded that the likelihood of the DNA sample coming from anyone other than the accused was one in 70 million.[103] This was a crucial finding by the expert and, as a result, the Director of Public Prosecutions charged the accused with murder. This finding would have been probative evidence that would have been adduced in examination in chief by the prosecution.

Some time later, however, and before the trial, the Gardaí also sent the same forensic expert samples of material taken from a bathroom mat where the victim had lain as the accused tried to revive him after strangling him outside the house. The expert carried out LCN testing on the mat and concluded that it also contained semen. Crucially, however, the expert held that this sample from the mat was not identical to the semen from the victim's hand. This led him also to revise his first analysis and he declined to give a statistical likelihood of the semen belonging to anyone other than the accused. In these circumstances, and though the evidence was still probative, the DPP did not tender the evidence at trial, given that it might undermine the accused's right to a fair trial, thus jeopardising the prosecution case. The effect of adducing such evidence at trial would have been out of proportion to its true value, given that it would have prejudiced the accused by making it very difficult for a jury to adopt an even-handed view of the facts. In sentencing the accused, the trial judge stressed that he had not taken this prejudicial evidence into account.

The Irish courts also have a long history of approaching certain categories of prosecutorial testimonial evidence with caution. For example, in any proceedings where the prosecution case is based wholly or substantially on accomplice testimony, the trier of fact must clearly bear in mind and be warned that it is dangerous to convict solely upon this uncorroborated evidence.[104] This is designed to safeguard against the danger of an accomplice fabricating or exaggerating culpability against the accused (Healy 2004: 150; O'Connor 1982b: 12). Similarly section 10 of the Criminal Procedure Act 1993 requires a mandatory corroboration warning requirement in any case on indictment where evidence of an uncorroborated confession is tendered by the prosecution.[105] It is also well established that visual identification evidence must be treated with circumspection. Given its shortcomings in terms of evidential accuracy – as numerous false-positive identification cases demonstrate[106] – Irish courts have attempted to provide direction for fact-finders on the need for caution before convicting on identification evidence, and on the need to have regard to the specific quality of the identification evidence (Carey 1999: 69; Lambert 2000: 11).[107]

The exclusionary rule in respect of hearsay evidence has also become firmly entrenched in Irish law.[108] This rule operates potentially to exclude some highly probative evidence. It provides that a witness may not testify as to the words spoken by a person who is not produced as a witness at trial, if the evidence is offered to prove the truth of the facts that it asserts (Ashworth and Pattenden 1986). The testimony, to be received, must be made orally by the maker of the statement in the trial of the accused. The rationale for excluding hearsay evidence flows from the absence of a number of procedural safeguards:[109] as to oath since the person making the statement is not present at the trial to testify; as to opportunity of the trier of fact to observe in the witness box the demeanour of the person who made the statement; and as to opportunity to cross-examine the maker of the statement by the party adversely affected by it (McGrath 2005: 216).

Indeed this latter procedural safeguard – the right of a party adversely affected to be allowed to cross-examine his accuser or witnesses for his accuser – is a constitutionally enshrined right under article 38.1 of the Irish Constitution,[110] and is also recognised under article 6(3)(d) of the European Convention on Human Rights. The hearsay rule can appear extremely harsh particularly when it mechanically[111] excludes what appears to be reliable and probative evidence that should be admitted for consideration. However, its foundation in fairness of procedures, especially the accused's right to test vigorously the prosecution case against him, means that any attempt to relax it significantly will be viewed as tipping the balance too far against the accused, thus breaching the Constitution and the ECHR. As regards cross-examination more generally, it is also the case that the trial judge should refrain from over-interfering in the conduct of the case, lest she make it impossible for the defence to cross-examine a prosecution witness properly and effectively, or convey the impression of a lack of impartiality to the jury or accused. Judicial interference of this kind may constitute grounds for quashing a conviction.[112]

It is also an exclusionary rule in Ireland that the previous bad character or convictions of an accused cannot be adduced at trial by the prosecution.[113] This rule is designed to protect the accused from 'no smoke without fire' type reasoning – that those with bad reputations or previous convictions have a greater propensity than others to commit crime. It has been held that using past misconduct or reputation as a proxy for helping to determine the merits of a criminal charge undermines the right of an accused to a fair trial and runs counter to 'the basic concept of justice inherent in our legal system'.[114] The danger is that such evidence might create a reasoning fallacy whereby too much significance is attributed to previous misconduct or reputation for which the accused is not being tried (Lloyd-Bostock 2000; Murphy 1998: 71). Current normative legal standards demand that the probative value of adducing such information – and bad character evidence and previous criminal records are often manifestly probative (Redmayne 2002: 684) – is outweighed by its possible prejudicial effect on the accused. An accused, for the most part, can only be tried on the criminal acts with which he is charged, not on the suspicions generated by a Kafkaesque trawl through his life that reveals his propensity to be *a* 'bad man' rather than *the* 'bad man'.

The accused, like any other party, also benefits from the privilege that attaches to communications with his lawyer at any time when that communication involves the giving or receiving of legal advice.[115] The right to communicate with a lawyer in an uninhibited and confidential manner is now regarded by the Irish courts[116] and the European Court of Human Rights[117] as a key element in the proper administration of justice (McGrath 2001: 126). The information disclosed during such communications need not be revealed, however probative it may be in discovering the truth about a crime. As succinctly expressed by Knight-Bruce LJ in *Pearse v Pearse*:[118]

> Truth, like all other good things, may be loved unwisely – may be pursued too keenly – may cost too much. And surely the meanness and mischief of prying into one's confidential relations with his legal adviser, the general evil of infusing reserve and dissimulation, uneasiness and suspicion, and fear into those communications which must take place, and which, unless in a condition of perfect security, must take place uselessly or worse, are too great a price to pay for truth itself.

Evidence obtained as a result of official illegality is seen as 'fruit of the poisonous tree' in Ireland and usually cannot be produced against an accused in court. This has the effect, of course, of impeding the truth-finding function of the trier of fact by preventing highly probative and relevant evidence from being adduced at trial. The criminal will often therefore 'go free because the constable has blundered'.[119] Specifically, any evidence obtained as a result of a 'deliberate and conscious' breach of constitutional rights will be inadmissible save in extraordinary excusing circumstances;[120] such circumstances would include 'the imminent destruction of vital evidence or the need to rescue a victim in peril'.[121] The doctrinal basis for this exclusionary rule is premised on three considerations (Ashworth 1977: 723; Martin 1992: 1). First, it is founded on a vindication of constitutional rights, such as the right to liberty, inviolability of the dwelling, and access to a lawyer. As was noted in *People (AG) v O'Brien*,[122] 'the vindication and the protection of constitutional rights of the citizen is a duty superior to that of trying such citizen for a criminal offence'. Secondly, it also has an instrumental aim of promoting institutional compliance on the part of the Gardaí. By excluding probative evidence obtained as a result of unconstitutional conduct, it sends a signal to 'those in authority over the crime prevention and detection services of the state to consider in detail the personal rights of the citizens as set out in the Constitution, and the effect of their powers of arrest, detention, search and questioning in relation to such rights'.[123] Finally, it is argued that to admit unconstitutionally obtained evidence at trial would provide judicial *imprimatur* for the conduct that produced the evidence. This would bring the administration of justice into disrepute and would breed contempt for the rule of law. It is suggested therefore that 'it is a less evil that some criminals should escape than that the Government should play an ignoble part'.[124]

A recent example of a high-profile case where a breach of an accused's rights led to the exclusion of very probative evidence was *People (DPP) v Brian Curtin*.[125] In August 2001 the Gardaí received information from Interpol about a search of a premises in Fort Worth, Texas, which revealed details of alleged customers of a company offering access to child pornography websites. The Gardaí commenced an operation (Amethyst) in relation to Irish persons allegedly identified as customers of the American company. One such alleged customer was a Circuit Court judge, Brian Curtin. On foot of a seven-day search warrant provided for under the Child Trafficking and Pornography Act 1998, the Gardaí conducted a search of his house on the afternoon of 27 May, 2002 and seized his computer, along with other materials, which allegedly contained images of child pornography. He was charged with knowingly having in his possession child pornography. At trial, however, counsel for the accused contended that the fruits of the search were inadmissible as evidence as they had been obtained in breach of his constitutional rights.

It appears that the search warrant itself was issued at 3.20 on 20 May 2002 and had a lifespan of seven days including the day of issue. Thus the warrant was only acted upon on the eighth day and had, unknown to the Gardaí, expired when the search of the house was carried out. This breached the accused's constitutional right to inviolability of the dwelling under Article 40.5. The question for the court was this: what were the consequences of the search warrant being spent when it was acted upon? The court ruled the evidence contained on the computer was inadmissible as it had been obtained in breach of constitutional rights. The accused, accordingly, was acquitted. Though the exclusion of such evidence may benefit an 'undeserving applicant',[126] it was, the court recognised, 'an anomaly which the system would have to tolerate'.

The courts are also conscious of the dangers of over-reliance on the suspect as an inculpatory source. This is not surprising given that confession evidence is such a powerful and compelling weapon in making the state's case. In order to protect the moral legitimacy and the integrity of the criminal justice system and to minimise the risk of an innocent person making a false self-incriminating statement, a number of safeguards have been set down about the reception of such evidence.[127] First, the statement must be voluntary in the sense that it has not been procured either 'by fear of prejudice' or 'hope of advantage'.[128] It is the state that bears the burden of proving beyond reasonable doubt that any inculpatory statement it wishes to adduce in evidence was voluntarily made.[129] Furthermore, if a confession is obtained in breach of the constitutional rights of the accused – including rights to privacy, bodily integrity, liberty and reasonable access to a lawyer – then the fruits of the violation will ordinarily be excluded at trial. Finally, the courts also retain a 'residual discretion' to exclude a confession if it does not accord with basic or fundamental fairness of procedures (McGuckian 1999). As noted by Griffin J in *People (DPP) v Shaw*:[130] 'The reason for exclusion here is not so much the risk of an erroneous conviction as the recognition that the minimum standards must be observed in the administration of justice.'

## Post trial: the sentencing and appeal stages

At sentencing stage, a number of safeguards also exist for the individual found guilty of criminal misconduct. It is clear, for example, that where a sanction is to be selected for a person found guilty at trial, it is a matter solely for determination by the judiciary and not by the legislature that has prescribed the range of penalties. Any encroachment upon the exercise of this power would be struck down on the basis that it would unconstitutionally interfere with judicial independence and the doctrine of the separation of powers. As was noted in *Deaton*, 'the individual citizen needs the safeguard of the Courts in the assessment of punishment as much as in his trial for the offence'.[131]

An offender is also constitutionally entitled to individuated justice. In *People (DPP) v WC*, for example, the accused pleaded guilty to raping his girlfriend on 31 December 1991. Both the accused and the victim had been in a relationship for five months. Though acknowledging that the offence of rape was one of the most serious on the criminal calendar and that it would be rare for a prison sentence not to apply to anyone found guilty of the offence, the trial judge determined that a suspended sentence of nine years was appropriate in the circumstances. He grounded his decision on the constitutional principle of proportionality, which made it clear that 'the imposition of a particular sentence must strike a balance between the particular circumstances of the commission of the relevant offence and the relevant personal circumstances of the person sentenced'.[132] The individual circumstances that persuaded the judge not to impose a prison sentence included the following: his youth, his lack of previous convictions, his good family background, the unlikelihood of further criminal misconduct, his early guilty plea, the level of remorse shown, his manifest intention to rehabilitate himself in society, the character evidence of witnesses, and favourable reports from a consultant psychiatrist and the probation service. As such Irish courts, when faced with a convicted person for sentence, adopt an individualised approach (treat 'different-cases-differently intuition') whereby the 'the sentence to be imposed is not the appropriate sentence for the crime, but the appropriate sentence for the crime because it has been committed by the accused'.[133]

It is also the case that a convicted person has the right to be punished only in accordance with the law existing at the time the offence was committed.[134] He also has a constitutional guarantee of procedural fairness in sentencing proceedings including the right to make a plea in mitigation[135] and the right to know the reasons for a sentencing decision.[136] Furthermore, an individual cannot be sentenced in respect of offences with which he was neither charged nor convicted and a trial judge is not permitted to speculate as to what other charges may have been brought.[137] Nor can an individual convicted of an offence be sentenced to any punishment that is too wide or indiscriminate.[138] There is also a lack of reciprocity between the prosecution and the defence in terms of the submissions that can be made regarding the appropriate sentence. While the defence is afforded considerable latitude to make such submissions, the prosecution generally refrains from offering any view as to what the appropriate sentence is in any particular case.[139] Finally, there is also a general lack of symmetry between the state and the accused in the appeal process following a criminal trial. If the accused is acquitted, the state has no general right of appeal,[140] whereas if the accused is convicted, he is allowed to appeal that conviction.[141]

## Conclusion

In Chapter 3 we documented the emergence of a number of the constituents of the modern criminal process including the state monopolisation of investigative and prosecutorial functions; the lawyer-isation of the trial process; an increased emphasis on certainty, proportionality and safeguards for the accused; and the gradual phasing out of 'justice as accommodation'. This chapter has sought to demonstrate how these values and policy choices – particularly as they relate to those accused of crime – became more embedded in Ireland's criminal process throughout the twentieth century. Facilitated by constitutional rights jurisprudence, we have witnessed a gradual concretisation of the rights of the accused. This process is still, to some extent, ongoing. For example, the presumption of innocence, the right to silence, the privilege against self-incrimination, the right of access to a lawyer, and the right to proportionality in punishment were all only given constitutional status in the 1990s at a time when many western jurisdictions were meant to be experiencing more control-oriented justice and streamlined pain delivery. Moreover, the European Convention on Human Rights, affording another level of protection for those accused of crime, was only incorporated into Irish law in 2003, albeit at a sub-constitutional level.

The institutionalised nature of these accused rights has ensured that they cannot be easily 'trumped' for collective policy reasons such as security and public protection (Dworkin 1977: 93–4). They remain very much part of the topography in the criminal process, carrying a 'threshold weight' (1977: 92) 'which the government *is* required to respect case by case, decision by decision' (Dworkin 1988: 223). This is particularly true of the cases involving possible or actual sexual misconduct that have been highlighted in this chapter. The judgments in *Curtin* (the right to have unconstitutionally obtained evidence excluded), *CC* (the right not to be criminalised for mentally blameless conduct), *O'Donoghue* (the right to have evidence excluded because its possible probative value is outweighed by its prejudicial effect on the accused), and *WC* (the right to individuated justice) all demonstrate the continued resonance of accused rights, and their capacity to continue to compete for priority and act as a counterpoint to the supremacy of the paradigm of control. An explicit appeal to crime control alone cannot therefore give meaning to all events and decisions in the Irish criminal justice system.

Of course in recent years it is arguable that Ireland has also witnessed the emergence of many crime control tendencies in its approach to serious offending. In relation to sexual offences, this includes increases in the maximum sentences available for sexual assaults, the introduction of a tracking system with notification requirements, civil provisions for the making of sex offender orders, mandatory obligations to provide employers with information on previous sexual offences in certain circumstances, a lack of treatment programmes, and a failure to release an individual after the law upon which he was found guilty had been declared unconstitutional (Kilcommins *et al.* 2004: 149).[142] In a sense, and as we shall see more fully in Chapter 6, a focus on Ireland's approach to serious offences like those involving sex offenders reveals a contradictory duality at play between the embedded nature of older modernising commitments and newer orthodoxies of control, security and public protection.

The problem with discourse on the control elements inherent in the criminal justice system is that it takes for granted the privileged, unifying position of public protection and security over the rights of those accused of crime. There is a tendency in such dystopian discourse to accept unconditionally the arrival of 'unvarnished authoritarianism', and the notion that 'protection *from* the State' has been replaced by 'protection *by* the State' (Garland 2001: 12; Feeley and Levine 2001). In painting this picture of the criminal process, control theorists concentrate almost exclusively on legislative function (acting upon policy considerations) and ignore the sometimes conflicting narrative of judicial craft (very often acting in 'hard cases', upon 'principle' and the protection of rights against governmental interference). Both are qualitatively and functionally distinct (Dworkin 1977: 82–92).[143] The significance of the distinction should not be underestimated, particularly in jurisdictions that accept that constitutional and human rights jurisprudence are higher up the hierarchical pecking order than parliamentary legislation. As Packer noted about the distinction:

> Because the Crime Control Model is basically an affirmative model, emphasising at every turn the existence and exercise of official power, its validating authority is ultimately legislative (although proximately administrative). Because the Due Process Model is basically a negative model, asserting limits on the nature of official

> power and on the modes of its exercise, its validating authority is the judicial power and requires an appeal to supra-legislative law, to the law of the Constitution. (Packer 1968: 173)

Control theorists have a tendency to elide the two in presenting this perceived drift towards more absolutist control.[144] In doing so, they fail to appreciate that arguments of policy, specifying what is perceived to be in the public interest, are normally the concern of the legislature, not the judiciary. Moreover, they also fail to appreciate that it is the provisions of the Constitution and judicial interpretation of same (and to some extent the European Convention on Human Rights) rather than the concerns of the legislature that are the overriding word in any dispute about the rights of the accused.[145]

Of course, in suggesting this, we should be very wary of pursuing a progressive agenda that views the judiciary with rose-tinted glasses, as the infallible protectors of rights. It is true, as we noted in the introduction to this chapter, that judges can, on occasion, engage in policy-making and interpret facts, principles, rules and rights in ways that support populist sentiments and control-oriented goals.[146] This will become more apparent in Chapter 6. But even in recognising this, we should still not close ourselves off from the continued appeal of constitutionalism, legalism, human rights, the internal logic of law and judicial craft, all of which remain strongly imbricated in the cross-currents of the Irish criminal justice system.

As far as Ireland is concerned, but one suspects this to be true more generally, control narratives are too unidirectional and one-dimensional, underplaying the embedded constituents of the criminal process. They have a tendency to do violence to the complexities being analysed, and engender a false and partial picture of the justice system.[147] We need to remain sensitive to the various nuances of the criminal process, its ideological functions and the different forms of knowledge upon which it is based. These nuances ensure to some extent that the culture of control society is only partially realised and not fully implemented. Nor at this juncture should they be seen as the dying sting of the modernist wasp, a preliminary step before the presentation of the culture of control society as a *fait accompli*. They are not simply insignificant anachronistic residues tossed up by the juggernaut of control as it bulldozes the edifices of modern criminal justice in Ireland. They remain deeply embedded and will require much in the way of negotiation at national and supra-national levels.

# Chapter 6

# Disaggregated justice

## Introduction

In previous chapters we outlined the various threads of the modern inculpatory model of justice. These threads include the emergence of a Leviathan state that monopolised investigative and prosecutorial functions and displaced its previous personalised and localised traits. It also includes the active embracement of adversarialism, the establishment of a fair state–individual balance, and the development of a process of 'criminalising abstraction' that emphasised egalitarianism, universalism and the rule of law. The key constituents of this justice network have been woven into the Irish criminal process in somewhat piecemeal legal fashion over the last 150 years. By the early twenty-first century, and keeping in mind the long past of state–accused relations, it can be said that a broad shadow has been cast by liberal assumptions and values – especially as common law and statutory principles became reinforced and expanded upon by constitutional and human rights jurisprudence – about the rights of the individual accused and the need for freedom from the tyranny of majoritarianism and executive arbitrariness. This logic remains deeply embedded in the justice system and continues to possess considerable epistemic and normative force.

In the past decade in Ireland, however, the hegemonic, unifying position of this model of justice has come under closer scrutiny. The justice system increasingly appears to be pulled in a variety of different directions by forces acting above, below and at state level. What is clear is that it is being renegotiated and reconsidered at various points. In this chapter we document how the delicate equilibrium between freedom from government and public protection is being unsettled by an anxious state determined to show strength by 'tooling up' in the fight against crime. Recent attempts at diluting due process rights appear semiotically designed to demonstrate to the public that something is being done about law and order, however ineffective the long-term results of such reforms will be. In addition to the normalisation of extraordinary laws, which we have previously looked at, and the tooling up of the state in the fight against ordinary crime, the renegotiation points also include the diffusion of the state into the civil sphere as a means of crime control, the criminalisation of regulatory arenas, and the accommodation of more stakeholders in the criminal process.

Justice in the early twenty-first century is thus becoming more disaggregated and more contradictory. It is more principled but also more repressive, more instrumental but also more expressive. It involves more normative legitimacy for rights-based discourse,[1] but also more normalisation of the 'sites of exception'. It continues to emphasise protection *from* the state, but increasingly also protection *by* the state. It is more inclusionary in seeking to accommodate victims, witnesses and local communities but also more exclusionary through, among other things, the expressive tone adopted in respect of offenders and those accused of crime. It embodies more authoritarianism but also more pluralism. It is more supra-national but also more local, more statist but also more globalised. It continues to emphasise adversarialism, but also encourages executive fact-finding and guilt determination in non-court settings. It involves more monopolised criminal control but also more fragmentation and blurring of boundaries. It is more focused on the poor and socially excluded but it also appears to be directing its gaze at white-collar crime. In this chapter we document the variety of ways in which the hegemonic dominance of the modern model of justice is being re-examined and renegotiated.

## Re-balancing state–accused relations

Ireland, as we have seen, has a long history of relying on emergency powers to combat the threat posed by paramilitarism on the island. This tradition of invoking extraordinary laws and creating special zones where normal laws do not apply has facilitated the partial advance of a crime control model of justice. In particular it has facilitated the creation of an environment where the public has become habituated to the employment of a crime control model of justice for paramilitaries and amenable – however fragile the evidence – to a similar instrumental logic of repression on the grounds of security being employed in the ordinary sphere. At the same time the 'normal' laws themselves, which increasingly only apply to low-risk groups of offenders, are often unconditionally championed as evidence of our unceasing commitment to civil liberties, human rights and due process concerns.[2] But even these civil liberties, as we shall see in this section, are not safe from reconfigurations that subtly tip, in accordance with dictates of efficiency, the state–accused balance more in favour of the former.

To begin with, recent changes in the law of search and seizure bear testimony to the current prioritisation being given to 'tooling up' the state and the concomitant hydraulic decline in the value placed on the primacy of the individual and limiting official power. The un-cuffing of the Gardaí in this regard is evident, for example, in the number of statutes that now permit search warrants to be issued internally by senior Garda officers in 'circumstances of urgency'. This more self-substantiating process circumvents the need for judges or peace commissioners to be independently satisfied that reasonable grounds exist for the crossing of thresholds.[3] It is also evident in the enactment of so-called 'hot pursuit' provisions that enable Gardaí to enter onto private property without a warrant when they are pursuing a suspected offender, diluting somewhat the sanctity of the inviolability of the dwelling as provided for in article 40.5 of the Constitution;[4] the authorisation of very broad Garda powers to seize any material in the circumstances of effecting a search;[5] the expansion in the number of bodily samples that can be taken without consent by the Gardaí;[6] and the introduction of far-reaching powers under the Criminal Justice Act 1994 in relation to drug trafficking and money laundering that provide for the issuance of access orders and search warrants against innocent third parties, such as solicitors and financial advisers, who may possess materials and documents that relate to suspected offences.[7] The Gardaí are also increasingly beginning to rely on more sophisticated methods of investigation that encroach upon the privacy rights of individuals and the sanctity of previously privileged relationships. These include the use of 'information reporters' such as banks, building societies, auditors and solicitors who are required to report various unlawful activities or suspicious transactions of their clients to the state;[8] the use of mass surveillance such as CCTV;[9] and the requirement that telephone companies and internet service providers retain data on their customers for the purposes of assisting the Gardaí with their investigations.[10]

The past 20 years has also witnessed dramatic increased powers of detention for the Gardaí. For example, the 1984 Criminal Justice Act made provision for the first time for the detention of 'ordinary suspects' for a maximum of 12 hours. Prior to this, the purpose of an arrest for an ordinary crime was to secure the suspect's presence in court. Provision had already existed in the terrorist domain for detention without charge.

Under section 30 of the Offences against the State Act, 1939, a suspect could be detained for a maximum of 48 hours without charge. The Offences against the State (Amendment) Act 1998, introduced following the Omagh bombing, extended this period of detention by a further 24 hours, when necessary. Returning to ordinary crime, under section 2 of the Criminal Justice (Drug Trafficking) Act 1996, an individual may be detained for a cumulative total of seven days on suspicion that the person has committed a drug-trafficking offence. The Leahy Report in 1998, drawing heavily on existing terrorist provisions, recommended extending the standard maximum period of detention (12 hours) to 24 hours, with provision for a further 24-hour period, if necessary, for certain specified offences such as murder, manslaughter, kidnapping and rape.[11] Section 9 of the Criminal Justice Act 2006 extends the maximum period of detention for ordinary, though serious, crime from 12 to 24 hours. There is thus a trend towards expanding the duration of pre-trial detention in Ireland. 'The whole centre of gravity of the criminal process', as Walsh has noted, 'is moving rapidly away from the open public forum of the court and into the private closed demesne of the police station' (Walsh 2005a). The same author noted: 'Increasingly guilt will be determined by executive processes in the closed secrecy of the police station rather than by judicial processes in the public transparency of the courtroom. Judicial territory is being ceded to the police to achieve a further streamlining and bureaucratisation of the criminal process' (2006: 4–5). Unfortunately, this trajectory has never been justified or framed in empirical terms – when, for example, does the legitimate tactic of interrogation reach a point of diminishing returns? Such concerns are amplified by a number of related issues.

First, the system has increasingly demonstrated a complacent attitude to the right of a detained suspect to have access to a lawyer. This right of access is worth further consideration given that it is one of the most basic of all procedural fairness rights. The legal and constitutional right to reasonable access to a lawyer is well established in Ireland.[12] Such a prophylactic requirement, however, has been narrowly construed so as to mean that a detained suspect only has a right of access to his or her solicitor for one hour during every four to six hours of detention. Moreover, and provided the Gardaí have made *bona fide* attempts to contact a solicitor, they are entitled to question the detained suspect. Even if contact is made with a solicitor, and assuming that she is available to come to the station, there is nothing to prevent the Gardaí questioning the detained suspected in the interim period before the solicitor's arrival. Moreover, even when the solicitor presents herself at the station, she is not entitled to sit in on the interrogation – the right to reasonable access does not extend to have a solicitor present during the interrogation. Nor is the solicitor entitled to have an audio-visual recording of the interviews (assuming they are available) or to see the interview notes during her client's detention. The stark lack of protection afforded to a detained person regarding access to a solicitor – and narrow judicial and Garda constructions as to what constitutes reasonable access – raises, as one commentator noted, questions about the commitment of the institutions of the Irish state 'to the protection of basic human rights and to the dignity of its citizens as human persons' (White 2000: 17).[13] Increasingly, the presence of a solicitor in a Garda station is seen as an internecine impediment to the pursuit of the truth rather than as a vital safeguard designed to dispel the compelling atmosphere inherent in the interrogation.

Secondly, significant inroads have also been made into the pre-trial right to silence. Sections 18 and 19 of the Criminal Justice Act 1984, for example, allow adverse inferences to be drawn from an accused's failure to account for objects, marks, or substances in his or her possession, and a failure to account for one's presence at a place at or about the time a crime was committed, respectively. Similarly section 7 of the Criminal Justice (Drug Trafficking) Act 1996 enables inferences to be drawn from a failure to mention certain facts when questioned which are later relied upon in defence at trial. All of these inferences have corroborative value only.[14] As noted in Chapter 4, the seminal case in Ireland on the right to silence is *Heaney v Ireland*. Unlike the High Court, which located the right in the guarantee of a fair trial under article 38.1 of the Constitution, the Irish Supreme Court held that the right to silence is but a corollary to the right to freedom of expression under article 40 of the Constitution. If the latter right could be qualified, so too could the former. Aside from finding a constitutional locus for the right to silence in a weaker, more 'collective' rights domain, thereby permitting its abrogation on a wider basis, the Supreme Court went on to note that where a person was 'totally innocent of any wrongdoing … it would require a strong attachment to one's apparent constitutional rights not to give such an account when asked pursuant to statutory requirement'.[15] The notion that the right to silence is one in which an accused is guaranteed the right to remain silent unless he chooses to speak in the unfettered exercise of his own will is clearly undermined by the judgment in *Heaney*. Increasingly, the perception has emerged – echoing Benthamite and Posnerian reasoning[16] – that the innocent are the only persons for whom the egregious right could never be useful or advantageous. Along the way, the reified, purer form of the right, and the rationale underpinning it, has been replaced by the vapid notion that it is the 'first refuge of the guilty' (Healy 2004: 415). This is also borne out in a recent submission by the Gardaí to a Joint Committee on Justice, Equality, Defence and Women's Rights:

> The present status of the right to silence is an historical relic and harks back to a previous age when suspects were deemed to be of limited intelligence. It is untenable that in serious crimes such as murder and rape, theft or fraud, suspects can refuse to disclose their whereabouts when questioned and courts cannot draw inferences from this. It is not a question of compelling anyone to speak but rather informing the court of a refusal and empowering it to draw inferences and take appropriate note.[17]

Thirdly, there appears to be growing evidence of Garda malpractice (this is more fully documented in the next chapter). Such evidence includes:

- Threats and inducements by the interviewing Gardaí in the Paul Ward case, an individual who was suspected of the murder of Veronica Guerin.
- The alleged insertion of false information by two detectives into the notes of interviews with Colm Murphy, a person suspected of having been involved in the Omagh bombing in 1998.
- The miscarriage of justice perpetrated on Dean Lyons, a homeless drug addict, who has died subsequently, who was wrongfully charged in 1997 with a double murder after signing a false confession.
- The Morris Tribunal, established in March 2002 to investigate serious complaints of Garda abuse in Donegal including hoax explosives and bomb-making equipment finds, allegations of harassment and extortion, and abuses in custody.
- Claims of Garda mistreatment by the European Committee for the Prevention of Torture after visiting Ireland in 1993, 1998 and 2002.

Despite such Garda abuses,[18] there remains a strong commitment to 'thickening' the maximum periods of detention in Ireland, while also 'thinning out' the prerequisites surrounding the interrogation particularly as regards the rights to silence and access to a solicitor. Moreover, and aside from the extension of Garda powers of detention that facilitate the determination of guilt by executive rather than judicial processes, the executive itself has also been increasingly empowered to dispense 'low visibility justice' and encourage citizens to avoid traditional adversarial justice through the use of on-the-spot fines, penalty points and fixed penalty notices for certain offences. Although this emphasis on bureaucratisation and executive convenience is not necessarily always repressive, it does constitute evidence of the reconfiguration that is taking place in certain areas of the justice system (Walsh 2006: 8–9).

Furthermore, the system has witnessed the reduction in age for criminal responsibility in children for certain offences (from 12 years to 10 years),[19] and an expansion in the range of hybrid offences which, at the option of the prosecutor, curtail the right of an accused to a jury trial (Hamilton 2004: 158). It has also witnessed the introduction of a very broad (and vague) new offence under section 72 of the Criminal Justice Act 2006[20] of knowingly contributing to or participating in any criminal activity of a criminal organisation for the purpose of enhancing its ability to commit or facilitate a serious offence, whether in or outside the state.[21] The Irish Council for Civil Liberties has suggested that this provision is 'at odds with the Irish Constitution which protects individuals against the operation of vague and uncertain criminal laws. If the Gardaí believe someone is a member of a criminal gang, then they should use traditional investigation techniques such as surveillance.'[22] Indeed the Minister for Justice, Equality and Law Reform conceded that a successful prosecution for the offence 'will almost certainly require one of the participants in a criminal organisation to act as a supergrass' (Dáil Debates, 28 June 2006, vol. 622 col. 1323). Acceptance of such an approach to gathering information for the prosecution of offences under section 72 increases the risk of jeopardising the entire criminal process by admitting evidence that is highly susceptible to fabrication and exaggeration, and often incapable of being properly verified.

The issue of the right to bail has also become more contentious in recent years. It had been thought, as we noted in a previous chapter, that it would be unconstitutional to refuse bail simply on the ground that the applicant might commit further offences.[23] In *Director of Public Prosecutions v Ryan*,[24] Walsh J noted: 'The criminalising of mere intention has been usually a badge of an oppressive or unjust system.' A refusal of bail, accordingly, was only justified on two grounds: (a) where there was a possibility that the accused might abscond; (b) where there was a likelihood that the accused might tamper with evidence or interfere with witnesses. Following a bail referendum in 1996, the grounds for refusing bail have now been widened to include the commission of a serious offence (O'Higgins 1998).[25] This implicit recognition that public protection should trump an individual's liberty interests moves the bail laws out of the realm of merely ensuring the integrity of the judicial process and into the domain of legitimating preventive detention – and the consequent limitations on the presumption of innocence – on the basis of forecasted but unconsummated offences.

Moreover, the hallowed notion that proof beyond reasonable doubt is among the essentials of due process and fair treatment has now also begun to look a little hollow. The crystallisation of a legal burden of proof into a beyond reasonable doubt formula was, of course, designed to impress upon the prosecution the need for something approaching a state of certitude given the consequences at stake for the individual accused and the values at play in a free society. It was premised on the bedrock value determination that the *false negative* error (that guilty individuals should go free) was far outweighed by the *false positive* error (that innocent individuals be convicted). The notion that some innocent people might become enmeshed in the nets that ensnared the guilty was thought too unpalatable for free and democratic societies. Though the 'golden thread' principle has long been accepted in Ireland, small cracks have begun to appear in the form of judicial interpretations of statutory 'reverse onus' provisions. In *O'Leary v Attorney General*, Costello J noted:

> The Constitution should not be construed as absolutely prohibiting the Oireachtas [the Irish legislature] from restricting the exercise of the right to a presumption of innocence … It seems to me that the Oireachtas is permitted to restrict the exercise of the right because it is not to be regarded as an absolute right whose enjoyment can never be abridged.[26]

Finally, a partial reorientation of the structural properties governing sentencing has become evident in Ireland. There is increased evidence of attempts being made to reduce the art of sentencing in Ireland – which up to recently was relatively unstructured (O'Donnell 2000; O'Malley 2006a: 53) – to a Procrustean formula that mechanically fits punishment to crime. Increases in the maximum penalties allowed by statute for various types of offences, calls for sentencing policy to be founded on just deserts, provision for the Director of Public Prosecutions to appeal unduly lenient sentences imposed on conviction on indictment, and increased control of groups of offenders such as under the Sex Offenders Act 2001 all signpost the changes occurring in sentencing practices (Kilcommins *et al.* 2004: 142–201). Moreover, a scheme of presumptive sentencing was provided for under the Criminal Justice Act 1999.[27] The Act created a new offence (now section 15A of the Misuse of Drugs Act 1977) of possession of controlled drugs worth €13,000 or more with intent to supply. A person convicted of the new offence, other than a child or young person, would be sentenced to a term of at least ten years unless there were exceptional circumstances that would permit a derogation.[28]

Section 82 of the Criminal Justice Act 2006 creates the new offence of importation of controlled drugs of €13,000 or more (now section 15B of the Misuse of Drugs Act 1977). This offence also carries the ten-year presumptive sentence. Moreover, when the courts are considering if there are exceptional and specific circumstances to warrant a lesser sentence than ten years for these drug offences, they are now permitted to consider if the accused has a previous conviction for a drug-trafficking offence, and whether the public interest in preventing drug trafficking would be served by the imposition of a lesser sentence. The Act also provides that where a person, other than a child or young person, is convicted of a second or subsequent offence under section 15A or section 15B, or is convicted of a first offence under one of these sections and already has a conviction under the other, the court must specify a straight minimum sentence to be served of at least ten years.[29] Notification requirements, broadly similar to those used for sex offenders, have also been introduced under part 9 of the Criminal Justice Act 2006. These requirements relate to those convicted on indictment of drug-trafficking offences who have been sent to prison for more than a year.[30] The 2006 Act also introduces presumptive minimum and mandatory minimum sentences for firearms and related offences.[31] Increasingly, therefore, the demand for more mechanical justice and fixity of purpose in sentencing in Ireland requires that the severity of the punishment match ever more closely the seriousness of the offence. As Garland (2001: 120) noted:

> The shift of sentencing policy towards mandatory penalties, sentencing guidelines and just deserts … has the effect of focusing attention firmly upon process and away from outcome. When sentencing becomes merely the application of pre-existing penalty tariffs, it loses much of its former social purpose. It shifts away from the older framework in which sentencers aimed to bring about a social outcome – the reduction of crime through individualised sentencing – to one where the key objective (fitting the punishment to the offence) is well within the capacity of the courts, and much less likely to fail.

## Reconsidering the balance

The exigencies of law enforcement in Ireland, from what we have seen in this section, is showing some signs of drifting in the direction of an 'assembly line' model of justice in which the state–individual balance is increasingly tipped in favour of the former. This has been achieved by dismantling some of the previous 'ceremonious rituals' that cluttered up the process of justice and the search for truth (Packer 1968: 159). All of the changes are grounded in the need for greater public protection and security. So, for example, when the Offences Against the State Review Committee recently argued for the retention of the non-jury Special Criminal Court, it did so on the basis that the threat posed by organised crime alone is sufficient to justify its maintenance. No qualitative or quantitative evidence was provided; nor did any comprehensive debate take place as to whether such crime tipped the balance in favour of enhancing security or preventing the loss of liberties.[32] Much of the reasoning behind retaining the court was premised on the notion that 'there have been instances in recent times where it appears that attempts have been made to tamper with juries in high-profile criminal trials in the ordinary courts'. Permitting a permanent state of exception to envelop the constitutional right to a jury trial on the paltry nature of such consequentialist evidence seems to cast doubt on the very notion of the actual right. As Dworkin noted:

> those constitutional rights that we call fundamental … are supposed to represent rights against Government in the strong sense … I must not overstate the point. Someone who claims that the citizens have a right against the Government need not go so far as to say that the State is *never* justified in overriding that right … What he cannot do is to say that the Government is justified in overriding a right on the minimal grounds that would be sufficient if no such right existed. *He cannot say that the Government is entitled to act on no more than a judgment that its act is likely to produce, overall, a benefit to the community. That admission would make his claim of a right pointless, and would show him to be using some sense of 'right' other than in the strong sense necessary to give his claim the political importance it is normally taken to have.* (1998: 191–2, emphasis added)

On the other hand, the needs of public protection and security are of course 'essential goods', necessary for our self-preservation, well-being and happiness. They must be factored in to any consideration of the right to a jury trial. Interference with jury decision-making, for example, would threaten these goods by impairing the ability of citizens to enjoy the fruits of fair justice and public order. For these reasons alone, such occurrences must be considered in the context of security and the need to enable justice to take place in an environment that is free from the threat of injury or harm. Public protection and order are objectives, as Ashworth has noted, 'that we should all support, because what we want for ourselves, our families, our friends and indeed our fellow citizens is to be able to flourish in our lives without risk of assaults on our persons or property' (2004a: 516). In some respects the ideology of liberal legalism and constitutionalism seems ill-fitted to contend with the social and cultural transformations that have taken place in recent decades, particularly the long-term increase in crime rates that jeopardises our ability to flourish in our lives. As Loader (2006: 581) has noted:

> Liberal elitism made sense in, or was at least fitted to, a world where crime was less prevalent an act and more settled as a cultural category; a world where people evinced trust and deference towards social authority and had more patient expectations of government; a world marked by greater equality and solidarity and less ambient precariousness and insecurity. Such an outlook speaks less well to a society where crime has become a recurrent feature of everyday life; where the anxieties and demands it generates are widely and excitedly disseminated by the mass media; where reduced levels of trust in the institutions of government coincide with heightened public demands of them; where consumerism threatens to eclipse citizenship as the organizing political principle – and symbol of belonging – of the age.

In such an environment, there are solid reasons why the constitutive tenets of liberal legalism and constitutionalism should at least be revisited and challenged. Recently in Ireland, however, there clearly has been a drift towards a *micro* focus on technologies of protection and the repression of particular instances of criminal conduct at the expense of more *macro* analysis of how protection and security can best be maintained in a society that continues to respect individual rights. We need, as Hudson notes, 'to balance the description and analysis of the strengthening and deepening penetration of governance in the name of providing security, with the Enlightenment elaboration of theories of justice and boundaries of legitimate authority which … set limits to governance' (2001: 146).[33] The common currency now in Irish political, media and prosecution circles is that restrictions on due process rights will enhance security in keeping with the needs of the majority of good-living, decent Irish folk. As the Minister for Justice Michael McDowell recently suggested: 'Time and time again one hears repeated voicing of disquiet that the rights of society to be protected take second place in the quest to ensure fairness to the suspect – in other words that the balance has shifted too far in favour of the accused. I believe this is a legitimate concern which must be addressed' (Dáil Debates, 15 February 2005, vol.

597, col. 1276).[34] Indeed, in setting out his intention to establish a committee to consider how the criminal justice system might be rebalanced, the same minister, in a speech in Limerick in October 2006,[35] noted:

> I want … to raise the possibility that we, as a society, must now face up to difficult questions, not as a substitute for good and effective policing and criminal investigation, but as a means of ensuring that the scales of justice are held evenly between those who would break the law and those who would uphold it, between the accused and the prosecutor and between the criminal, the victim and the community.

The minister went on to suggest that in looking at the imbalance, particular attention should be given to the right to silence,[36] character evidence,[37] the exclusionary rule, modifications of the double jeopardy rule, the need for greater obligations to be imposed on the accused to disclose his defence to the prosecution before presenting it in court at the trial, and the need to expand the role of the prosecutor at sentencing stage.

Many of the arguments in favour of rebalancing, however, though strong on utility, expediency, 'othering',[38] emotional narratives of risk and safety (Hudson 2003: 73),[39] and appeals to common-sense authoritarianism and simple majoritarianism, are weak on evidence-based criteria and broader considerations of strategy implications. Is there, for example, and to paraphrase Ashworth, a simple hydraulic nexus between hardening the rules against those accused of crime and better protection of victims and citizens? Will a deliberate strategy of punitiveness better guarantee security? How much protection for individual citizens can the criminal justice system actually provide? Are their other mediums, such as those involving employment, education and housing, through which crime prevention can be orchestrated? (Ashworth 1996). To what extent can the right to security 'trump' other individual rights? When does this reified notion of security stop being a utility and start being a disutilty?[40] How much of our own social security depends on other considerations such as education, health, employment, transportation and the environment? How prepared are we to channel resources away from these areas into crime control? To what extent can rights secured by justice be subject to 'political bargaining or to the calculus of social interests'? (Rawls 1999: 3–4; Zedner 2005). In assuming that the majority of Irish citizens place little value on freedom from lengthy pre-trial detentions, downward pressures on standards of proof, restrictions on the right to silence, and increased powers of detention, is it correct to suppose that a clear demarcation exists between the criminal minority and the law-abiding majority?[41] Though the *'external preferences'* of Irish citizens may be for the assignment of more powers to the Gardaí against those accused of crime, are these also their *'personal preferences'* for themselves? For example, though the Gardaí have repeatedly called for more powers in the fight against crime, the very due process rights that they seek to dismantle against those accused of crime are also employed by them on occasion when the finger of suspicion is pointed at their own members. As P. J. Stone, General Secretary of the Garda Representative Association, noted about the Gardaí under investigation as a result of the Morris Tribunal findings: 'It is acknowledged that a small number of people have sullied the good name of the force *but these people have also to be dealt with according to due process and constitutionally afforded the right of every other citizen to account for their actions*' (*Irish Times*, 21 June 2005, p. 14, emphasis added). Such considerations are rarely, if ever, teased out.[42] Instead, justifications for the trade-off are purchased through the claim that the benefits of increased security will exceed and should trump lost freedom – this claim, more often than not, is buttressed by reference to the needs of the 'silent majority' of Irish people, and the hubristic assurance that the 'innocent have nothing to fear'.

Moreover, this erosion of institutional restraints and balances appears to be carved out on the back of political expediency, as a means of 'governing through crime' (Simon 1997).[43] The neo-conservative image of a strong sovereign state has been promoted and maintained in Ireland through, in part, the valorisation of law as a panacea for serious criminal ills. Increasingly the criminal law is viewed as the perfect conduit through which to direct collective and righteous demands for vengeance. The grammar of the law itself easily accommodates such a function. In keeping with its 'classical' genealogy, it has for the most part remained autonomous in orientation and has remained closely tethered to the formulaic individual subject – *homo juridicus* (Lacey 2001).[44] Whenever security or order is threatened within the state, it is almost always coercive law that is the medium called upon to provide a solution. This is all very much part of the 'acting out' strategem described by Garland. As he notes (2001: 134):

> Policymaking becomes a form of acting out that downplays the complexities and long-term character of *effective* crime control in favour of the immediate gratifications of a more *expressive* alternative. Law making becomes a matter of retaliatory gestures intended to reassure a worried public and to accord with common

sense, however poorly those gestures are adapted to dealing with the underlying problem.

The intense outrage produced by certain crimes, coupled with the demands for the state to reassert its power through the criminal justice system, has resulted in the rise of more repressive penal laws – premised on control rather than readjustment – that draw ever clearer lines between a fearful public and 'monstrous' criminals.

The collapse of the Liam Keane trial in the Central Criminal Court, for example, in November 2003 brought such a phenomenon in to sharp focus. The 19-year-old accused in the case had been charged with the murder of Eric Leamy. The Director of Public Prosecutions, however, directed that a *nolle prosequi* be entered after six prosecution witnesses denied making statements identifying the accused as being the man who stabbed the murder victim. The collapse of the trial, and the two-fingered salute given by Keane to the waiting press as he left the court, immediately led to claims about a 'crime crisis'; suggestions that the 'fabric of society … [was] at risk'; calls for more 'anti-terrorist type laws' ; and a recognition by the Taoiseach that the Gardaí 'cannot take on a crowd of gangsters with their *peann luaidhes* [pencils]' (*Irish Times*, 6 November 2003, pp. 6–7). Such claims signify the extent to which policy-makers in Ireland have recognised the capacity of criminal law to act as a catharsis for public anger and disquiet. Indeed, and as a direct consequence of the Liam Keane trial, part 3 of the Criminal Justice Act 2006 now makes provision for the admission of statements relating to arrestable offences before trial as proof of the truth of their contents.[45] Previously such out-of-court statements could only be admitted for the limited function of undermining the credibility of a witness, not to prove the truth of their contents.[46] This limitation was rooted in the traditional view that such statements 'suffer from the classic hearsay dangers of fabrication, distortion, mistake, misperception and inaccuracy', along with the fact that the part adversely protected is denied various procedural protections afforded by the adversarial process (McGrath 2006: 1).

A Meadian analysis of such developments would no doubt note that the law acts as a forum through which an 'emotional solidarity of aggression' can be expressed by the *conscience collective*. As Mead (1918: 590) notes: 'the majesty of the law is that of the sword drawn against the common enemy.'[47] In times of perceived crisis, calls are made for the sword to be sharpened – having been dulled by a liberalist agenda – so as to strengthen the solidarity and dominance of the group over the individual. This is particularly important in Ireland at a time when it is experiencing an identity shift from being a relatively homogeneous

Catholic society to a more fluid, heterogeneous mix of diversity.[48] Repressive laws directed at the outside 'enemy' (Radin 1936; Sparks 2006: 34) remain a glue that binds in a milieu that has witnessed the loss of many traditional solidarity identifiers.[49] Punishment, as Mead (1918: 580–1) suggests, 'provides the most favourable condition for the sense of group solidarity because in the common attack upon the common enemy the individual differences are obliterated'. From a political perspective, achieving an emotional and populist solidarity through more punitive laws that exclude the criminal *from the group* – however anodyne the impact long term of such laws on public protection – appears far less risky and requires far less commitment and justificatory evidence than a 'reconstructive attitude' that focuses on including the criminal *within the group* (through supportive policies on housing, employment, health, child care, etc.).[50] It is within this 'acting out'/'emotional solidarity of aggression' paradigm that we should begin to see the 'tooling up' of the state in Ireland and the dismantling of equality of arms provisions.

### 'Civil'ising crime

The employment of criminal law as the monopoly mechanism for dealing with deviant behaviour is also beginning to fragment and blur. In particular, the diversification and diffusion of the state into the civil sphere as a means of crime control is becoming more visible in Ireland. This move away from the traditional condemnatory 'prosecution-conviction-sentencing' approach to deviant behaviour may to some extent be seen (through a benevolent lens) as a willingness to move beyond the harsh consequences of criminalisation (Ashworth 2004b). It seems more likely, however, that the recent embrace of civil measures is more closely connected with the perceived ineffectiveness of the criminal law mechanism. The principled protections of the criminal process – premised on a criminal sanctioning model of justice – can more easily be circumvented by directing the flow of power into this parallel system of civil justice. Though this phenomenon is rapidly occurring, our due process defences have remained static, firmly fastened to the place inhabited by criminal law. They remain enmeshed in the fixity of definition and are incapable of contending with the plasticity and fluidity of the flow of power into civil spaces.[51]

Perhaps nowhere is this ruse of placing sanctioning powers in the civil rather than criminal realm more palpable than in relation to the enactment of measures by which the proceeds of crime can be confiscated. As we have already discussed, the Proceeds of Crime Act

1996 authorises the confiscation of property in the absence of a criminal conviction; permits the introduction of hearsay evidence; lowers the threshold of proof to the balance of probabilities; and requires a party against whom an order is made to produce evidence in relation to his or her property and income to rebut the suggestion that the property constitutes the proceeds of crime (McCutcheon and Walsh 1999). This practice of pursuing the criminal money trail through the civil jurisdiction – thereby immunising the state from the strictures of criminal due process embodied in the Irish Constitution – raises all sorts of civil liberty concerns about hearsay evidence, the obligations of discovery, the burden of proof, the presumption of innocence, and the redefinition of justice as the extraction of ill-gotten revenue. Moreover, and given the revenue-producing capacity of the Criminal Assets Bureau (CAB), the temptation, as Lea notes, 'to displace concerns of justice with those of revenue flows cannot be ruled out' (2004b).

Furthermore, under section 5 of the Criminal Assets Bureau Act 1996, CAB is also required to ensure that the proceeds of criminal activity or suspected criminal activity are subjected to tax.[52] In raising a tax assessment, CAB, in fully applying the Revenue Acts to the proceeds of criminal activity, has considerable powers to require a taxpayer to furnish details of earnings and assets,[53] and to obtain orders freezing monies and assets.[54] The taxpayer has 30 days within which to appeal the assessment.[55] Before an appeal can take place, however, the taxpayer must pay an amount of tax not less than the amount that would be payable on foot of his/her own tax returns.[56] Non-payment of this tax within the 30 days renders the assessment by CAB final and conclusive (Gallagher 2003).[57] In challenging the assessment, the question of whether or not the profits or gains were the result of criminal activity must be disregarded. Once the assessment becomes final and conclusive, CAB can then seek to enforce the assessment under various statutory powers. It may also seek to exercise the powers that it operates in conjunction with the DPP in relation to the criminal prosecution of revenue offences (knowingly or wilfully failing to make returns, or making incorrect returns).[58] In light of the strengthening of revenue powers and their far-reaching nature, the Revenue Powers Group (2003: 109–15) recently called for 'key restraints' on the use of such powers and for the need to enhance the protections and safeguards for taxpayers.[59] No rebalancing has, however, taken place and CAB appears to have come to rely more on its powers to tax than its power to seize the proceeds of crime, the former not requiring a seven-year period before finality, or causing the same complications with regard to third party rights (Considine and Kilcommins 2006).

Concerns about CAB's powers to seize and tax are counterpoised by the simple legal appeal to the civil as opposed to criminal design of the provisions. This reasoning, which has judicial *imprimatur*, is to some extent, however, an exercise in obfuscation. As was noted in another context: 'merely redefine any measure which is claimed to be punishment as regulation and, magically, the Constitution no longer prohibits its imposition'.[60] It is difficult to dislodge the perception that such devices permit the Irish state to achieve late-modern criminal justice goals – public protection, targeting, non-inflammatory stigmatisation, and threat neutralisation – in a more 'jurisprudentially unconstrained' civil setting (Zedner 2006: 1–19).

Such measures might best be described as falling under a schema of *criminal administration*, a cost-efficient form of legitimate coercion that jettisons the orthodox safeguards of *criminal law* (the requirements of criminal guilt,[61] proof beyond reasonable doubt, obligations of discovery in criminal proceedings, proportionality to offence seriousness, and the presumption of innocence), but continues to embody criminal indicia including the moral opprobrium associated with the prohibited conduct and the capacity of the measures to stigmatise. In addition to the absence of safeguards, this schema also, however, displays another important difference from the traditional criminal law. Provisions that seize or tax the proceeds of crime are not designed to reorientate human behaviour or to reintegrate those that are deviant. Instead, their focus is more 'apersonal' in orientation (albeit with the sanctioning potential to stigmatise and exclude), which is not surprising given that they are applied *in rem* rather than in *personam*. They are tailored to sweep up the material proceeds of the crime rather than fit the broad range of individuated circumstances of wrongdoers. They transform 'person punishment into threat neutralisation, and criminal law into criminal administration' (Dubber 2002: 150).

The introduction of anti-social behaviour orders under the Criminal Justice Act 2006 offers further evidence of this civilising strategy. It too can be viewed as a 'regulatory-disciplinary' approach to crime prevention that criminalises through 'the back door of civil injunctions' (Scraton 2004). The Act, *inter alia*, gives power to the Gardaí to issue a behaviour warning (which will remain in force for at least three months) to adults (under part 11) and to children (under part 13) who have behaved in an anti-social manner. As regards adults, there is no requirement that a member of the Gardaí must have witnessed the anti-social behaviour. Indeed the warning can be issued at any time within one month of the behaviour taking place.[62] Failure to comply may result in a senior member of the Gardaí applying to the District Court for an order prohibiting the person from engaging in certain defined behaviour (which can remain in place for a maximum period of two years). Such an order will be granted on the civil standard of proof (without the protections that normally apply to criminal proceedings), but breach of the order will constitute a criminal offence. Anti-social behaviour itself is defined in vague and very broad terms,[63] giving rise to the potential for arbitrariness, net widening and the promotion of exclusion (Kilkelly 2006: 185–7; Ashworth 2004b). As Walsh (2006: 10–11) argued about the employment of such orders for adults:

> Arguably the police are being used as a proxy to extend the reach of the criminal process into territory that traditionally had been the preserve of the civil process. Although they are a constituent element of the criminal process, they will be imposing severe restraints on the freedom of the individual to engage in behaviour which was not, is not, and probably never will be, criminal. It is tantamount to the development of a quasi-criminal process under the control of the police. For those affected it will appear as if they are being treated as criminals without the benefit of the traditional process. Their liberty is restrained not by reference to the publicly promulgated standards of the criminal law, but by what an individual member of the Garda deems to be anti-social behaviour. Moreover, the decision to impose the restraint is rooted in the low visibility exercise of executive discretion by a police officer on the ground, rather than in the public transparent environment of a court chaired by an independent judge.

Furthermore, we are increasingly witnessing the employment of civil standards by criminal courts. These include provisions for the imposition of sex offender orders where there are *reasonable grounds* for believing they are necessary; provisions for the refusal of bail where it is *reasonably considered necessary* to prevent the commission of further offences; provisions for the imposition of notification requirements on drug-trafficking offenders where the *interests of the common good so require*;[64] and provisions for the confiscation of a criminal assets post conviction on the *balance of probabilities*. These are all indicative of increased support for a risk management standard, premised on efficiency rather than certainty, as opposed to a more traditional criminal standard that placed a premium on accuracy and was designed to afford individuals every possible benefit of law. Such measures are no longer driven by respect for due process values and civil liberty safeguards that guarantee some element of parity between the state and defendants in the criminal arena.

Instead they are organised around a desire to maximise efficiency, enhance control and minimise risk.

## The rise of the regulatory Irish state

In examining the contours of the penal complex, criminologists and penologists are often drawn to traditional 'real crime' (homicides, violent assaults, organised crime, sexual offences, requirements of *mens rea* and *actus reus*, and general defences) while ignoring regulatory offences that are often enforced by specialist agencies. They have tended to be preoccupied with the punitive regulation of the poor – a project closely tied to a police-prisons way of knowing – that focuses on 'crime in the streets' rather than 'crime in the suites' (Ashworth 2000; Braithwaite 2003: 7). The narrow exclusivity of this approach is a mistake because regulatory criminal law is becoming increasingly influential, not least because criminalisation is now more than ever viewed as a panacea for almost any social problem (Mann 1992: 1798). More and more we are witnessing the increasing and extensive use of regulatory strategies by the Irish state. In areas such as competition law, environmental protection, health and safety law, and consumer and corporate affairs, there has been a move towards using criminalisation as the last-resort strategy when compliance through negotiation and monitoring has failed.

Distinctions have traditionally been drawn between regulatory crimes and ordinary crimes on the basis that the former are *mala prohibita* (prohibited wrongs) and the latter are *mala in se* (moral wrongs). Regulatory crimes, it was suggested, should be thought of in 'instrumental means-ends terms', as not embodying quasi-moral 'values such as "justice, fairness, right, and wrong"' (Lacey 2004: 145). They were viewed as a 'quasi administrative matter' that did not attract significant moral opprobrium or stigmatise those convicted (McAuley and McCutcheon 2000: 341).[65] It has also been argued that regulatory crimes are more likely to be victimless (or at least not have a readily identifiable victim). Thirdly, and as noted above, it is suggested that regulatory offences for the most part do not embody a punitive or sanctioning model of justice, preferring instead to favour compliance strategies.

There are a number of interesting characteristics about the current use of these regulatory strategies in Ireland. First, the emergence of this regulatory criminal framework is significantly different from the unified monopolies of centralised control underpinning policing and prosecution in the modern state. Arguably these new techniques and strategies can be seen as part of a pattern of more (rather than less) governance, but taking 'decentred', 'at-a-distance' forms. Prior to the nineteenth century, the institution of local policing was heavily oriented towards the 'creation of an orderly environment, especially for trade and commerce' (Braithwaite 2005: 13–14). It did not focus exclusively on offences against persons and property, but also included the regulation of 'customs, trade, highways, foodstuffs, health, labour standards, fire, forests and hunting, street life, migration and immigration communities' (Braithwaite 2000: 225). Throughout the nineteenth century, however, and as we noted in a previous chapter, the state very gradually began to monopolise and separate the prosecutorial and policing functions, particularly for serious crimes. In terms of policing, this meant the following:

> Uniformed paramilitary police, preoccupied with the punitive regulation of the poor to the almost total exclusion of any interest in the constitution of markets and the just regulation of commerce, became one of the most universal of globalised regulatory models. So what happened to the business regulation? From the mid-19th century, factories inspectorates, mines inspectorates, liquor licensing boards, weights and measures inspectorates, health and sanitation, food inspectorates and countless others were created to begin to fill the vacuum left by constables now concentrating only on crime. Business regulation became variegated into many specialist regulatory branches. (Braithwaite 2005: 15–16)[66]

Similarly, and as noted earlier, during the course of the nineteenth century conflicts were no longer viewed as the property of the parties most directly affected. Previously strong stakeholder interests in the prosecution process, such as victims and the local community, were gradually colonised in the course of the nineteenth century by a state apparatus that acted *for* rather than *with* the public.

Now, however, the Office of the Director of Public Prosecutions is, to some extent, increasingly losing its monopoly role. The number of administrative agencies that have entered the criminal justice arena, colonising the power to investigate regulatory crimes in specific areas and to prosecute summarily, has increased dramatically in Ireland in recent years. They include the Competition Authority, the Director of Consumer Affairs, the Environmental Protection Agency, the Health and Safety Authority, and the Office of the Director of Corporate Enforcement. Significantly, the agencies have *both* investigative and prosecution functions, with each pursuing their own agendas, policies and practices. All of this represents more criminal regulation by the state (as well as of the state), rather than any 'hollowing out' of the state (Braithwaite 2005: 26). This enlargement in scope, however, is fragmented in nature, occupying diverse sites and modes of operation. Despite extensive powers to share information, there is no unifying strategy across the agencies or with other law enforcement institutions such as the DPP or Gardaí. Staffing levels, resources, workloads and working practices vary from agency to agency. Indeed, and apart from respective annual reports, there is little in the way of an accountability structure overseeing the policy choices of the various regulatory agencies, the manner in which they invoke their considerable investigative and enforcement powers, or the way in which information is shared between them and with the Gardaí.

Secondly, many aspects of regulatory crime operate in opposition to the general trend of paradigmatic criminal law which permits general defences, demands both a conduct element and a fault element, and respects procedural standards such as a legal burden of proof beyond reasonable doubt. Pure doctrines of subjective culpability and the presumption of innocence are increasingly abandoned within this streamlined regulatory framework 'to make up for expected difficulties of proof in difficult cases' (Goldstein 1992: 1899). It remains a matter of speculation the extent to which the instrumental mentality underpinning much of the regulatory framework will seep into paradigmatic criminal law and be employed to undermine further the doctrinal reasoning that supports many of the due process protections operating in that domain. But we should certainly remain alive to the possibility of the normalisation of some of the more repressive, consequentialist aspects of this regulatory framework into the ordinary criminal justice system.

The increasingly instrumental nature of criminal legal regulation is evident, for example, in the introduction of 'reverse onus' provisions that require the accused to displace a presumption of guilt. Section 100(2) of the Company Law Enforcement Act 2001, for example, states that an officer of a company *shall be presumed to have permitted a breach by the company* unless he can establish that he took all reasonable steps to prevent it or that by reason of circumstances beyond his control he was unable to do so. Previously section 383 of the 1963 Companies Act required the prosecution in such cases to prove that the officer 'knowingly and wilfully' authorised or permitted the default refusal or contravention (Bohan 2002). Similarly section 81 of the Safety, Health and Welfare at Work Act 2005 now provides that in any proceedings for an offence under the Act consisting of a failure to comply with a duty or requirement to do something so far as is reasonably practicable, *it shall be for the accused to prove* that it was not reasonably practicable to do more than was in fact done to satisfy the duty or requirement.[67]

It is also evident in the instrumental fault element requirements of criminal regulation. The attachment of subjective mental element to wrongdoing in paradigmatic criminal law is often severed in the regulatory criminal arena where objective standards of culpability apply. Section 100(3) of the Company Law Enforcement Act 2001, for example, states that it is the duty of each company to ensure that they comply with all the requirements of the Companies Acts. As such, officers are personally responsible for ensuring compliance. If it is demonstrated that a company has committed a criminal offence, the officer must prove that he has not permitted the breach and has taken all reasonable steps to prevent it. Similarly, section 58 of the Criminal Justice (Theft and Fraud offences) Act 2001 also provides that any company officer or any person purporting to act in that capacity may be convicted of an offence under the Act (such as false accounting, suppression of documents) if it is proved that the offence was carried out with his consent, connivance, or is attributable to his neglect. Under health and safety law, where a health and safety offence has been committed by a body corporate, and that offence is shown to have been committed with the consent or connivance of, or to have been attributable to any neglect on the part of any director, that person may be prosecuted in addition to the corporate body.[68]

In some instances these agencies demand that individuals or institutions are required to become 'information reporters'. Solicitors, for example, are required to report clients' suspicious transactions to the Revenue Commissioners and the Gardaí under section 6 of the Criminal Justice Act 1994 (section 32) Regulations 2003 on the Prevention of the use of the Financial System for the purpose of Money Laundering. Similarly, section 192(6) of the Companies Act 1990, as amended, requires that where a disciplinary tribunal of a recognised body of accountants has reasonable grounds for believing that an indictable offence has been committed by a person while the person was a member of the body, the body shall inform the Director of Corporate Enforcement. A similar provision exists under section 194(5) of the 1990 Act, as amended, as regards the auditors carrying out an audit of the accounts of a company.[69] Section 56 of the Company Law Enforcement Act 2001 also requires every liquidator of a company to file a report to the Director of Corporate Enforcement detailing the impact of the behaviour of the officers of the company in the ultimate liquidation.

Thirdly, very wide powers of entry, inspection, examination, search, seizure and analysis are given to some of these agencies. For example, under section 64 of the Health and Safety Act 2005, health and safety inspectors are, *inter alia*, entitled to enter any place with the consent of the occupier or with a warrant and enquire into, search, examine and inspect the place and any work activity; require records to be produced; inspect and take copies of such records; remove and retain records; and require the employer or any employee to give the inspector any information that the inspector may reasonably require for the purposes of any search, examination, investigation, inspection or inquiry.

Similarly, section 45(4) of the Competition Act 2002 permits the Competition Authority to obtain a search warrant to enter by force and seize from a premises of suspected undertakings (and the homes of individuals involved in their management) any books, records and documents relating to the activity of an undertaking.[70] Persons on the premises may also be required to answer certain questions relating to the activity engaged in by the undertaking. Since individuals questioned in this manner are not in custody, they do not have the right to legal representation.[71] The Competition Authority also has the power to summon persons to appear before it to answer questions and to produce certain documentation. Such persons will be examined on oath. It is an offence not to produce documents, or to answer the questions to which the Competition Authority may legally require an answer.[72] In conjunction with the Director of Public Prosecutions, the Competition Authority also operates a Cartel Immunity Programme, which provides immunity from criminal prosecution for suspected individuals who are willing to cooperate and testify on behalf of the prosecution (Gorecki and McFadden 2006).[73]

Fourthly, there is also some evidence of a possible drift towards a more punitive approach to regulation (Baldwin 2004). Traditionally it had been said that the focus of the sanctions for many of these regulatory offences was more 'apersonal' in nature than their ordinary counterparts. The argument was that 'these were not real crimes to which stigma should attach, but were rather in the nature of administrative regulations with non-stigmatising penalties such as fines' (Lacey 2004: 161). The traditional lack of a *mens rea* requirement operated as the 'doctrinal marker of these defendants less than fully criminal status from a social point of view' (2004: 161). But regulatory agencies have increasingly grown considerable teeth as regards prosecution.[74] For example, section 78 of the Safety, Health and Welfare at Work Act, 2005 now imposes on conviction on indictment for an offence under the Act a fine not exceeding €3 million or imprisonment for a term not exceeding two years, or both. On conviction on indictment for competition law offences, undertakings are liable to a fine not exceeding whichever of the following amounts is the greater, namely €4 million or 10 per cent of the turnover of the undertaking in the financial year ending in the 12 months prior to conviction. Individuals are subject to the same fine limits and/or a term of imprisonment not exceeding five years.[75]

Though all of this constitutes evidence of a drift towards the greater use or threatened use of criminal sanctions, it should not be pushed too far. The area of regulatory crime still, by and large, remains predominantly oriented towards a compliance model of enforcement. This is facilitated by a wide range of strategies that favour the employment of negotiation, consultation and persuasion, rather than an exclusively sanctioning approach that would potentially polarise the various parties involved (Gray 2006). These strategies include audits, warning letters, notices, injunctions, guidance, binding directions, and the suspension and revocation of licences. All of these ensure that prosecutions remain relatively rare, employed as a last resort mechanism.

Finally, another striking feature of this regulatory infrastructure is the proliferation of hybrid enforcement mechanisms that can be employed by the agencies or, on occasion, by private parties. These mechanisms have also contributed to a more general 'blurring of legal forms' (Ashworth 2000: 237), conflating the functional distinctions that exist between criminal and civil law and between regulatory wrongdoing and ordinary wrongdoing. For example, and apart from the possibility of a criminal prosecution by the Competition Authority, private parties can seek to initiate civil enforcement of competition law under section 14(1) of the Competition Act 2002. Section 8(10) of the same Act provides that an action under section 14 may be brought whether or not there has already been a criminal prosecution in relation to the matter concerned and, in addition, a section 14 action will not prejudice the initiation of any future prosecution. Indeed the Competition Authority itself can also seek to bring a civil action under section 14(2) of the Act. This fragmentation in responses to a breach of a regulatory offence can give rise to difficulties having regard to the principled protections generally afforded to those accused of crime. To give one instance, the Revenue may proceed against a tax defaulter through the criminal courts under section 1078 of the Taxes Consolidation Act 1997 while also exercising its considerable civil powers to collect tax and impose civil penalties (fixed penalties and tax geared penalties) under section 1053 of the same Act. The latter penalties are available 'without prejudice to any other penalty to which the person may be liable'. This, as O'Malley notes, can pose a 'problem for any sentencing system claiming to be guided by proportionality standards' (2000b: 128).

For example, in *People (DPP) v Redmond*,[76] the defendant, who had previously worked as a senior official in local government in Dublin, had been charged with ten counts of failing to make tax returns between 1989 and 1997. The prosecution case was that the defendant failed to disclose about £249,000 of income during this period. The defendant was found guilty and the trial judge imposed a total fine of £7,500 in respect of the ten counts. The Director of Public Prosecutions appealed on the basis that this sentence was unduly lenient having regard to the gravity of the offences. In determining the proportionality of the punishment, the Court of Criminal Appeal noted that the defendant had, since his arrest, settled his civil revenue liability by paying a total sum of £782,000 to the Criminal Assets Bureau which was acting for the Revenue Commissioners. This figure constituted the tax liability owing in relation to the criminal charges and other unspecified liabilities including interest and penalties. In order to meet this civil liability, Redmond had to sell the family home. The Court of Criminal Appeal noted that this full settlement figure was not broken down into various headings including the amount claimed in penal interest or revenue penalties. This was regrettable since information of this kind was important in determining the appropriate criminal sanction. In refusing to increase the criminal penalty, the court noted:

> Since proportionality is a key principle of sentencing, the court would endeavour to consider the cumulative sum of penalties in assessing the amount of the final one. The revenue penalties may vary, in particular with whether default in compliance is negligently or fraudulently caused. Such penalties in certain circumstances can exceed three times the difference between the tax paid and the tax actually payable … [T]hese are penalties which will be imposed on top of the primary obligation of every tax payer to pay the correct amount of tax. Similarly, a penal rate of interest may be applied where income tax has not been paid as a result of a fraud or neglect of the tax payer. This, too, is in the nature of a penalty. It is plainly not possible for a sentencing court in a case such as this to ignore the fact that other penalties, which may be much greater in amount than the cumulative sum of the maximum fines for these charges, have already been paid. It is therefore most unfortunate that the evidence does not extend to a statement, even approximate, to the amount of penalties so paid, or the defaults in respect of which they were imposed.

The court was attempting to maintain some sort of harmony between punishments to ensure that the overall quantity of punishment was not proportionately excessive. As justice becomes disaggregated, this task becomes more difficult to achieve as numerous organisations possess prosecutorial powers. They interpret and refract the world according to their own concerns rather than society as a whole even if they assume that their interests coincide with the wider society. Such organisations are akin to what the seventeenth-century philosopher Gottfried Leibniz termed monads, distinct substances whose internal workings are not fundamentally altered by everything external to them: there is 'no way in which it could make sense for a monad to be altered or changed internally by any other created thing' (Leibniz 1998: para. 7). Monads can be extrinsically affected by objects external to them, like vessels bobbing in the water after a ripple, but they are not intrinsically affected. While regulatory agencies are dependent upon a central state for their establishment and continued flow of resources (Shipan 2003), the criteria that underlie their operations are largely internally derived (Black 2005). Monads comprehend the universe from their own distinct perspective and their representation of events 'can only be distinct with respect to a small part of things' (Leibniz 1998: para. 60). According to Leibniz, only God could contain the plenitude of the universe and ensure that each monad remains in harmony with the others.

We are increasingly living in a monadic society in which individuals are bound by weak ties, brushing up against each other and then recoiling. Social collisions are '"problems" to be *managed*, not moral lapses for which one is held accountable ... Events happen; the task is to manage the aftermath effectively and efficiently' (Feeley 2006: 221, italics in original). Use of civil powers and the extension of regulatory powers indicate that the management of criminality is becoming demoralised. Emphasis shifts away from developing an intrinsic change within individual offenders whereby they renounce previous habits and towards adjusting their outward behaviour. As the moral sheen of criminal law dulls, it blends into instrumental regulation.

Regulatory agencies, like monads, are relatively oblivious to events beyond their stipulated purview but societies need some assurance that regulators' actions are congruent with the public good as well as the narrower organisational perspective. The problem is that contemporary societies cannot invoke God as a guarantor of order however much some people might like to ascribe divine qualities to the judiciary. A new institutional arrangement, a new architecture of justice is needed that can encompass the growing complexity of a monadic society and maintain it in some state of harmony rather than allow it lapse into a state of mutual repulsion.

We often ascribe to the 'state' the capacity to regulate thus but as it becomes more disaggregated this assumption is cast into doubt. What we are witnessing is the emergence of 'complex sovereignty' as organisations that stand apart from a monistic state increasingly influence people's lives (Rosanvallon 2006); people themselves are understood in an increasingly diverse way as they attempt to define themselves in terms of particular interests – victim, child, woman – rather than the more general category of citizen, and even these specific identities are capable of being further disaggregated.

## Justice as accommodation

The story of criminal justice for much of the nineteenth and twentieth centuries might best be told as the rise of institutionalised justice whereby the state gradually monopolised investigative and prosecutorial functions and colonised 'ownership' of the wrongfulness of criminal wrongdoing. This also entailed the steady development of an 'equality of arms' framework, designed to offset the power vested in an increasingly Leviathan state and offer some protections and safeguards to those accused of crime. Within such a depersonalised, bureaucratised system, the victim was displaced, confined largely to the bit-part role of reporting crime and of adducing evidence in court as a witness, if needed (Rock 2004). These foundational principles of modern Irish justice are now beginning to creak and strain, however, as newly 'discovered' competing narratives emerge. These narratives are increasingly undermining the fixity of criminal law and its tendency to organise justice around the central axis of the State and the accused/offender. Justice is thus gradually being reconstructed in Ireland as it demonstrates, among other things, an increased sensitivity to previously excluded voices and a willingness to accommodate a range of standpoints rather than engage in debilitating stereotyping.

To begin with, a growing number of victims' rights advocacy/support groups and victim surveys[77] have increasingly made victims more visible again and highlighted the ways in which they are marginalised or further scarred by the process (Carney 2007: 11–12).[78] In Ireland, for example, a Victim's Charter was produced by the Department of Justice, Equality and Law Reform in 1999 'reflecting the commitment to giving victims of crime a central place in the criminal justice system'. A Commission for the Support of Victims of Crime was established in 2005 to disburse funds to individual victim groups and to establish an appropriate national framework of services.[79] The Director of Public Prosecutions has recently given undertakings to have regard to the views expressed by victims of crime when making decisions in specific cases whether or not to prosecute and to facilitate pre-trial meetings to explain the trial process.[80] The Gardaí too have given a number of commitments to victims of crime including the provision of information on the progress of a case and the prosecution process (Office of the DPP 2006: para. 2.12; Rogan 2006b).

These changes have been augmented by developments in the European Union. In March 2001, for example, the Council adopted a framework decision on the Standing of Victims in Criminal Proceedings that provides minimum rights for those victimised by crime.[81] The courts,[82] the legislature and politicians[83] are also beginning to take more account of the interests of victims of crime and there has been an expansion in service (welfare) and procedural (participatory) rights. These rights include: the employment of intermediaries, live television links and video testimony for witnesses and victims of crime; the abolition of the mandatory requirement on judges to warn juries of the dangers of convicting on the basis of uncorroborated or unsworn victim/witness testimony; the removal of wigs and gowns when conducting an examination in chief or cross-examination of child witnesses; restrictions on the admissibility of the prior sexual history of victims; the protection of the identity of victims in sexual offence cases; separate legal representation for rape victims where an application is made to admit previous sexual history; the reduction of victim alienation through the use of victim impact statements; the ability of the DPP to appeal unduly lenient sentences; and provisions for the payment of compensation to victims in respect of any personal injury or loss caused by a crime (Kilcommins *et al.* 2004: 150–3; Rogan 2006a).

The previously fossilised exclusionary assumptions underpinning the perception of some victims/witnesses in our justice system is evident, for example, in the law on the corroboration of sexual complaints. In the past the evidence of a complainant in a sexual offences case required a mandatory warning to the jury on the dangers of acting on such evidence alone. This rule was justified 'by the fear that complaints of sexual offences may sometimes be the product of spite, jealousy, psychological denial of having consented, or a reaction to having been jolted; that women with nothing to lose might seek to subject a man of high social standing to blackmail; and that the accusation of rape is easily made, but difficult to defend' (Healy 2004: 157).[84] More recently, however, these essentialised notions about the traits and motives of sexual complainants have largely been abandoned[85] and the trial judge now has a discretion whether or not to give such a warning to the jury.[86] This point was picked up upon by McGuinness J in *PC v DPP*:[87]

> In years gone by, accusations of rape or any kind of sexual assault were treated with considerable suspicion. The orthodox view was that accusations of rape and sexual assault by women against men were 'easy to make and hard to disprove' and judges were required

> to give stern warnings in their charge to the jury of the need for corroboration and of the dangers attached to convicting on the evidence of the complainant alone. No-one today would support the orthodoxy of the past and there has been a great increase in the psychological understanding of sexual offences generally.

The same is true of the traditional common law approach to the previous sexual history of a complainant. Such evidence was previously admissible provided it was relevant. Once relevant, a trial judge was obliged 'to allow unpleasant charges to be made against the complainant in connection with her past'.[88] If admitted, such evidence of sexual reputation was employed to cast serious doubt on the trustworthiness of a female complainant, the probative link between sexual reputation and suspicion about the veracity of a complaint being fixed and clear. The destructive assumptions entrenched in the common law – particularly the reinforcement of sexist stereotypes – were thus employed to undermine the credibility of victims as witnesses especially on the question of consent. But the dynamics have changed in more recent times and the legislature has attempted to counteract such 'folkloric' and sexist assumptions. Section 1 of the Criminal Law (Rape) Act 1981, as amended by section 13 of the Criminal Law (Rape) (Amendment) Act 1990, now imposes tighter restrictions that offer victims better protection against unnecessary and distressing information being raised about their sexual histories. No evidence may now be adduced or question asked on cross-examination by the defence about any sexual behaviour of the complainant beyond the circumstances of the alleged offence without leave of the court. The law on marital rape was also imbued with sexist ideology. A husband was previously exempted from liability for the rape of his wife. This was premised on a rule enunciated by Hale that a husband could not be guilty of rape 'committed by himself upon his lawful wife, for by their mutual matrimonial consent and contract the wife hath given herself up in this kind unto her husband which she cannot retract' (quoted in Temkin 1982: 407). The marital rape exemption was abolished in Ireland in 1990.

Similarly, the previous mandatory requirement of corroboration for a young child's testimony[89] – again premised on the often untested assumption that such evidence was inherently unreliable – has now also been removed. In more recent years the system has also witnessed a far less rigid approach to the circumstances in which the spouse of an accused is competent to testify for the prosecution in criminal proceedings;[90] a greater awareness of the reasons why a complainant may not have made a complaint of a sexual offence at first reasonable opportunity but still avail of the doctrine of recent complaint,[91] a relaxation of the exclusionary rules on opinion evidence in certain circumstances;[92] the introduction of a provision that makes it clear that the absence of resistance by a victim in a rape case does not equate with consent;[93] and, a more secular, intelligibility-driven approach to the determination of certain witnesses' competence to testify at the trial of an accused.[94]

The introduction of restorative justice in Ireland can also be seen as a response to the dissatisfaction experienced by victims under the ordinary adversarial justice system. Part of the attractiveness of restorative justice is its potential to refocus the problem of crime on to the harms caused to individual victims and local communities. By divesting the state of ownership of the crime problem and through dismantling the 'equality of arms' conflict approach, the restorative justice process is designed to empower victims and local communities to give their accounts in their own terms free from the strictures of formal adversarialism.[95] As Hudson (2003: 210) notes: 'it incorporates the principles that justice should be discursive, that it should be responsive to the circumstances of the particular case rather than subsuming individual acts and actors under general classes, and that it should allow a plurality of voices within the discourse'. Though restorative justice initiatives are only in their infancy in Ireland, their inclusionary potential, particularly their capacity to emphasise the standpoints of victims and local communities, has ensured that they are being embraced.[96]

Driven largely by an inclusionary logic – flowing from many streams – the Irish criminal process is thus increasingly accommodating the previously excluded voices of victims of crime. In the last three decades the status of the crime victim has gradually altered from being perceived as a 'nonentity' or 'hidden casualty' to a stakeholder whose interests and opinions matter (Christie 1977). Crime victims are being anchored once again as key constituents in the criminal justice landscape and criminal justice agencies are having to rework their relationships with them. Some commentators argue that this shift in the status of the victim will contribute to a reprioritisation of commitments resulting in a recalibration of the scales of justice that further hollow out the rights of an increasingly dissociated accused (Ashworth 2001: 186; Henderson 1985). As Garland (2001: 143) has noted, 'the sanctified persona of the suffering victim has become a valued commodity in the circuits of media and political exchange'. These concerns about the exclusionary potential of victim discourse are, of course, real. We should be wary of the possibility of political or media manipulation, or the depiction of the criminal justice system as a 'zero-sum game' where gains for victims must be at the expense of those accused of crime. That said, we should also be mindful that victim ideology is not just the manifestation of a sinister state or the product of media exaggerated alarm about law and order. Instead its recent emergence must be seen much more as a response to a previous scandalous neglect, as a justified attempt to correct an imbalance in which the victim was constituted as a 'silent abstraction, a background figure whose individuality hardly registered' (Garland 2001: 179).

## Conclusion

The organising motifs of the modern inculpatory model of justice included a commitment to adversarialism; the state monopolisation of violence through the conduit of criminal law; the restriction of public and victim interests to that of a central axis between the state and the accused/ offender; and a belief in the primacy of the individual and the need to curtail executive power, victim vindictiveness, and public passions. In recent years, this model of justice has become more of a battleground, a site for struggles and competing claims about security, liberty, humanity, governance, accommodation and instrumental effectiveness. Elements of rupture are increasingly thrown into the mix with older orthodoxies such as the commitment to liberal values and principles and the continued incorporation of enunciated rights into domestic law. These newer elements are in many instances more instrumental, emotionally charged and exclusionary, but also may be more democratic, accommodating and inclusionary. They include, for example, the normalisation of measures employed in respect of terrorism. As we have seen, Ireland has a long tradition of invoking extraordinary laws and creating 'sites of exception' where normal laws do not apply. These 'sites', which facilitated a redistribution of institutional power relations in certain limited areas, have now infiltrated institutions and culturally, acting as a yardstick for the public against which it can measure its ability to counteract the threat posed by other non-terrorist pariahs. They also include the embrace of hybrid enforcement mechanisms, the criminalisation of regulatory arenas, and the accommodation of more stakeholders in the criminal process. The principled, deontological elements of the constitutional state thus increasingly jockey for position with newer orthodoxies that emphasise security, embrace civil and emergency models of justice, and seek to accommodate a greater range of standpoints.

All this is reminiscent of O'Malley's argument, reviewed in Chapter 2, that punishment is becoming more volatile and contradictory. But O'Malley was unable to provide an explanation for this, save for the curiously self-referential one that such changes are attributable to a change in discourse. As to what promotes this change in discourse, we are left unenlightened. We would argue that the increased volatility is explained in part by the emergence of sites of justice beyond the state, above and below it, that may jar with how the state has defined and administered justice. We are not making the mistake of presuming that the nation-state has been supremely sovereign in its borders until recently, as the reliance on emergency law that we have documented shows this to be a fallacy. What is different is that the legitimacy of these alternative sites is much harder to dismiss than the terrorist threat since justice above and below the state promises, in very different ways, to promote further democratisation.

## Chapter 7

# Justice beyond the nation-state

Usually the emergence of the rule of law coincided with a reduction of the executive's reliance on arbitrary powers. Ireland's experience, as both a colony and independent state, has been different as its fractious and unsettled society curbed this movement away from emergency powers. That these developments all occur within a single jurisdiction seems too obvious to note except for the fact that it encourages the nation-state as the container of society (Beck 2005: 338). On this view, nation-states are autonomous of each other and therefore executives within them have the greatest power to engineer change while remaining relatively impervious to other influences. Even if it is acknowledged that states are increasingly subject to influences and events beyond their borders, the power to change how the rule of law operates belongs to each of them alone or acting in conjunction.

This rather atomistic and undifferentiated view of nation-states is contested by the advent of alternative sources of political rule that have emerged above and below the nation-state in the form of supra-national influences and local communities, a phenomenon known within European Union studies as multi-level governance (Bache and Flinders 2004). This occurrence signals the 'de-statization of the political system' (Jessop 2004: 65), whereby actors other than the sovereign national state emerge to further projects that necessarily involve states but are not reducible to them. Therefore the state as some unified political entity is not the only actor, perhaps not even the primary actor, in the initiation and execution of policy in an era of multi-level governance. This should not be taken as some preliminary to some neo-liberal rhetoric about the demise of the state; in fact, recent times have seen an intensification of state activity, albeit that the state is far more splintered (Cerny 1999) than is recognised within criminology and the activity is not necessarily punitive.

It is a commonplace within criminological thought that states emphasise repressive policies when they feel themselves under threat (Garland 1996). Yet this portrayal could be said to be offering up a rather partial and anachronistic model of the national territorial state that sees political rule as a bilateral relationship between citizen and state. But the multi-level governance perspective refers to new governmental and civil society actors that may push politics in another direction. Multi-level governance alters the internal quality of the nation-state so that 'whatever constitutes "society" and "politics" becomes in itself questionable, because the principles of territoriality, collectivity and frontier are becoming questioned' (Beck 2000: 87).

Beck's account queries whether relations between state and citizen have already altered so that a return to the *status quo ante* of the sovereign-state era is impossible. More specifically, the frames of reference that citizens use to assess the actions of the state may have been altered by the emergence of alternative sources of political affiliation to the extent that people may make demands that sit uneasily with the agendas of states.

In this chapter, we examine how justice is being reformulated as a result of influences above and below the nation-state. First we examine how greater European integration has affected the dispensation of justice, noting how this field has become more pivotal to the work of the European Union. A discourse and practice of security has been promoted since the 1990s and lent a stronger impetus in the light of the terrorist attacks in New York, Madrid and London. European states have attempted to make their criminal justice systems work more harmoniously together by avoiding many of the judicial strictures that had governed legal relations between them. There is a fear then that the Europeanisation of criminal justice, haunted by terrorism, will diminish the rights of those within the European Union through an increased emphasis on security that is matched by stricter border controls directed against would-be migrants and that the systems for managing both security and migration are merging. We contend that this possibility remains contested through the existence of recalcitrant due process values at the national level and liberal freedoms promulgated at the European level. European integration has enabled nations to affiliate around certain 'shared norms and values to operate collective arrangements' (Wallace 2000: 377–8) such as the European Convention on Human Rights (ECHR) that may be equally effective at the national level and circumscribe state action (Vaughan and Kilcommins 2007). We show how human rights norms have been accessed and downloaded to circumscribe police powers.

We also detail how justice at the local level is being reconfigured through greater involvement of representatives and local government in policing. Rather than seeing this as a sop to populism, we note how it may help moderate some of the excess into which community justice can descend, as demonstrated by our account of citizen-led policing against drugs in Dublin during the 1980s and 1990s.

## European justice

Although cooperation in policing matters among European nations extends as far back as the nineteenth century, it was not until the 1970s, after several countries had experiences with domestic terrorism, that European ministers for justice and home affairs formed the Trevi group to coordinate their anti-terrorist efforts (Anderson *et al.* 1995). A number of *ad hoc* working groups were added in the 1980s and 1990s to address issues such as drug trafficking and judicial cooperation.

Increasing political integration also had an effect on cooperation in security matters. The Schengen Agreement of 1985 between France, Germany and the Benelux countries removed border controls in an effort to create a common European space. Relaxing these controls brought forth compensatory measures in the form of greater police cooperation, and the storing of personal data on computer systems. The extension of Schengen-type arrangements also stimulated greater fears about illegal migration and provided for a merging of internal and external security. By 1992, the Maastricht treaty explicitly recognised the sphere of justice and home affairs as a third pillar of the European Union to be managed by inter-governmental processes rather than directed by the Commission as a community matter. The European Police Office or Europol was established under German bidding although it did not meet their expectations of a European FBI, having no operational powers. Participation by members of the EU became mandatory and all states appointed liaison officers to share information. Initial concerns were about trafficking activities of serious crime networks although this remit has expanded with time. During the 1990s, this field became one of the busiest arenas of the EU and it was identified as one area in which Europe could be made more relevant for its citizens. In the words of the Amsterdam Treaty (1997), the European Union has committed itself to 'provide its citizens with a high degree of safety within an area of freedom, security and justice' (Article 29).

Cooperation was intensified after the Tampere summit in Finland in 1999, the first European Council meeting explicitly dedicated to justice and home affairs. Tampere set three objectives. The first pertains to harmonisation of laws so that behaviours contrary to common European values, such as human trafficking and money laundering, should be prosecuted and punished in the same way everywhere in the EU. Moves are also afoot to approximate certain aspects of criminal procedure, for instance the standing of victims (see Chapter 6). The second relates to mutual recognition, which was recognised as the mainstay of judicial cooperation. Mutual recognition arises when a member state agrees to recognise as valid a decision taken in another jurisdiction even if that decision might have been taken differently or had another outcome in the first jurisdiction. This allows for a greater recognition of the diverse ways through which different jurisdictions can secure justice but does run the risk of inconsistencies in procedural justice arising. For example, a European Evidence Warrant, which allows for the acquisition of objects or data, must be issued by a judge in some jurisdictions whereas in others the relevant authority would be a police officer. The third objective has been fulfilled by the creation of coordination bodies. Perhaps one of the most notable is Eurojust, composed of one judge from each of the 27 member states, whose aim is to improve the cooperation between national personnel investigating and prosecuting serious crime.

The Tampere accord was accelerated and augmented by the terrorist attacks of 9/11 and later in Madrid and London. Previously, terrorism was viewed largely as a matter of domestic concern but the perceived transnational nature of Al Qaeda instilled a desire to have more effective methods of prosecution across borders. In 2002, the European Council assented to a European Arrest Warrant (EAW) which came into force in Ireland on 1 January 2004. This warrant effectively depoliticises the procedure of extradition and is sent directly from one judicial authority to another. Those in receipt of the request take the *bona fides* of the case in good faith. Unsurprisingly, the European Arrest Warrant has been described as 'the first, and most symbolic, measure applying the principle of mutual recognition' (European Commission, quoted in House of Lords 2006: para. 29). Many other fundamental accretions to the third pillar have also been made so that there are preliminary grounds for fearing for that a rampant securitisation without appropriate oversight is under way. Yet, just as the judiciary can check emergency measures of the national executive, so too can they impede measures agreed between governments, as has occurred with the Polish and German constitutional courts (Komarek 2007).

In April 2005, the Polish Constitutional Tribunal annulled implementation of the European Arrest Warrant framework because it conflicted with the constitutional prohibition on extraditing Polish nationals. The Tribunal held that the individual liberties contained within the Polish constitution 'indicate a minimum and unsurpassable threshold which may not be lowered or questioned as a result of the introduction of Community provisions' (quoted in Komarek 2007: 3) The Federal Constitutional Court of Germany argued that the strict principle of mutual recognition 'cannot restrict the [national] constitutional guarantee of fundamental rights' (2007: 13) and found implementation of the EAW to be unconstitutional. The Polish case touched on the matter of the primacy of EU law under the third pillar whereas the German case challenges the very principle of mutual recognition, since it refused to take on trust the *bona fides* of foreign judicial systems. Instead, it insisted that in every individual case a review of the requesting country's judicial system must be made to see if they conform to German constitutional requirements.

Both decisions point to the importance of the judicial *habitus* in tempering decisions taken by national executives operating in relatively closed circumstances in conjunction with officials of the European Union (Loader 2002). This lack of accountability has often been criticised for its potential to undermine the legitimacy of decisions taken. Yet this criticism is partial in that it ignores how the judicial *habitus* is forced to negotiate between two different legal orders, one deriving from national constitutions and one emergent from international agreements, the so-called state of constitutional pluralism (Walker 2002). In moderating between these two influences, the judiciary explores and substantiates its and the European Union's commitment to the abstract principles of liberty, democracy, respect for human rights and fundamental freedoms, and the rule of law (article 6 of TEU) (Kumm 2005). A recent ruling from the European Court of Justice (C-303/05 *Advocaten voor de Wereld*) supports this interpretation. It considered that the 'Framework Decision [establishing the EAW] does not seek to harmonise the criminal offences in question in respect of their constituent elements or of the penalties which they attract' (para. 52), which would rebuff the German interpretation of reviewing every case afresh. Instead of confidence being secured by consistent interpretation of criminal offences and similar practices throughout the European Union, the Court also insisted that, by virtue of article 6 of the Treaty of the European Union, member-states are bound to observe the rule of law and ensure that they respect fundamental rights as articulated in the European Convention on European Rights. How much convergence this entails remains open and can only be explored by examining in greater detail how the process of Europeanisation operates. Before exploring one example of how European norms have infiltrated national discourses around police accountability, let us be clearer about how this might be achieved.

## Europeanisation and the negotiation of domestic change

What this indicates is that the process of securitisation is by no means inevitable nor is the only domestic change inspired by European integration, a process known as Europeanisation (Olsen 2002; Vink 2003) that should be of interest to criminologists. This transformation extends beyond institutional change to encompass cultural beliefs, for example, in the importance of the environment or due process. Norms inspired by Europeanisation should not be construed simply as a behavioural constraint since they may provide 'domestic agents with basic understandings of interests' (Checkel 2001: 196) that were previously muted (Schmidt and Radaelli 2004), an argument that reiterates Beck's view that interconnectedness between nation-states alters the internal quality of that state and the accompanying society. In an area as contested as due process rights, it may well be that the introduction of novel norms may impede or destabilise customary ways of working as well as helping others to reformulate their interests. What this involves is a 'process of institutionalisation in which new rules of the game are constructed' and since 'these rules are wide in scope they are interpreted and edited by national actors so that they fit into the domestic political context' (Morth 2003: 173). Therefore, Europeanisation does not necessarily entail convergence – monetary union is an exception and even here countries have responded to stringencies of a single currency in different ways – and moreover usually involves diversity given that countries are starting from different positions. Translation of these norms is dependent on local circumstances and does not happen automatically with the promulgation of rights at a European level.

What are the conditions for activation? Most obviously, there must be some mismatch between European and domestic policies, processes and institutions from which there is no obvious exit point for the member state in question. Probably the most important factor in capitalising upon this potential for change is the existence of what Börzel and Risse label *norm entrepreneurs*, who form an advocacy coalition to press for change usually after 'critical policy failure or in perceived crises and situations of great uncertainty' (2003: 67). The bombings of 9/11, Madrid and London are obvious examples of events that call into question accepted procedures. Recognition of a mismatch is not automatic and even after it occurs, there is no guarantee that successful adaptation to European norms will occur. In some respects, the limits to Europeanisation will lie in the lack of specificity about what these norms entail or the degree of ambiguity attaching to them. As policy transfer is facilitated by 'anchorage to best practice or EU desirable models' (Radaelli and

Schmidt 2004: 373), the process may be disrupted by the capacity of actors to define the 'implications of EU models via appropriate discourse' (2004: 373) that ensures it fits with the *status quo*. Therefore, the main enabler of Europeanisation will be the enunciation of a convincing narrative about why change is necessary and the production of ideas that show how that change can be induced and sustained. It is not enough, as Börzel and Risse (2003) contend, that a scandal emerges that apparently stands in stark contrast to European norms and values. Norm entrepreneurs also must produce a narrative of change, explaining why the heritage of the past must be revoked and how a new future can be secured. So rather than regarding Europeanisation as some kind of 'objective, external constraint' (Wincott 2004: 355) that automatically intrudes upon the national, analysis should concentrate on how European influences are modulated to fit national circumstances and how downloading them affects the perceptions of domestic situations.

In this respect, Risse and Ropp's (1999) spiral model of human rights change is useful. It involves several distinct stages, the first of which is *repression*, whereby the state enjoys sufficient power to impose its will, irrespective of the quality of its actions. Hegemony is almost always contested and groups within a state may be able to publicise violations of human rights. If such information seeps out, the state may well *deny* not just the charges but also the very validity of international human rights norms and may sanctify the principle of non-interference in domestic affairs. Even though the Irish state ratified the ECHR in 1953, it did not incorporate it until 2003, so that a dualist system pertained whereby the ECHR applied to Ireland but not within it, at least until expressly integrated by an Act of Parliament (O'Connell 2000). As the state becomes increasingly entangled in international affairs, it may become more difficult to disavow human rights norms and the state may begin to make *tactical concessions* to forestall further criticisms, a process of 'controlled liberalisation' (Risse and Ropp 1999: 238). In 2003, the Irish state incorporated the ECHR at a sub-constitutional level, which meant that domestic legislation or the act of a public body could be declared incompatible with the ECHR. The Irish state is only under an onus to put this declaration before Parliament and is not required to take any remedial action (O'Connell 2004). The last stage is where norms gain a *prescriptive status*, their validity is no longer challenged and states attempt to institutionalise them domestically. It is a stage in which all relevant players accept the new rules of the game. One possible way this could happen in the Irish situation is that the judiciary will strive to render compatible the provisions of the Irish Constitution and the ECHR. Rather than end up in the *cul-de-sac* of incompatibility, they may 'simply tire of the whole rigmarole' (Hogan 2004: 33) and declare legislation or actions unconstitutional under the 1937 Constitution, drawing upon the ECHR as support. The net effect is to copper-fasten a transnational judicial conversation (McCrudden 2000) as ECHR jurisprudence is subsumed into domestic constitutional law (Hogan 2004).

The process outlined above is neither automatic nor irreversible. For example, states may alternate from making *tactical concessions* to *denial* that concessions granted are not adequate to prevent further human rights abuses. Kick-starting the process again requires determined efforts to draw upon novel resources to negate the denials offered by the state. We will now illustrate just such a process by documenting how police accountability was tactically controlled by the Irish state until a change in domestic conditions made the accessing of a cosmopolitan discourse of rights more attractive.

## Police perpetrating harm

It may seem perverse that after referring to influences of a transnational nature, we should turn to a small part of Ireland, the county of Kerry, that represents the essence of the Irish nation in many people's eyes. In that county in 1984, Joanne Hayes gave birth to a child fathered by a married man, which would have caused notoriety in a still conservative country. The child died and was hidden on the family farm. Around the same time, another infant was found washed up on the shore 15 miles away that had been fatally stabbed. The murder squad of the Irish police, An Garda Síochána, descended on the region to investigate. When the Hayes family were interrogated, they confessed soon afterwards to being responsible for the death of the stabbed infant to whom Gardaí believed Ms Hayes had recently given birth. She was charged with murder and her family with concealment of the crime. Shortly afterwards, the corpse of Hayes' baby was discovered on the farm and it was shown to possess a different blood group from the murdered infant. The Gardaí did not wish to countenance the possibility that Hayes may not have been responsible for the death of the stabbed infant. They insisted that she had been impregnated by two different men and given birth to twins, each of whom had a different biological father, thus explaining the difference in blood types. According to the Gardaí, one baby was thrown into the sea and another was buried close to the family farm. The Director for Public Prosecutions refused to accept this explanation and the charges against the Hayes family were dropped. But the Garda file was leaked to the press and then Joanne Hayes claimed that her confession had been coerced. She claimed:

> 'It was the Guards that made the statements. We just agreed with them at the end. They convinced themselves that we did do it. They were saying the statements and we were just agreeing with them' (quoted in Inglis 2003: 47).

These claims were being revealed at the same time as the Irish government was proposing to extend the powers to the Gardaí in the form of the Criminal Justice Bill 1983. This legislation represented a realignment of the relationship between citizen and state as the police would have enjoyed 'powers over all citizens which previously they enjoyed only over subversive suspects' (Walsh 1998: 261). In the context of persistent allegations about Garda coercion of confessions since the onset of violence in Northern Ireland in the 1970s (Kilcommins *et al.* 2004: 208–10), many were reluctant to give the police *carte blanche* powers. One senator expressed the view that:

> For ten or 12 years there has been talk about heavy gangs [the term used to designate the cohort of Gardaí specialising in the interrogation of murder suspects and who regularly produced confessions] of one sort or another in the Garda. For a long time I believed that these stories or reports were the inventions of an imaginative media. I find now that my belief was wrong ... There have been many cases in which statements have been made, apparently voluntarily, which afterwards have been proved without question to have been wrong. People have admitted committing crimes they did not even commit and obviously could not have committed given all the circumstances available to the courts (Deputy Moloney, Dáil Debates, 11 December 1984, vol. 354, col. 2174)

An internal Garda inquiry into what became known as the Kerry Babies affair proved inconclusive after both Gardaí and the Hayes family refused to give direct evidence. A tribunal was set up in December 1984 to inquire into the circumstances leading to criminal charges being laid against the Hayes family and the allegations of abuse against Gardaí. The sole judge in charge of the tribunal claimed that the family had made these allegations to explain their confessions, whereas the Garda defence of the confessions was a mere 'gilding of the lily', the elevation of suspicion into fact.

While some criticised these findings for their timidity (Inglis 2003), awareness of the potential harms that could arise from police actions to secure order stabilised in public discourse. It became politically impossible to offer greater enforcement powers to the Gardaí without counterbalancing it in some way. The enactment of the Criminal Justice Bill 1983 was frozen until a new complaints mechanism was introduced (another requirement was the creation of comprehensive regulations for the treatment of persons in Garda custody). Previously, complaints made by members of the public had been dealt with as an internal disciplinary matter within the Gardaí.

In 1985 the Garda Complaints Bill was published. In the ensuing debate, many political representatives accepted that some Gardaí could have engaged in conduct that was 'oppressive, irregular or otherwise unacceptable' (Deputy Woods, Dáil Debates, 28 January 1986, vol. 363, col. 753). The main issue was how independent the new Garda Complaints Board should be as the Bill proposed that Garda personnel would still carry out investigations, albeit with civilian oversight. The Minister for Justice at the time argued that the level of independence should not interfere with the need for the commissioner of the force to maintain 'discipline and morale amongst its members' (Deputy Noonan, Dáil Debates, 28 January 1986, vol. 363, col. 729). The prospect of a number of independent investigators, a 'second police force', was warranted neither by the 'scale nor seriousness of the problem' and would have been 'far more costly' than the solution proposed by the minister (cols. 732–3). In addition, the low visibility and contestability of the incidents leading to complaints meant that investigation by a nominally independent body – a representative of the Garda commissioner sits on the board – would be 'just as effective as investigation by a fully independent person' (col. 733). In the following decades, this level of equanimity about the effectiveness of the complaints body dissipated as it was seen to be incapable of preventing the police perpetrating illegitimate harms.

When the Act was reviewed in 1991, the 'whole question of drug-related criminal activity' had become 'the subject of widespread and justifiable public concern' (Noel Treacy, Dáil Debates, 13 June 1991, vol. 409, col. 1917) and justified the retention of the 1984 Act as necessary to deal with drug-related crime (ICCL 1993). Furthermore, the same minister contended that the new safeguards such as custody regulations and the Garda Complaints Board had resulted in a 'virtual disappearance of complaints of physical ill-treatment or threats of violence' (col. 1928). This sanguine outlook would be tested in the decade ahead as policing powers were scrutinised and assessed against international human rights standards.

## Opening up policing to Europe

The Committee for the Prevention of Torture (CPT) first visited Ireland between 26 September and 5 October 1993. One of its main findings was a consistent allegation from people detained in custody that they had been 'physically ill-treated' (Council of Europe 1995: para. 13). As a result of their investigations, the CPT considered that 'persons held in certain police establishments in Ireland run a not inconsiderable risk of being physically ill-treated' (para. 20). The composition of the Garda complaints Board also drew adverse comment since its composition meant that it was unlikely to be considered as impartial and its capacity to deal objectively with complaints was put in doubt (para. 55). A system of independent inspection of police stations was also recommended.

The response of the state to these criticisms, which directly contradicted its own opinion about the 'virtual disappearance' of police complaints, might charitably be described as dilatory. The CPT report was published in December 1995, over two years after the initial visit. In their response to the 1993 visit, the Irish government committed itself to a review of the complaints mechanism.

Following a second visit in 1998, the CPT reiterated concern about the persistent allegations 'regarding the use of excessive force by police officers' (Council of Europe 1999: para. 14). It reminded the Irish government of its previous recommendation, that one of the main bulwarks against such allegations was the existence of an impartial and independent complaints mechanism. The CPT also suggested that there had been no 'significant augmentation of the intensity' (para. 18) with which senior police officers were exercising oversight of custody arrangements. The government's response indicated that it hoped to introduce 'procedural change' (Irish Government 1999: para. 27) to the Board by 2000 as it was 'generally satisfied with the operation of the Complaints Act and the board' (Minister for Justice, Dáil Debates, 18 October 2000, vol. 524, col. 776). And in response to the issue of the independent inspection of Garda stations, the government believed such a system 'would be difficult to operate' (Irish Government 1999: para. 41).

So far, the story is reassuringly state-centric as a sovereign government resists attempts to regulate effectively one of its core functions, the potential exercise of violence. If the story was left here, it might well chime with ideas of states intent on coercion and show up the limits of Europeanisation in operating as a buffer against authoritarian policing. Despite evidence to the contrary, the Irish state denied that the regulatory apparatus of policing needed systemic reform, indicating that the pressure of European norms was insufficient to move the Irish state beyond denial. However, conditions internal to the island of Ireland and, in particular, the downgrading of the conflict in Northern Ireland, created new resources with which norm entrepreneurs could agitate for change.

## A contagion of rights in Ireland

When the broader significance of Northern Ireland has been evaluated, it has usually been in terms of how the exceptional powers granted to criminal justice agencies to counter a paramilitary threat would eventually become part of the normal apparatus to deal with ordinary crime. This 'contagion' thesis predicts that the attractiveness of emergency powers, with their capacity to slip free from normal due process restraints, will prove irresistible to state actors in their 'fight against crime' (Kilcommins and Vaughan 2004; Mulcahy 2005). Our own narrative demonstrates this possibility but also indicates how it may be resisted, namely through the judicial *habitus* attuned to the primacy of rights that cannot be sacrificed before popular anxieties. So while it is possible that we have increased normalisation of the exception, a countervailing tendency in the form of greater normalisation of human rights is also prevalent.

While criticism of An Garda Síochána was a sporadic, occasional affair, disputes about policing matters in Northern Ireland have been far more vociferous and persistent. Many nationalists and Catholics either rejected policing as the extension of an illegitimate state or denounced it for aggressive tactics. Even if some nationalists accepted that police in Northern Ireland could act fairly, they were consistently less supportive of the organisation than Protestants, particularly on the issue of impartiality of treatment. This perception of inequity ensured that fundamental reforms to policing were vital for any political settlement (Mulcahy 2006).

The Belfast Agreement of 1998, which laid the basis for a formal cessation of paramilitary violence, recognised that policing was an 'emotive' issue and that any new arrangements needed to be actively supported by the entire society of Northern Ireland. An independent commission, which became known as the Patten Report after its chairman, was established to outline the desired new policing arrangements. The purpose of the Patten Report was to reorientate 'policing towards the support of active and equal citizenship rather than the support of a sovereign statehood' (Walker 2001: 246). To adapt Jessop, this entailed a 'de-statization' of the rationale for policing, to be replaced by 'protection and vindication of the human rights of all' (Patten Report 1999: para 4.1).

These developments affected policing in the Republic of Ireland in a number of directions. In the Belfast Agreement, the Irish government committed itself to strengthen protection of human rights in its jurisdiction, by examining the feasibility of incorporating the ECHR and setting up a Human Rights Commission to oversee state practice regarding human rights. Human rights developments acted like a magnet, pulling the institutions of the Republic along to the level reached in Northern Ireland.

As paramilitaries desisted from their campaign of violence, this had a destabilising effect on policing in the Republic. As late as 1997, the Gardaí insisted that their primary role was 'to ensure the security of the state' (An Garda Síochána 1997: 2) against paramilitary threats. This rationale provided the pretext for the Gardaí to invoke emergency powers against 'ordinary' criminals and to negate due process values (Kilcommins and Vaughan 2004). While the Troubles in Northern Ireland persisted, the Irish state was less than willing to regulate the conduct of policing (Mulcahy 2002), only doing so grudgingly once a scandal erupted, as with the Kerry Babies case.

Just as the Irish state was contending with the fact that a fundamental threat to its sovereignty had diminished, a policing scandal emerged that called into question many of the Garda tactics used in the struggle against criminals. In 1996, members of the McBrearty family in a rural part of north-west Ireland were falsely accused of being involved in a fatal hit-and-run incident. Disputed confessions were obtained from this family, yet charges were never produced against them. In the aftermath, 160 summonses over licensing and public order offences were laid against their business premises, yet the Director of Public Prosecution dropped these. The McBrearty family hired a team of private investigators to validate their claims of police harassment and sought damages from the state. The publicity attracted media attention, forcing an inconclusive Garda inquiry which reported in 2001. In 2002, a tribunal of inquiry, known after its chairperson Judge Morris, was set up to investigate various claims relating to Garda corruption.

What has emerged so far from the Morris Tribunal is evidence that Gardaí claimed credit for the discovery of paramilitary explosives that they had concealed; used informants in a totally unregulated fashion to gain evidence against suspects; and planted arms and explosives in two separate cases to incriminate citizens. Allegations of Garda abuse of suspects in custody are now being investigated. Judge Morris dismissed the notion that these events might have been a statistical blip (Morris

2005: 664) since they were indicative of a wider management failing to maintain effective oversight from the Department of Justice, through to Garda headquarters and divisional command. What Morris has disclosed are the secrets of Ireland's 'dirty tricks'[1] against terrorism and how it had gone unchecked as long as the Irish state was thought to be under threat. The Morris Tribunal found this lack of oversight to be 'contrary to modern theories of risk management' and that new practices were necessary to 'interpose a barrier of distrust and to engage in the process of management assuming that fault, deceit, negligence and cover-up will occur' (Morris 2004: 457). Without some level of independent oversight, it becomes likely that greater weight will be placed on the 'needs of the Garda operation or investigation' and lesser consideration will be accorded to the rights of the citizen, as stipulated both by the Irish Constitution and the ECHR (Morris 2006: 268).[2]

The combination of these revelations and the process of policing reform in the North made it difficult for politicians in the Republic of Ireland to resist proposals for systems of oversight detached from police control. Calls to emulate the examples of a police ombudsman and police board in Northern Ireland were made more and more frequently by political representatives and campaigning groups in the Republic of Ireland. These demands were initially resisted on the basis that the 'situation in Northern Ireland in relation to policing differs substantially from the position which has obtained in this jurisdiction' (Minister for Justice John O'Donoghue, Dáil Debates, 15 November 2000, vol. 526, col. 74 ). While police reform predicated upon the protection of human rights may have been suitable for Northern Ireland, it was not appropriate for the Republic of Ireland where the Gardaí comprised part of a 'blessed trinity' of communal control in rural Ireland, the others being the priest and school teacher (P. McGrath, Dáil Debates, 20 April 2005, vol. 600, col. 1571).

In contesting these positions, norm entrepreneurs made several points. Stressing that Northern Ireland was a unique situation ignored how the Patten recommendations for reform were largely, in the words of a commission member, a 'statement of international best practice as far as policing is concerned' (quoted in Mulcahy 2006: 164). Northern Irish policing reforms were largely cosmopolitan rather than provincial in their origins. And emphasising the affinity between Irish citizens and their police force overlooked how the structures of the police force were 'not appropriate to the rights and freedoms individual [Irish] citizens now demand' (Brendan Howlin, Dáil Debates, 28 March 2002, vol. 551, col. 937). Bolstering their case, norm entrepreneurs drew out the implications of the ECHR that was being incorporated into Irish domestic law. The implications of various cases of alleged unlawful killing by state agents in which the European Court of Human Rights had found that article 2 (right to life) of the ECHR had been violated as these cases had had not been independently investigated[3] was discussed in parliament. The inference was that compliance could not be achieved by 'tinkering with the Garda complaints legislation' but only 'in a more fundamental way by establishing an independent investigative authority' (Brendan Howlin, Dáil Debates, 23 May 2001, vol. 536, col. 1418). The then Minister for Justice conceded that the judgments in the cases cited above had 'implications for this jurisdiction, *prima facie*. In the circumstances, it appears that change will be required' (col. 1417).

In recognising the validity of these objections, the government conceded 'recognition of the crucial importance of the standards set by international human rights bodies' (Irish Human Rights Commission 2002: 7). Furthermore, the Irish Human Rights Commission reminded the Irish government that under the Belfast Agreement it had committed itself to the principle of equivalence of human rights protections in both parts of the island of Ireland. Following the model of cosmopolitan policing, based around the protection of human rights, was increasingly difficult to avoid for the Irish state despite protestations that Northern Ireland was a unique situation. Coupled with the facts emerging from the McBrearty affair, the government felt compelled to concede the inadequacy of the Garda Complaints Board and announced, in July 2002, that a Garda Inspectorate would be established to deal with police complaints.

The Irish Human Rights Commission insisted that there was a basic incompatibility between an inspectorate and ombudsman, with the former being more concerned with efficiency and the latter oriented around human rights values. The Minister for Justice conceded that the Commission had a 'legitimate point' (Dáil Debates, 6 February 2003, vol. 560, cols. 1406–7) and this distinction was realised through the distinct offices of a Garda Inspectorate and a three-person Ombudsman Commission, being introduced in the final version of the Bill that was passed into law, the Garda Síochána Act 2005. Further controls include the creation of an internal standards unit and the establishment of local policing committees to liaise with the public (Vaughan 2005). Most attention and criticism has focused on the alleged inadequacy of the powers granted to the Ombudsman Commission in comparison to its counterpart in Northern Ireland, especially the possible impediment that the trump card of state security could play in restricting investigations (Walsh 2004b). While the Minister for Justice has tried to rebut the impression that 'everything that we do down here [in the Republic of

Ireland] is second-rate in comparison' to developments in Northern Ireland (Dáil Debates, 23 June 2005, vol. 605, col. 111), this has not prevented interested parties pressing home the differences in the two jurisdictions.

Opposition political parties have proposed that an Independent Garda Authority be established to sustain the public accountability of the Irish police. The government has resisted these moves on the grounds that it would impair democratic accountability as realised through parliament, although a new security and policing committee will be established (M. McDowell, Dáil Debates, 29 November 2006, vol. 628). To paraphrase Gerry Adams, President of Sinn Féin, the debate on Garda oversight and accountability 'hasn't gone away, you know'.[4] And the reason why it refuses to go away is that the normative power of human rights is difficult to contest – 'no one could be against human rights', in the words of the Minister for Justice (Dáil Debates, 23 June 2005, vol. 605, col. 113) – so that it stands in persistent contrast with the allure of a model that emphasises security for the majority, law-abiding populace. A possible counter to this entrenchment of human rights is the strategy of making policing more answerable to local communities that might well encourage the police to prioritise the security demands of the majority.

## Policing below the state

One of the problems with policing becoming so intertwined with the defence of the Irish state is that it became relatively unresponsive to certain communities. From the 1950s on, the Irish police were esteemed as 'Irish in thought and action' (McNiffe 1997). Just as the Irish Prime Minister, Eamon de Valera, considered that if he wished 'to know what the Irish want, I [need only] look into my own heart', so too the Gardaí did not see any need to develop formal modes of liaison with the Irish people. Tight affiliation with the public was made possible by the rural nature of Irish society that fostered a low crime rate and enabled the Gardaí to concentrate on non-crime duties. Conversely, if social conditions changed, it was more likely that the Gardaí would encounter problems in maintaining their bond with Irish communities.

We have already alluded to how the Gardaí had to adjust to a rising crime rate in the 1960s. Perhaps one of the biggest influences was the stark rise in drug consumption in the early 1980s, particularly in relatively deprived areas of Dublin. Senior Gardaí estimated that drugs had been 'the biggest single influence on the crime profile during their time of service', exceeding even the impact of the Northern Ireland conflict

(Mulcahy and O'Mahony 2005: 10). However, the resources of the state were directed primarily towards managing this conflict rather than the drugs issue, leading to accusations of neglect from many communities. Rather than rely on the state to take action against drug-dealing, communities decided to take action themselves, overthrowing many of the presumptions of the rule of law.

From 1982, groups in different neighbourhoods began to organise themselves against drug-dealing. By 1984, these groups had coalesced into Concerned Parents Against Drugs (CPAD). The *modus operandi* of CAPD involved patrolling neighbourhoods to keep drug-pushers out, gathering information from the community and the accumulation of *prima facie* evidence of drug-dealing or consumption (Lyder 2005). This evidence could be gained by citizen patrols or more intensive investigation, either through time-consuming surveillance or via people in the normal course of their occupational interactions, such as taxi-drivers or milkmen (Bennett 1988). Information secured in this fashion was passed from various districts through to what was known as the Central Committee, made up of two representatives from each area. The information was conveyed orally and written records were introduced in 1986. Data about suspects were used in the 'single greatest institution of the CPAD, the public meeting' (1988: 27). People were named as drug-dealers or 'pushers' and asked to come to a subsequent meeting to reply. If a person confessed to being a pusher, they were asked to desist. The parallels with the former Garda practice of inviting someone to a location to assist with enquiries are obvious, as are the dangers that a person might wrongly inculpate himself under pressure. As Bennett notes, 'once the flow of testimony has begun in a locality, a great deal of what then occurs is actually made up of confessions or the defence of innocence' (1988: 28), just as happened with the exculpatory system of communal trials in the eighteenth and early nineteenth centuries. Opinions differ on the accuracy of these methods. Bennett starkly declared that CPAD were 'always right because their procedures result in a requirement of absolute proof before any sanction can be activated' (1988: 39). If the alleged dealers were less than receptive to the evidence presented at these 'trials', they may have been the subject of a march by community members before their own residences. Other observers were less than convinced about the correctness of proceedings, believing that often people could be mistakenly identified as 'pushers' (Murphy-Lawless 2002).

CAPD forbade the neighbourhood groups to cooperate with the Gardaí. Groups that ignored this stricture were disaffiliated from CAPD although this was not always consistently applied (Lyder 2005). In turn, Gardaí denigrated the activities of CPAD as 'vigilantism' (Bennett 1988:

39) to register the allegedly unlawful nature of this group. However, it seems that CPAD fulfil Johnston's (2000: 150) definition of vigilantism as the practice of autonomous citizens engaged in civil policing. For Johnston, this form of policing has five features. It involves planning and preparation rather than simply reactive violence; it is undertaken by private citizens; it retains the potential to use force; it attempts to re-impose social order; and it accomplishes this through a guarantee of security. Consequently, 'vigilantism is a mode of policing – a strategy for offering guarantees of security – located neither in the state apparatus (public policing) nor in the market place (commercial security) but in the sphere of civil society' (2000: 152). CAPD represented one of the first undertakings in Ireland to break the state monopoly of policing in an effort to provide a sense of protection to a local community that could not be obtained otherwise. This is not to deny that vigilantism as civil policing is not guilty of excesses, but as we have seen this is equally true of policing conducted by the state. The strategies used by CAPD, such as use of hearsay evidence and reversal of the burden of proof, reoccur in the state administration of justice in the 1990s and beyond.

The Irish state attempted to sequester the potential policing powers of civil society by introducing a type of community policing in the form of Neighbourhood Watch. In 1983, the Garda Commissioner Laurence Wren had warned that 'the gardaí need to start building bridges back to the community unless we are to find ourselves in trouble' (quoted in Kilcommins *et al.* 2004: 217). Neighbourhood Watch was a mechanism by which Gardaí could communicate messages about crime prevention to the public and receive information about suspicious activities. It suffered the fate of many community policing initiatives, namely that many of the most troubled areas were least interested since they enjoyed an often fraught relationship with the police. Some believed that in the 1980s the Gardaí operated a policy of containment in relation to these areas, preventing local residents from coming out and 'robbing the gaffs [houses]' in nearby genteel areas (Mulcahy and O'Mahony 2005: 11). So it would seem that two forms of policing, one below the state and the other through the state, existed simultaneously; but they were superseded in the late 1990s by a new policing initiative, joint policing committees, that set up formal structures of consultation for the first time.

These new committees had their origins in the desire of communities afflicted by drug trafficking to improve their situation. It has been suggested that there is less militancy on the part of Sinn Féin representatives in their dealings with the gardaí (Mulcahy and O'Mahony 2005: 12), a move towards normalisation inspired by the diminution of conflict in Northern Ireland referred to earlier. Equally important has been the development of the second of a twin-track approach to illegal drugs, the first of which has been the repressive legislation described in Chapter 6. The second approach was the development of a locally-based, inter-agency approach to implement anti-drugs strategies. Eleven local drugs task forces were set up, with all but one in Dublin. These task forces drew representatives of state and community closer together, and some of these linkages formalised in community policing fora (Joint Committee 2005) that have been favourably reviewed (Connolly 2002).

When instigating reform of the Gardaí through the publication of the Garda Síochána 2004, the experience of the policing fora were noted and incorporated into a proposal for joint policing committees. Although initial proposals excluded community representatives, lobbying from several quarters ensured that they could serve on it. The primary function of these committees is to 'review patterns of crime and disorder' and provide appropriate advice on how best to prevent such activity. It is envisaged that there will be 114 such committees eventually. Whether they institute a credible form of local accountability remains to be seen. These groups are also supposed to evaluate claims from communities for the installation of CCTV systems in public places, subsidised by the government to a maximum of 200,000 euros. By the end of 2007 it is envisaged that there will be 26 Garda CCTV systems, 24 community-based ones and 12 in housing schemes occupied by older people (Department of Justice Press Release, 30 March 2007).

## Conclusion

Although the effect of supra- and sub-national influences is to increase the accountability placed upon policing, these do not necessarily operate in mutually consistent ways. The effect of drawing upon cosmopolitan discourses of human rights and establishing organisations to oversee their observance by the police is to reinforce a level of morality that is essential to the due-process model. This is not only in tension with the trends outlined in the last chapter but may also jar with the idea of allowing the community to have a greater say in policing and its modes of surveillance. Of course, this latter option may be less morally arbitrary and more open to contestation than other forms of policing that have been undertaken by communities. The future is uncertain and the best we can do is set out these competing trends to understand the complex configuration of negotiated justice that may now be emerging.

## Chapter 8

# Conclusion: The war on terror and campaigns for rights

Essential ambiguity between rule by law and the rule of law is the theme of this book. Recurrent forces push the state towards authoritarian rule but competing influences hamper this trend. Criminologists have devoted most of their attention to the former by concentrating on the media clamour for less tolerance to be shown to criminal suspects and offenders and by extensive analysis of executives' guarantees of greater security. Unwittingly, this strategy articulates a 'criminology of the present tense' that passes over the persistence of the past particularly through the judicial *habitus* that is steeped in classical legal principles, such as due process and proportionality. If neglect of the past is one factor that leads to claims about the novelty of our times, effacing the distinctiveness of particular national cultures is another. Putting so much emphasis on forces that encompass the planet – worldwide terror, international crime networks, global insecurity – means that the specific nature of responses within individual countries can be underplayed. Paraphrasing Braudel, we might call this phenomenon 'jurisdictional time', the different rates at which countries adjust to these global forces via the habitus formed through the *longue dureé* of legal time.

In recent times, many governments have tried to curb this *habitus* by, for example, structuring sentencing rather than leaving it to individual judges. But there are limits to the extent to which executives can guide the judiciary without breaching the separation of powers doctrine and so a space always exists to resist executive encroachment. This book has tried to demonstrate that acts of judicial resistance still manifest themselves, despite the greater prominence given to public protection, be it from terror, crime or both. We hope not to have succumbed to either romanticising the role of the judiciary or reifying the past. The judiciary can be too deferential to the executive, bowing before the trump card of national security or being too credulous before claims about a threatening form of criminality. Equally, we do not wish to align ourselves with what Loader and Walker (2007: 12) label the liberty lobby, which sees the coercive capacity of the state as a perennial danger to be regulated by strict adherence to due process. One consequence is that the liberty lobby operates largely as a 'negative, oppositional force ... that evacuates the terrain that the security lobby so effectively and affectively occupies' (2007: 14). Retreating thus, the liberty lobby insists on the inviolability of due process procedures despite them having originated in specific social conditions that might be changing, as we have tried to document. Assumptions about the relative weakness of offenders *vis-à-vis* community and state and the reliability of certain kinds of witness may no longer be tenable today and may necessitate a reconsideration in how certain kinds of offences are investigated and prosecuted.

At best, we have provided some evidence that such changes should not be deplored outright but we have not been able to stipulate the normative principles that would justify this kind of alteration (for a beginning, see Vaughan 2007). The discourse on human rights, at least as it figures in debates on crime, too often involves the 'selective privileging of the value of the individual over the collective, especially where the latter takes the form of the State' (Woodiwiss 2006: 1). By accentuating the priority of the individual, rights discourse elevates the autonomy of the individual over the interdependence within which people as social beings are enmeshed. Emphasising this latter component restores the importance of reciprocity and contributes to the 'democratization of the rule of law' (2006: 11) by including previously suppressed voices into legal practice. The capacity of human rights to escape any definitive categorisation ensures that they are always capable of challenging the *status quo* despite being dependent on a state for their activation. The force of human rights has spilt over the boundaries of individual states, obliging them to take more seriously the impact of their practices upon these rights.

This is an unusual step for states to take since most of their practice is concerned with defending their own territorial integrity, even at the cost of deviating from the normal model of inculpatory justice. The legitimacy of the earlier exculpatory model had become increasingly devalued before the mass of the population, and its effectiveness slowly expired, itself a rebuke to instrumentalists who believe that moral norms have no power. *Realpolitik* did intrude when outright threats to the state emerged in the form of republican paramilitaries and persists as serious crime networks have joined terrorism as one of the primary threats to state and society.

Popular voices, particularly as enunciated through the media, demand greater protection from the state but this call is rendered in two distinct tones. People overtly wish for more forceful forms of state security that dampen the protections afforded to those suspected of criminality, in the way that the state has dealt with terrorism. Muffled amid this clamour, an alternative campaign presses the state to impose greater regulation and oversight upon its own apparatus of justice to prevent possible abuses of power – people want to be protected *from* rather than simply *by* the state. This campaign for rights is boosted by underlining the international obligations that the Irish state has ratified and incorporated as part of its self-image as a 'civilised' European nation. Norm entrepreneurs gripped the opportunity offered by dawning peace in Northern Ireland and the diminishing importance granted to state security to emphasise the need to offer enhanced protection from the state through independent oversight bodies. Establishing an independent Ombudsman Commission as a conduit between the grievances of citizens and the police force is an example of what Tilly called 'protected consultation', extending the democratisation of the rule of law.

This process of democratisation has been cognitively resourced by notions of cosmopolitan justice that emphasise the primacy of human rights over the nation-state rather than seeing the former as bestowed by the latter. It would be a mistake to view this as an unrelenting process of transposition of international norms to the national level. Acknowledgement of these norms' validity does not entail effacement or replacement of rights as defined by nation-states – monism does not replace the previous state of dualism. Instead, the judicial *habitus* is engaged in a delicate process of translation, examining rights defined at both levels to see how they can be made congruent with each other and with the commitment to concepts such as liberty, democracy and human rights. European integration is often thought to have inspired a process of securitisation that fortifies borders against the 'unwanted', particularly migrants who cannot lay claim to national citizenship of the European nations, and fosters a culture of unease within a national population (Bigo 2002). Securitisation has been supposedly further promoted by measures to extend a common space of freedom, security and justice within the European Union. This reading is too monochromatic, failing to note that the necessary translation of both securitisation and democratisation processes at national level clears an opening for interpretation, contestation and hence moderation.

Considering this irresolvable tension between national and transnational levels should discommode notions of state sovereignty upon which so much criminological thinking still depends. There are other facets of Europeanisation that should add to the discomfort, particularly those related to the growth of regulatory agencies. Although we have not been able to trace their individual origins, we have pointed to the significance of their legal powers and the fact that many of them are able to undertake prosecutions without reference to the Director of Public Prosecutions. One of the principal reasons for the establishment of these agencies has been the process of deepening European integration, a project infamous for its capacity to overlook popular wishes. Realising this, it would be foolish to interpret their development as some sort of straightforward process of democratisation. And their insulation from the public is only exacerbated by the emphasis on expertise, their operational distance from government and lack of populist input. And yet their existence is testimony to the possibility of extending the understanding of crime beyond that usually defined by the 'normal' criminal justice system. Progress is not without its costs and the insulated operation of these regulatory agencies shield many difficult questions. Do they strike a fair balance between the rights of the accused and prosecution? Do they inappropriately blur the lines between criminal and civil measures? And does their understanding of harms correspond with the wider public?

Enquiring about the appropriate balance between different values is usually the preserve of security concerns, especially those around terrorism or serious crime. Politicians talk of tilting the 'balance' back towards the victim, and striking a 'balance' between new security measures and maintaining liberties. Some (e.g. Zedner 2005) think that the notion of 'balancing' is spurious, suggesting that it reconciles disparate values too easily and is a euphemism for imposing the wishes of the majority. Even these critics admit that societies need to mediate between competing goods and elaborate some institutional means for doing so. Zedner (2005: 533), for instance, nominates a 'culture of critical judicial scrutiny' allied to a resolute belief in due process.

Although this strategy is meant to combat the executive's fixation with security, it accepts too readily the terms of the debate. Pitting the judiciary against the executive can elide the former into the liberty lobby with little capacity to connect with public fears. A more hopeful strategy might be to stop treating security as an end in itself but rather as a means to other goods (2005: 532). We expect the executive, through the criminal justice system, to produce security as a means of ensuring our physical safety and yet safety encompasses the work of bodies like a health and safety inspectorate and even an entity like the Environmental Protection Agency. Regulatory agencies are what Vibert (2007) calls 'unelected bodies' and 'affect the way we are able to deal with life's accidents and chances, fortunes and misfortunes' (2007: 7), all of which are essential to the notion of security. Expanding the notion of safety allows us to dilute the importance given to a notion like security, defined via the non-occurrence of crime or terror, by relating it to a broader set of goods and so 'civilizing security' (Loader and Walker 2007). Broadening the security debate helps us to surpass the executive–judiciary polarity with which so much of this book has been concerned, as the judiciary are no longer the sole organisation tasked with protecting human rights. Instead, this task falls on to an extensive alliance of interests, making up what Slaughter (2004) calls a disaggregated state, comprising state officials, NGOs, human rights commissions, judges and concerned citizens forming an advocacy coalition to ferment change on this subject. What this amounts to is a new separation of powers that transcends judiciary superintending the executive and involves a range of expert organisations regulating specialised sectoral areas and being invigilated by the disaggregated state.

In Ireland, the long nineteenth century of criminal justice has been punctuated by a struggle to establish a system based on procedural justice. Perceived states of exception have held up this process by the introduction of 'emergency law' that filtered into the 'normal' system of criminal justice. Just at a time when this contamination may be arrested, popular insecurity may be unleashing new states of exception that demand incursions upon procedural justice. Greater awareness of human rights and acceptance of their legitimate force may block this hostility. The prime feature of the long nineteenth century, the rule of law, mediates between rights and the states of exception that menace them. What has altered is that this struggle no longer occurs between two primary actors – the executive and judiciary – and at one level – the national. Instead, the contest has splintered as many other actors claim to have a role in the acknowledgement and activation of rights that are being unbound from a national order.

Demands for greater public involvement in the dispensation of justice have often been worriedly characterised as populist and pitted against the 'establishment'. Resentment at the foisting of 'elitist' values on to matters that fundamentally affect the population is thought to be one of the defining features of this kind of populism. Since resentment is understood in negative terms, encapsulating bitter feelings of enmity, it is thought best to maintain the marginal involvement of citizens in matters of justice either by establishing tokenistic restorative justice initiatives or by endorsing victims in a zero-sum game with offenders.

It is possible to view resentment in a more positive light, directing attention to matters that have been unfairly marginalised and seeking an explanation for this neglect. Furthermore, public involvement in matters concerning risk is not always viewed in a negative light. When we examine the work of regulators and their stress on risk management, the lack of public deliberation around the criteria chosen is often seen as a matter of concern to be resolved by a new politics of accountability (Black 2005, 2006). Given the temptation for the criminal justice system to emulate the tactics of regulatory agencies that pay scarce heed to due process rights (Considine and Kilcommins 2006) – 'the normalisation of regulation' – deliberating upon the appropriateness of targets selected and powers deployed by regulators becomes compelling.

One of the reasons why this has not become an urgent matter of concern is that the forces of the criminal justice system appear to be the most obvious manifestation of the oppressive capacity of the state. Thus, the liberty lobby is prepared to resist dramatic additions to this capacity. Greater powers are sought for anti-terrorism measures and the resistance of civil libertarians often goes up a level too. Much of this book has been devoted to tracing this dialectic and how the struggle against terrorism can fundamentally alter due process principles within ordinary criminal justice systems. We have tried to indicate that this is neither a *fait accompli* nor should it always be deplored, since it may point to the dissolution of a constrictive arrangement between state and accused that leaves little space for others. Normalisation of extraordinary measures is not the only lesson to draw from Irish experience, although it has the oldest pedigree. Regulatory activities that curb due process may affect more people than anti-terrorism strategies but since they are not directed at obvious criminals they provoke little attention. Even the scholars of responsive regulation who do take these developments seriously analyse these organisations on an individual basis to see if they abide by dialogue or opt for command-and-control. Omitted is any consideration of what the proliferation of these agencies means for the governance of justice so that what Rosanvallon (2006: 28–9, our translation) calls the 'unpolitical', 'the lack of a global understanding of the problems faced in organising the common good' forcefully emerges. Previously, jurisdictions have relied on the separation of powers between legislature, executive and judiciary to deliberate and realise the common good. Legislatures have become unwilling to closely interrogate executive proposals to diminish the manifestation of terror in various forms and elevate security, leaving this task to judges. While this is not as hopeless as many believe, there are reasons for doubting that individual judicial decision-making – Dicey's third feature of the rule of law – is capable of regulating matters for the common good, given the complexity of contemporary monadic societies.

What we need is a new architecture of justice that can articulate this common good in an era of diversity and pluralism within both state and society to preserve the other two features of the rule of law, non-arbitrariness of government and equality of relations. There is some evidence that these two principles are embedded more strongly in criminal justice and that it is from the civil side that the threat to the rule of law might appear. Thanks to this mixed verdict, it would appear that the long nineteenth century of criminal justice has not yet concluded.

# Notes

## Chapter 3

1 Indeed Ireland acted as somewhat of a laboratory for England and Wales in the fields of education, police, prosecution, prisons and public health. As one commentator noted in the nineteenth century: 'Experiments are made in that country [Ireland] on so large a scale, and pushed to their extreme consequences with such disregard to the sufferings which they inflict, that they give us results as precious as Majendie [Francois Magendie, the physiologist, noted for his dedication to the live vivisection of animals that spurred a landmark bill banning animal cruelty]' (quoted in MacDonagh 1976: 206).

2 See also Beattie (1986: 39) who suggested: 'Informal means of dealing with offenders, including direct and immediate physical punishment, must often have been preferred to a formal and troublesome prosecution, especially in a small community in which a court case might well be disruptive of social relationships.'

3 As Langbein (2003: 278) notes, 'in a system that emphasized capital punishment, the right to remain silent was literally the right to commit suicide'.

4 Indeed Edmund Burke, commenting to the House of Commons in 1794, denied that there was any such thing as the law of evidence: 'It is true, something has been written on the law of evidence, but ... [it was] very general, very abstract, and comprised in so small a compass that a parrot he had known might get them by rote in one half hour, and repeat them in five minutes' (quoted in Allen 1931: 277). On the lack of a law of evidence in the eighteenth century more generally, see Langbein (1996).

5 As Stephen remarked: 'When the prisoner had to speak for himself, he ... could not, without tacit admission of guilt, insist on the inconclusiveness of

the evidence against him. The jury expected from him a clear explanation of the case against him; and if he could not give it, they convicted him' (Stephen 1863: 194–5).

6 See also *Entick v Carrington* (1765) 19 State Trials 1030 at 1066.

7 See also Hale who suggested in 1736: 'That in favour of life great strictness's have been in all times required in points of indictments, and the truth is, that it grows to be a blemish and inconvenience in the law, and the administration thereof.' (1971: 193).

8 Alternative systems of law were often employed to resist the colonizing process. As Laird (2005: 127) notes: 'Subversive law in the form of boycotting, "unwritten law", Repeal Association arbitration courts, Ribbon Association courts, Land League courts, National League courts and United Irish League courts attempted to fill the gap created by an official system of law which rarely sought and never attained the kind of widespread support that its successful administration required.'

9 P. Hillyard, *The War on Terror: Lessons from Ireland* available at www.liberty-security.org/IMG/pdf/The_War_on_Terror_lessons_from_Ireland.pdf. Extraordinary legal responses had also from time to time been employed in England as evident in the state response to Chartism in the summer of 1842.

10 As Hobbes (1651: 226–8) noted: 'The finall cause, End or Designe of Men … is the foresight of their own preservation, and of a more contented life thereby; that is to get themselves out from that miserable condition of Warre … [T]he agreement of these creatures is Naturall; that of men, is by covenant only, which is Artificall; and therefore it is no wonder if there be somewhat else required (besides Covenant) to make their Agreement constant and lasting; which is a Common Power, to keep them in awe, and to direct their actions to the common benefit. The only way to erect such a common power … is to conferre all their power and strength upon one man, or upon one assembly of men, that may reduce all their wills … unto one Will … This is the generation of that great Leviathan.'

11 Beccaria noted, for example: 'Punishments that exceed what is necessary for protection of the deposit of public security are by their very nature unjust, and punishments are increasingly more just as the safety which the sovereign secures for his subjects is the more sacred and inviolable, and the liberty greater' (1995: 121).

12 Hobbes, Locke, Rousseau and Rawls all employ such an analytic framework. Other writers such as Bentham and Hume, however, explicitly reject social contractarianism.

13 But see Foucault (1991: 222) who would suggest: 'Historically, the process by which the bourgeoisie became … the politically dominant class was masked by the establishment of an explicit, coded and formally egalitarian framework … But the development and generalization of disciplinary mechanisms constituted the other, dark side of the process. The general juridical form that guaranteed a system of rights that were egalitarian in principle was supported by these tiny, everyday, physical mechanisms, by all those systems of micro-power that are essentially non-egalitarian and asymmetrical that we call the disciplines … The contract may have been regarded as an ideal foundation of

law and political power; panopticism constituted the technique, universally widespread, of coercion ... The "Enlightenment", which discovered the liberties, also invented the disciplines.'

14 It is important, however, not to underemphasise the hostility to executive control of policing which remained deeply embedded in England in the early to mid nineteenth century. A Report of the Select Committee on the Police of the Metropolis in 1822 noted that it was difficult to 'reconcile an effective system of policing with that perfect freedom of action and exemption from interference which are the great privileges and blessings of society in this country, and your Committee think that forfeiture or curtailment of such an advantage would be too great a sacrifice for improvements in police, or facilities in detection of crime, however desirable in themselves' (Report of the Select Committee on the Police of the Metropolis (1822) [440] Vol. IV, p. 11).

15 The Prisoner's Counsel Act of 1836 enabled an accused felon to be fully represented by a lawyer.

16 Stricter divisions, for example, became evident between examination-in-chief and cross-examination.

17 As Stephen (1883: 354) noted: 'In the present day the rule that a man is presumed to be innocent till he is proved to be guilty is carried out in all of its consequences. The plea of not guilty puts everything in issue, and the prosecutor has to prove everything that he alleges from the very beginning.'

18 Private prosecutors could still initiate proceedings. See *People (DPP) v Killen* (1958) ILTR 182; *The People (Attorney General) v Boggan* [1968] IR 67. See also Osborne (1993: 119).

19 See also Nietzsche (1956 205) who noted: 'whenever a community gains in power and pride, its penal code becomes more lenient, while the moment it is weakened or endangered the harsher methods of the past are revived. The humanity of creditors has always increased with their wealth; until finally the degree to which a creditor can tolerate impairment becomes the measure of his wealth. It is possible to imagine a society so flushed with such a sense of power that it could afford to let its offenders go unpunished.'

20 We are grateful to Anthony McGrath for this point.

21 In time, more subjective principles of criminal responsibility would develop around concepts such as intent, recklessness, belief and knowledge (Lacey 2002).

22 This perception of offending rested on two assumptions: first, that all actions were free-willed, and; secondly, that free-will existed to like extent for all actors (Saleilles 1968: 64). For an earlier version of this perception, see, for example, J. Bentham, (1952–4) *Jeremy Bentham's Economic Writings, III*: 434.

23 See also Havelock Ellis (1890: 232) who noted: '[This conception] of punishment was founded on the assumption of the normality of the criminal: he was a normal person who had chosen to act as though he was not a normal person ... no regard [was had] to the varying nature of the offender; he was regarded as a constant factor.'

24 This must be seen as part of a broader matrix of rationalisation that was occurring during the period in question. In addition to the desire to have a more structured trial process and a fixed code of penalties proportionate to the

offence and administered with certainty, rationalisation was also evident in attempts at combating disease (Dobson 1987: 17), in the need to establish work rhythms and systematise production in factories (McKendrick 1961), in the reform of policing after 1829, and in the organisation of the workhouse system after 1834 (Driver 1993: 65).

25 For fuller accounts, see Garland (1985), Wiener (1999), Friedman (1993: 149–261), and Rothman (1983).

26 See also Rothman (1979: 10) who, in describing the transformation in late nineteenth and early twentieth century America, noted the following: 'No word was more popular in the lexicon of Progressive reformers than "individual". Again and again, they insisted that the criminal law had to respond to each individual offender, not to uniform categories of offences. As one of them put it: "In the old system, the main question was, what did he *do*? The main question should be, what *is* he?" As the most popular slogan of the period phrased it, "treat the criminal, not the crime".'

## Chapter 4

1 The Public Safety (Powers of Arrest and Detention) Temporary Act 1924, and Public Safety (Punishment of Offences) Temporary Act 1924.

2 Military courts operated where there was some doubt but where a person was caught, for example, in possession of firearms, they were brought before a committee and had no opportunity to consult a legal representative.

3 Eamon Broy was Garda commissioner at the time and the designation of Harriers was meant to signal an affinity with the Black and Tans, who also took their name from a hunting pack. Even today, the term operates as a political form of abuse to indicate too close an affiliation between police and government (see Joe Costello, Dáil Debates, 21 June 2005, vol. 604, col. 700).

4 [1979] IR 85. See also *People (DPP) v Shaw* [1982] IR1, where such Garda practices were described as 'no more than a euphemism for false imprisonment'.

5 The Offences against the State (Amendment) Act 1998, introduced following the Omagh bombing, increased this maximum period of detention to 72 hours.

6 The relevant provision of the Act, section 4, did not, however, come into operation until 1987, a year in which 2,854 persons were arrested under section 30 (Hogan and Walker 1989: 180–1). See also *Report of the Committee to Review the Offences against the State Acts, 1939–1998, and Related Matters* (Stationery Office 2001), para. 7.12, which noted: 'While the provisions of that legislation [the 1939 Act] was intended to afford the Gardai specific powers in cases where the security of the State was threatened, they were routinely applied in cases of which came to be described as "ordinary crime".'

7 These are the only years for which such figures are available.

8 See the long title to the Offences against the State Act 1939. For a different view, see *People (DPP) v. Quilligan* [1986] IR 495.

9 Offences currently scheduled include those under the Explosive Substances

Act 1883 and the Firearms Acts 1925–1971.

10 See *Report of the Committee to Review the Offences against the State Acts, 1939–1998*, dissenting views of Professor Dermot Walsh.

11 [1986] IR 495. See also *People (DPP) v Walsh* [1988] ILRM 137; see also Walsh (1989: 1099–1102).

12 [1989] ILRM 629.

13 Irish Council of Civil Liberties, *Submission to the Committee to Review the Offences against the State Acts, 1939–1998, and Related Matters*. Available at http://iccl.ie/DB_Data/issues/CriminalJustice_10007_Publications.htm.

14 The Irish Council for Civil Liberties suggests that the 'level of paramilitary violence has declined more than tenfold since the mid 1970s and the threat of paramilitary violence now comes largely from very small splinter groups with virtually no popular support' (Irish Council of Civil Liberties *Submission to the Committee to Review the Offences Against the State Acts, 1939–1998, and Related Matters*. Available at http://iccl.ie/DB_Data/issues/CriminalJustice_10007_Publications.htm.

15 Available at http://iccl.ie/DB_Data/issues/CriminalJustice_10007_Publications.htm.

16 See *Kavanagh v Ireland*, Human Rights Committee of the United Nations, 4 April 2001 (CCPR/C7D/819/1998). See, for example, the Report of the UN Human Rights Committee in 1993 which suggested that 'it did not consider that the continued existence of that court is justified in the present circumstances'. Report of the Human Rights Committee, Official Records of the General Assembly, 48th Session, Supplement No. 40, 1993, (A/48/40), Part 1, pp. 125–8.

17 Much of the reasoning behind the justification to continue with the court was premised on the notion that 'there have been instances in recent times where it appears that attempts have been made to tamper with juries in high-profile criminal trials in the ordinary courts' (*Report of the Committee to Review the Offences against the State Acts, 1939–1998*, 2001). To be content to justify the continuance of a non-jury, extraordinary court on the fragile, somewhat whimsical, evidence of 'instances' – without feeling the need to present any qualitative or quantitative verification, or to engage in any debate as to whether such evidence tipped the balance in favour of enhancing security or preventing the loss of liberties – raises serious questions about the state's commitment to the values enshrined by the Irish people in its Constitution.

18 The Proceeds of Crime (Amendment) Act 2005 reduces this period to three years if both parties consent.

19 See Cassidy and Law Society of Ireland (2003: 8). Other causal determinants would include legislative initiatives in the United States in the early 1970s and a number of international conventions on drug trafficking, money laundering, confiscation of the proceeds of crime in the late 1980s and early 1990s.

20 [1988] IR 326.

21 This relates to the hearsay provision in the Proceeds of Crime legislation.

22 Section 21 of the Offences against the State Act 1939 makes it an offence to be a

member of an unlawful organisation. The relevant section does not, however, properly define what constitutes 'membership' or 'organisation'. Moreover, and as referred to in the text, a number of evidential techniques are permitted to provide evidence that an individual is a member of an unlawful organisation. Section 3 of the Offences against the State (Amendment) Act 1972 provides that evidence of oral or written statements, the conduct of the accused, or the opinion evidence of a chief superintendent in the Gardaí may be admitted to prove membership. Section 24 of the Offences against the State Act 1939 also allows evidence of incriminating documents to be adduced to prove membership of the unlawful organisation.

23 See section 18 of the Offences against the State Act 1939. In cases where the Proceeds of Crime Act 1996 has been subject to constitutional challenge, the state, *inter alia*, has also relied on the constitutional support provided by the decision in *Clancy*. See *Michael Murphy v GM, PB, PC, GH; John Gilligan v CAB, Revenue Commissioners, the Garda Commissioner, Ireland and the Attorney General* [2001] 4 IR 113. See also *Gilligan v Criminal Assets Bureau* [1998] IR 326.

24 McCracken J. in *People (John Gilligan) v DPP* (Unreported, CCA, 8 Auguse 2003) noted the following about the witness protection programme: 'There are certainly some very disturbing factors in the way in which the authorities sought to obtain the evidence ... This was the first time that a witness protection programme had been implemented in this State, and one of the most worrying features is that there never seems to have actually been a programme. There ought to have been clear guidelines as to what could or could not be offered to the witnesses. This was not done, and instead there was an ongoing series of demands by the witnesses, most of which, it must be said, were rejected, but the position was kept fluid almost right up to the time when they gave evidence ... [T]he authorities appeared at all times to be open to negotiation, but this is something which certainly ought not to have been allowed to happen.'

25 See *Irish Times*, 6 November, 2003: 6–7.

26 See *Gilligan v Criminal Assets Bureau* [1998] 3 IR 185; Murphy (1999: 165).

27 *Irish Times*, 13 December 2006.

## Chapter 5

1 For examples in the penal arena, see Kilcommins (2003), Smith (1989), McAuley (1993), Osborough (1975), O'Sullivan (1997) and Carroll Burke (2000).

2 The European Convention of Human Rights entered into force in Ireland on 3 September 1953. Due, however, to Ireland's dualist position, the Convention did not form part of domestic law until the European Convention of Human Rights Act 2003, which was introduced at a sub-constitutional level. Though the incorporation of the Convention may result in 'some leveling down as well as leveling up of rights' in Ireland, it should also be noted that there is a 'very high degree of overlap' between the Constitution's guarantees and those of the ECHR. See Hogan (2004); Hogan (1999b: 208–9); and Ni Raifeartaigh (2001:

111).

3 See O'Mahony (1998), Kelly (1980: xxx–xxxi), Casey (2000: 25), and Barrington (1987). More generally see Gwynn-Morgan (2003).

4 See Packer (1964, 1968: 164–7). See also Dworkin (1981). For criticisms of Packer's two models of justice, see Ashworth and Redmayne (2005: 38–40), Goldstein (1974) and Griffiths (1970).

5 The right of access to a lawyer, for example, which has only relatively recently been elevated to constitutional status, has been very narrowly construed by the judiciary. This is discussed more fully in Chapter 6. See also O'Connell *et al.* (2006) which notes the lack of impact that the incorporation of the European Convention on Human Rights has had on the Irish judiciary.

6 More generally, see Hunt (1986), Douzinas (2000) and Gearty (2006: 60–98). For a feminist critique of liberal rights, see Mullally (2006: 1–26).

7 More generally, see Harvey (2004: 306–7).

8 See *Kennedy v Ireland* [1987] IR 587 at 593 where Hamilton P noted that 'the dignity and freedom of an individual in a democratic society cannot be ensured if his communications of a private nature, be they written or telephonic, are deliberately, consciously, and unjustifiably intruded upon and interfered with'. See also *People (DPP) v Dillon* [2002] 4 IR 501. See also article 8 of the European Convention on Human Rights and *Malone v United Kingdom* (1984) 7 EHRR 14 and *Khan v UK* (2001) 31 EHRR 45. The constitutional right to privacy is not absolute. See, for example, section 2(1) of the Interception of Postal Packets and Telecommunication Messages (Regulations) Act 1993.

9 A *habeas corpus* application can be made under article 40.4.2° to challenge the legality of any detention. See also Costello (1988). See also article 5(4) of the European Convention on Human Rights.

10 See *State (Bowes) v Fitzpatrick* [1978] ILRM 195; *Trimbole v Governor of Mountjoy Prison* [1985] ILRM 465.

11 See *People (DPP) v Lynch* [1982] IR 64.

12 See *People (Attorney General) v White* [1947] IR 247. See also *Re O'Laighleis* [1960] IR 93 where it was stated: 'We accept it as settled law that in the case of an arrest without the production of a warrant the arrest will not be lawful unless the person being arrested is told why he is being arrested ... The reason for the rule is not far to seek. Arrest must be for a lawful purpose; and since no one is obliged to submit to an unlawful arrest the citizen has a right before acquiescing in his arrest to know why he is being arrested.'

13 See, for example, section 5 of the Criminal Law Act 1997.

14 See *People (DPP) v Walsh* [1980] IR 294.

15 See McCutcheon (1987) and Ryan (2000).

16 For an exception, see, for example, section 20 of the National Monuments (Amendment) Act 1987.

17 See *DPP v Rooney* [1992] 2 IR 7.

18 See *People (DPP) v McFadden* [2003] 2 ILRM 201; *Farrelly v Devally* [1998] 4 IR 76.

19 *O'Callaghan v Ireland* [1994] 1 IR 555.

20 Article 40.5 of the Constitution states that the dwelling of every citizen is inviolable and shall not be forcibly entered save in accordance with the law. But see *DPP v Delaney* [1998] 1 ILRM 536. See also section 6(2) of the Criminal

Law Act 1997 which enables a Garda to enter a dwelling for the purpose of effecting an arrest without a warrant in limited circumstances.

21 In *Simple Imports Ltd v Revenue Commissioners* [2000] 2 IR 43, it was noted: 'Search warrants ... are powers which the police and other authorities must enjoy in defined circumstances for the protection of society, but since they authorise the forcible invasion of a person's property the courts must always be concerned to ensure that the conditions imposed by the legislature before such powers can be validly exercised are strictly met.'

22 See *Creaven v Criminal Assets Bureau* [2004] 4 IR 434. But see now section 180 of the Criminal Justice Act 2006.

23 See *Byrne v Grey* [1988] IR 31; *DPP v Yamanoha* [1994] 1 IR 565.

24 See section 4 of the Criminal Justice Act 1984, section 2 of the Criminal Justice (Drug Trafficking) Act 1996 and section 30 of the Offences Against the State Act 1939.

25 See *People (DPP) v Boylan* [1991] 1 IR 477.

26 See *People (DPP) v Reddan* [1995] 3 IR 560.

27 See section 4 of the Criminal Justice (Drug Trafficking) Act 1996, section 10 of the Criminal Justice Act 1984, and section 30 of the Offences against the State Act 1939.

28 See Keane (1997), McLaughlin (1981). See also article 5(1)(c) and 5(3) of the European Convention on Human Rights. See also *Brogan v UK* (1989) 11 EHRR 117; *K-F v Germany* (1998) 26 EHRR 390.

29 The latter provision is governed by the Criminal Justice Act 1984 (Electronic Recording of Interviews) Regulations 1997.

30 See *People (DPP) v Spratt* [1995] 1 IR 585.

31 For acceptance of the rules in Ireland, see *People v Cummins* [1972] IR 312 at 317–18.

32 See *People v Farrell* [1978] IR 13. The Rules relate, *inter alia*, to the need for a Garda to caution a suspect in custody before questioning; to caution a suspect before questioning him once a decision has been made to charge the suspect with the crime; to caution a suspect before he volunteers a statement; to not cross-examine a suspect when he is making a voluntary statement; and, to ensure that a statement is in writing and signed.

33 See section 2(5) of the Criminal Justice (Forensic Evidence) Act 1990, as amended.

34 See O'Connor and Cooney (1980), and Ring (1997).

35 See *Heaney v Ireland* [1994] 3 IR 593, and Hogan (1999a).

36 See *Murray v UK* (1996) 22 EHRR 29; *Funke v France* (1993) 16 EHRR 297; *Saunders v UK* (1997) 23 EHRR 313; *Condron v UK* (2001) 31 EHRR 1; and *Bacik* (2004: 162–7).

37 See *Attorney General v Durnan* (No. 2) [1934] IR 540; *People (DPP) v Lynch* [1982] IR 64. See also the Judges' Rules which provide guidance on the questioning of suspects as set out in *People (AG) v Cummins* [1972] IR 312 at 323.

38 See *People (DPP) v Finnerty* [1999] 4 IR 364.

39 More generally, see McGrath (2005: 623–30); Roberts and Zuckerman (2004: 408–25)

40 *Re National Irish Bank* [1999] 3 IR 145 at 153.

41 *Re National Irish Bank* [1999] 3 IR 145 at 153.
42 See *Heaney v Ireland* [1996] IR 580 at 585.
43 378 U.S. 478, 84 S.Ct. 1758 12 L.Ed.2d. 977 1964.
44 See *Heaney v Ireland* (2001) 33 EHRR 12 at para 40.
45 *Miranda v Arizona* 384 U.S. 436, 86 S.Ct. 1602, 16 L.Ed.2d. 694 (1966).
46 See *Averill v UK* (2001) 31 EHRR 36; *S v Switzerland* (1991) EHRR 670.
47 *People (DPP) v Madden* [1977] IR 336. See also section 5 of the Criminal Justice Act 1984 and the Criminal Justice Act (Treatment of Persons in Custody in Garda Síochána Stations) Regulations 1987.
48 *People (DPP) v Healy* [1990] 2 IR 73; see also *People (DPP) v Buck* [2002] 2 IR 268.
49 See *People (DPP) v Darcy* (Unreported CCA, 29 July 1997).
50 See *O'Brien v Director of Public Prosecutions* (Unreported, SC, 5 May 2005).
51 See *People (DPP) v Finnegan* (Unreported, CCA, 15 July 1997).
52 *Dunne v Clinton* [1930] IR 366. Provision can be made for police bail, provided the accused enters a recognisance to attend the Court within 30 days. See section 3 of the Criminal Justice (Miscellaneous Provisions) Act 1997. The Gardaí must set a bail sum which is reasonable in all the circumstances. See *People (Attorney General) v O'Callaghan* [1966] IR 501. The accused is also protected by the fact that a decision to prosecute cannot be influenced by improper motives or policies. See *State (McCormack) v Curran* [1987] ILRM 225.
53 *People (Attorney General) v O'Callaghan* at 517. See *also McDonagh v Governor of Cloverhill Prison* (Unreported, SC, 28 January 2005); Walsh (2002: 491–555); and O'Higgins (1998).
54 *Braddish v DPP* [2001] 3 IR 127 at 133.
55 *Swaine v DPP* (Unreported, SC, 26 April 26 2002); *DH v Judge Groarke* (Unreported, SC, 31 July 31 2002). See also Dwyer (1993: 66). On disclosure by the defence, see Walsh (2002: 916–18). The accused's right to see relevant prosecution evidence prior to trial is also protected under article 6 of the European Convention on Human Rights. See *Barbera, Messague and Jabardo v Spain* (1988) 11 EHRR 360; *Edwards v United Kingdom* (1993) 15 EHRR 417. Prosecution obligations in respect of disclosure are more relaxed in respect of summary criminal proceedings. See *DPP v Doyle* [1998] 2 IR 286.
56 See *People (DPP) v Nevin* (Unreported, CCA, 14 March 2003).
57 *People (DPP) v McSweeney* [2001] 4 IR 102 at 109-110 *per* Geoghegan J.
58 See also the reasoning of Mr Justice Brennan in the US Supreme Court case of *In Re Winship* 397 U.S. 358, 90 S.Ct. 1068, 25 L.Ed. 2d 368 (1970).
59 [1935] AC 462.
60 But see Smith (1987).
61 See *A.G. v O'Connor* [1935] Ir. Jur. Rep. 1; *A.G. v Berber and Levy* [1944] IR 405; *Attorney General (Comer) v Shorten* [1961] IR 304; *People (Attorney General) v Oglesby* [1966] IR 162; *People (Attorney General) v Byrne* [1974] IR 1.
62 [1993] 1 IR 102 at 107.
63 The right, which is not absolute, is implicit in article 38.1 of the Irish Constitution. See also *People (DPP) v DO'T* [2003] 4 IR 286. See also article 6(2) of the European Convention on Human Rights which provides that 'everyone charged with a criminal offence shall be presumed innocent until proven guilty according to law'.

64 See *CC v Ireland, Attorney General and Another; PG v Ireland, Attorney General and Another* [2005] IESC 47 *per* Denham J. See also *People (DPP) v Murray* [1977] IR 360. More generally, see McAuley and McCutcheon (2000: 309–12).

65 [2006] IESC 33.

66 Section 2 of the same Act provided that where the girl was aged under 17 at the time of the intercourse, the offence was punishable by up to 5 years' imprisonment for a first offence and up to 10 years' for a subsequent offence.

67 See *Attorney General (Shaughnessy) v Ryan* [1960] IR 181 and *Coleman v Ireland* [2004] IEHC 288.

68 See *Regina v City of Sault Sainte Marine* (1978) 85 DLR 161 *per* Dickson J. See also *Hess and Nguyen v The Queen* [1990] 2 SCR 906 *per* Wilson J. In Ireland, see also Law Reform Commission (1990: para. 4.14).

69 Hardiman J also noted that to 'jail perfectly respectable people on the basis of an event over which they had no control … is so complete a negation of their rights to liberty, due process, equality and respect for human dignity that it cannot be contemplated no matter what the benefits'.

70 On the application of strict liability to regulatory offences more generally, see Hanly (2006: 91–3).

71 For the position of the impecunious accused prior to 1965, see Greer (1969: 270).

72 See *Poitrimol v France* (1993) 18 EHRR 130; *Artico v Italy* (1980) 3 EHRR 1; Bacik (2004: 167).

73 [1976] IR 325. See also Henchy J (at 354) who noted: 'A person who has been convicted and deprived of his liberty as a result of a prosecution which, because of his poverty, he has had to bear without legal aid has reason to complain that he has been meted out less than his constitutional due. This is particularly true if the absence of legal aid is compounded by factors such as a grave or complex charge; or ignorance, illiteracy, immaturity or other conditions rendering the accused incompetent to cope properly with the prosecution; or an inability, because of detentional restraint, to find and produce witnesses; or simply the fumbling incompetence that may occur when an accused is precipitated into the public glare and alien complexity of courtroom procedures and is confronted with the might of a prosecution backed by the State. As the law stands, a legal aid certificate is the shield provided against such an unjust attack.' See also Casey (1987: 41); Walsh (2002: 558–63), and Ryan and Magee (1983: 224).

74 On the need for legal representation to be effective under the European Convention on Human Rights, see *Daud v Portugal* (2000) 30 EHRR 400.

75 *State Healy v Donoghue* [1976] IR 325 at 348–9 *per* O'Higgins CJ.

76 *State (Walsh) v Lennon* [1942] IR 112; *Enright v Ireland* [2003] 2 IR 321. See also Article 7(1) of the European Convention on Human Rights.

77 *King v Attorney General* [1981] IR 233.

78 *Attorney General (OMaoinigh) v Fitzgerald* [1964] IR 458. As was noted in *Green v United States* (pp. 187–8): 'the underlying idea, one that is deeply ingrained in at least the Anglo-American system of jurisprudence, is that the State with all its resources and power should not be allowed to make repeated attempts to convict an individual for an alleged offence, thereby subjecting him to

embarrassment, expense and ordeal and compelling him to live in a continuing state of anxiety and insecurity, as well as enhancing the possibility that even though innocent he may be found guilty. This underlying notion has from the very beginning been part of our constitutional tradition. Like the right to trial by jury, it is clearly "fundamental to the American scheme of justice".' This statement was quoted with approval by Henchy J in the Irish Supreme Court in *People (DPP) v O'Shea* [1982] IR 384.

79 See *Attorney General v Cunningham* [1932] IR 28.

80 Nobody should be a judge in his own case. See *People (Attorney General) v Singer* [1975] IR 408. See also article 6(1) of the European Convention on Human Rights. See also article 40.3 of the Constitution.

81 See also 6(3)(a) of the European Convention on Human Rights.

82 *The State (Howard) v Donnelly* [1966] IR 51. See also article 6(3)(b) of the ECHR.

83 See *State (O'Connell) v Judge Fawsitt* [1986] ILRM 639. In *Re Singer* 97 ILTR 130, Maguire CJ noted: 'The rule that an accused person should be returned for trial to the first competent tribunal is in accordance with the fundamental and well recognised principle that justice should not be delayed. There seems to be no clearer illustration of the truth of the maxim that justice delayed is justice denied than the case of an accused person who is not given an opportunity of establishing his innocence at the earliest opportunity.' Delays in proceeding with a prosecution in cases that involve sexual abuse of children or young people fall into a special category. See *B v DPP* [1997] 3 IR 140; *J'OC v DPP* [2000] 3 IR 122; *H v DPP* (Unreported, SC, 31 July, 2006). See also Fennell (2001). See also article 6(1) of the European Convention on Human Rights and cases such as *Portington v Greece* [1998] HRCD 856.

84 See *D v DPP* [1994] 2 IR 465. See also article 6(1) of the European Convention on Human Rights.

85 See *Shelly v District Justice Mahon* [1990] 1 IR 36.

86 See, for example, *People (DPP) v McGinley* (3 Frewen 251 at 252 *per* Hederman J) where it was noted: 'By virtue of the obligation under the Constitution, and in order to ensure that justice is done, a criminal trial must be held in public; and the accused should always be present during all of a criminal trial on indictment which includes sentencing. It is not in accordance with law that any part of a criminal trial should be held in a judge's chambers and in the absence of the accused ... Justice must be administered in an open court and everything pertaining to a criminal trial and to the sentencing of a person who has been convicted must be in open court.' For exceptions, see Walsh (2002: 952–3).

87 See *de Burca and Anderson v Attorney General* [1976] IR 38 at 74 *per* Henchy J. See *O'Callaghan v Attorney General* [1993] 2 IR 17 at 25.

88 *People (DPP) v O'Shea* [1982] IR 384 at 342.

89 See section 25 of the Criminal Justice Act 1984. A majority verdict would include 10 from 12, 10 from 11, or 11 out of 12.

90 Persons concerned with the administration of justice, members of the defence forces or persons of insufficient capacity are ineligible to serve.

91 A person with a previous criminal record may be disqualified from sitting on a jury.

92 See *People (DPP) v Tobin* [2001] 3 IR 469.
93 See section 21 of the Juries Act 1976.
94 See *Melling v O'Mathghamhna* [1962] IR 1.
95 See *People (DPP) v Mark Davis* [1993] 2 IR 1. A judge can give his opinion to the jury as to his or her views of the facts, but it should never be expressed as a direction as to what the jury should do as regards the determination of guilt or innocence.
96 [2006] IECCA 128.
97 Nally was acquitted by a jury in the retrial.
98 [1982] IR 384 at 438 *per* Henchy J.
99 Section 1 of the Criminal Justice (Evidence) Act 1924. If an accused person is jointly charged with other co-accuseds, he is competent but not compellable for any of these co-accused. He is not competent or compellable for the prosecution against them as long as he is jointly charged. See *Attorney General v Joyce* [1929] IR 526.
100 See *People (DPP) v Finnerty* [1999] 4 IR 364; *People (AG) v Reynolds* (1958) 1 Frewen 184; *People (DPP) v Connolly* [2003] 2 IR 1.
101 See O'Connor (1985), Jackson (1989), Jackson (1993), Law Reform Commission (1985).
102 See *People (AG) v O'Neill* [1964] Ir. Jur. Rep. 1. See also *People (DPP) v Meleady* (Unreported, CCA, 20 March 2001 at p. 26) where Geoghegan J. stated: 'A judge, as part of his inherent power, has an overriding duty in every case to ensure that the accused receives a fair trial and always has a discretion to exclude otherwise admissible prosecution evidence if, in his opinion, its prejudicial effect, in the minds of the jury, outweighs its true probative value.'
103 Employing statistical probability of DNA matches between the crime stain and the accused also raises the danger that an improper conclusion might be drawn from such data. This is known as the 'prosecutor's fallacy'.
104 See *Dental Board v O'Callaghan* [1969] IR 181; *People (DPP) v Hogan* [1994] 2 ILRM 74
105 See Pattenden (1991).
106 See *People (DPP) v Meleady* [1995] 2 IR 517.
107 The courts have developed a practice of giving a warning to the jury in all cases that depend substantially or wholly on such evidence.
108 See *Cullen v Clarke* [1963] IR 368; *Eastern Health Board v MK* [1999] 2 IR 99.
109 The rule, for the most part, is concerned with prosecution evidence but it can also operate potentially to exclude an accused's probative evidence of innocence. See *People (Attorney General) v O'Brien* (1969) 1 Frewen 343; *Sparks v R* [1964] AC 965.
110 *State (Healy) v Donoghue* [1976] IR 325. See also *In re Haughey* [1971] IR 217 at 261 where O'Dalaigh CJ noted: 'an accused person has a right to cross-examine every witness for the prosecution, subject, in respect of any question asked, to the court's power of disallowance on the grounds of irrelevancy. An accused, in advance of cross-examination, cannot be required to state what his purpose in cross-examining is.'
111 To alleviate the harshness of the rule, a complex, somewhat incoherent, mosaic of exceptions has been developed that permits hearsay evidence to be

admitted.

112 See *People v McGuiness* [1978] IR 189.

113 For exceptions, see McGrath (2005: 469). See also Murphy (2003: 115–68).

114 See *King v Director of Public Prosecutions* (Unreported, 24 October 1978) where McWilliam J stated: 'It is one of the concepts of Justice which the courts have always accepted that on a criminal trial evidence of character or previous convictions shall not be given except at the instigation of the accused, as this could prejudice the fair trial of the issue of the guilt or innocence of the accused ... The provisions that evidence may be given of the known character of the accused and that no evidence need be given of any act showing or tending to show intent are contrary to the concept of justice which is implicit in the Constitution.' See also *DPP v Keogh* [1998] 1 ILRM 72; Healy (2004: 188).

115 *Smurfit Paribas Bank Ltd v AAB Export Finance Limited* [1990] 1 IR 469. Though normally the privilege attaching to the relationship is always privileged, it may be abrogated, it seems, in circumstances where the innocence of an accused is at stake. See the Canadian case of *R v Dunbar* (1983) 138 DLR 9 (3d) 221.

116 See *Bula v Crowley* (No. 2) [1994] 2 IR 54; *Miley v Flood* [2001] 2 IR 50.

117 *Niemitez v Germany* (1992) 16 EHRR 97; *Campbell v United Kingdom* (1993) 15 EHRR 137.

118 (1846) 1 De. G and Sm. 12 at 28–9.

119 See *People v Defore* 242 NY year at 21 *per* Cardozo J.

120 See McAuley and McCutcheon (1981).

121 *People (AG) v O'Brien* [1965] IR 142 at 170 *per* Walsh J. This exclusionary rule operates in accordance with the 'absolute protectionist principle': a 'good fault' exception, where the police are unaware that they are breaching constitutional rights, is not permitted. See *People (DPP) v Kenny* [1990] 2 IR 110. If the evidence is illegally obtained, as opposed to unconstitutionally obtained, the court has a discretion to admit or exclude it. See *DPP v McMahon* [1987] ILRM 87. See also Healy (2004: 329-31). For an analysis of evidence obtained in breach of the European Convention on Human Rights, see McGrath (2005: 362–5). More generally, see O'Connor (1982a) and Friedman (1993).

122 [1965] IR 142 at 170.

123 *People (DPP) v Kenny* [1990] ILRM 569 at 578 *per* Finlay CJ.

124 *Olmstead v United States* 277 U.S. 438, 48 S.Ct. 564, 72L. Ed. 944 (1928) *per* Holmes J. In the same judgment, Brandeis J (at 485) stated: 'If the Government becomes a lawbreaker it breeds contempt for law; it invites every man to become a law unto himself; it invites anarchy. To declare that in the administration of the criminal law the end justifies the means – to declare that the Government may commit crimes in order to secure the conviction of a private criminal – would bring terrible retribution.'

125 Unreported, CC, 23 April 2004.

126 The judge in the case declined to say whether Brian Curtin was a deserving or undeserving applicant.

127 More generally, see White (2000a, 2000b), Costelloe (2001).

128 See *Ibrahim v R* [1914] AC 599 at 609 *per* Lord Sumner, as adopted in Ireland by Kennedy CJ in *AG v McCabe* [1927] IR 129. See also the Supreme Court decision in *Re National Irish Bank* [1999] 3 IR 145 at 186–7 where Barrington J stated: 'It

appears to me that the better opinion is that a trial in due course of law requires that any confession admitted against an accused person in a criminal trial should be a voluntary confession and that any trial at which an alleged confession other than a voluntary confession were admitted in evidence against an accused person would not be a trial in due course of law within the meaning of article 38 of the Constitution and that it is immaterial whether the compulsion or inducement used to extract the confession came from the Executive or from the Legislature.' See also O'Connor (1980).

129 See *State v Treanor* [1924] 2 IR 193. Other safeguards, as noted above, also exist for accused persons in custody. They include the Judges' Rules, as set out by Walsh J in *People AG v Cummins* [1972] IR 312, the Criminal Justice Act 1984 (Treatment of Persons in Garda Custody) Regulations of 1987, and the Criminal Justice Act 1984 (Electronic Recording of Interviews) Regulations of 1997.

130 [1982] IR 1 at 61.

131 *Deaton v Attorney General and Revenue Commissioners* [1963] IR 170. See also O'Malley (2000a).

132 See *People (DPP) v WC* [1994] ILRM 321 at 325. See also *State (Healy) v Donoghue* [1976] IR 325 at 353; *People (DPP) v M* [1994] 3 IR 306 and Kilcommins *et al.* (2004: 183–5).

133 *People (DPP) v McCormack* [2000] 4 IR 356.

134 See *Enright v Ireland* [2003] 2 IR 321. See also article 7 of the European Convention on Human Rights and O'Malley (2006a: 69–70).

135 See *McGrane v Coughlan and DPP* (ex tempore, HC, 20 June 2005).

136 At present this right is more emphatically guarded through the European Convention on Human Rights than through the domestic courts. See *Garcia Ruiz v Spain* (2001) 32 EHRR 589. See also *People (DPP) v Cooney* (Unreported, CCA, 27 July 2004).

137 See *People (DPP) v Gilligan* No. 2 [2004] 3 IR 87.

138 *Cox v Ireland* [1992] 2 IR 503. See also O'Malley (2006a: 434).

139 See *People (DPP) v Sheedy* [2000] 2 IR 184 at 190.

140 But see section 34 of the Criminal Procedure Act 1967, as amended by section 21 of the Criminal Justice Act 2006, which enables the AG or the DPP, after an accused has been acquitted (whether in respect of the whole or part of an indictment), to appeal a point of law to the Supreme Court. This is without prejudice to the verdict or decision returned in favour of the accused. Section 2 of the Criminal Justice Act 1993 also permits the DPP to appeal unduly lenient sentences to the Court of Criminal Appeal. See O'Malley (1994).

141 See, for example, the Seventh Protocol to the European Convention on Human Rights.

142 See *A v Governor of Arbour Hill Prison* [2006] IESC 45. A High Court judge posthumously criticised the judgment. He stated: 'The lengths to which the Supreme Court went to obfuscate the fact that the continued detention of a prisoner in an Irish jail (in fact the re-arrest of a released prisoner) for an offence that did not exist in law at the date of his conviction smacks of an attempt to curry favour with a potentially hostile media' (*Irish Times*, 3 January 2007). More generally, see Simon (1998, 2000).

143 Cross-fertilisation does, however, occur in that the legislature can from time to time engage in the protection of rights and the judiciary can also engage in policy-making.
144 As Zedner (2002: 343–4) has noted, they also have a tendency to elide 'discourse with practice' and mistake 'talk for action'. On the capacity of classical legalism to act as counterpoint to the control paradigm, see Vaughan (2000: 33).
145 There is, of course, scope for Irish society to change a constitutional provision through a referendum.
146 See also Kilcommins *et al.* (2004: 174) and Fennell (1993a: 8).
147 O'Sullivan and O'Donnell (2007) have recently made a similar argument about imprisonment in Ireland and the extent to which it fits with the control thesis.

## Chapter 6

1 This is occurring across many areas including education, welfare, mental health, employment law, consumer protection and freedom of information. It is also occurring in the criminal justice arena through the incorporation of the European Convention on Human Rights.
2 For example, in April 2003, the Minister for Justice, Equality and Law Reform, Michael McDowell, could suggest that Ireland was the only 'member state of the EU in which individual citizens are guaranteed the constitutional right to due process, exclusion of illegally obtained evidence, to trial by jury in all non minor cases, to fair bail, to the presumption of innocence, to *habeas corpus*, and the right to have any law invalidated in the courts which conflicts with his or her rights and the right not to have any of these rights altered except by referendum' (*Irish Times*, 24 April 2003).
3 See section 14 of Criminal Assets Bureau Act 1996, section 8 of the Criminal Justice (Drug Trafficking) Act 1996, and *People (DPP) v Byrne* (Unreported, CCA, 30 October 2003). See also section 5(3) of the Criminal Justice Act 2006, which empowers a Garda of superintendent rank or higher to issue a direction designating a place as a crime scene. This authorises Gardaí to search for and collect evidence at the crime scene (including a dwelling) and to impose restrictions on persons present or seeking to gain entry into the crime scene. Under section 5(7), this direction lasts for 24 hours, but can be extended by 48 hours on application to a District Court judge. Such an extension may be granted on three consecutive occasions under section 5(9).
4 See section 6(2) of the Criminal Law Act 1997 and section 39(1) of the Road Traffic Act 1994.
5 See section 9 of the Criminal Law Act 1976; see also section 7 of the Criminal Justice Act 2006.
6 Section 14 of the Criminal Justice Act 2006 reclassified saliva as a non-intimate sample, enabling the Gardaí to take a sample without the person's consent.
7 See sections 63 and 64 of the Criminal Justice Act 1994. In *Hanahoe v Hussey* [1998] 3 IR 69 at 94–6, Kinlen J in the High Court noted that hitherto search

warrants were only ever issued in respect of proposed respondents to any investigation. The learned judge went on to note: 'we live in an era of fantastic and intrusive invasion of privacy. The State, the media and many electronic devices have combined in a growing and worrying assertion that the invasion is allowable because of the battle against crime and corruption and also based on the alleged "public's right to know".'

8 Solicitors, for example, are required to report clients' suspicious transactions to the Garda Síochána and the Revenue Commissioners under section 6 of the Criminal Justice Act 1994 (section 32) Regulations 2003 on the Prevention of the use of the Financial System for the purpose of Money Laundering. Similarly, section 73 of the Company Law Enforcement Act of 2001 provides that whenever disciplinary tribunals of accountancy bodies have reasonable grounds for believing that an indictable offence has been committed by one of their members it must report the suspicion to the Director of Corporate Enforcement.

9 Garda CCTV schemes were first introduced in Dublin in 1995. The Minister for Justice, Equality and Law Reform also launched a community-based CCTV scheme in June 2005. This initiative was designed to facilitate communities to press ahead with their own local CCTV systems. The scheme operates in accordance with section 38 of the Garda Síochána Act 2005. We are grateful to Dorothy Appelbe for this point.

10 In April 2002, the Minister for Public Enterprise issued the direction under section 110(1) of the Postal and Telecommunications Services Act 1983. See also section 63 of the Criminal Justice (Terrorist Offences) Act 2005, and article 15 of the EU Directive on Privacy and Electronic Communications (Directive 200/58/EC). We are grateful to Elizabeth Campbell for this point.

11 *Report of the Expert Group on changes to the Criminal Law* (1998). See also Keane (1997: 1–17) and Ryan (2000).

12 See Chapter 5.

13 See also *DPP v Buck* (Unreported, Court of Criminal Appeal, 6 December 1999); *Lavery v The Member in Charge, Carrickmacross Garda Station* [1999] 2 IR 390. See also McFadden (2002) and Costelloe (2001).

14 For similar corroborative inferences in the terrorist realm, see sections 2 and 5 of the Offences against the State (Amendment) Act 1998. Section 7 of the Criminal Justice (Drug Trafficking) Act, 1996 and section 5 of the Offences Against the State (Amendment) Act 1998 will be repealed by a proposed new Criminal Justice Bill which will restrict the right to silence at a more general level.

15 [1996] IR 580 at 586. See Hogan (1999).

16 See Lewis (1990) and Posner (1999).

17 Joint Committee on Justice, Equality, Defence and Women's Rights (Dublin, 8 December 2003). See also the comments of Garda Commissioner Noel Conroy at the annual conference of Garda sergeants and inspectors in Kilkenny in March 2005 where he noted: 'Recent reporting of high profile cases suggests a criminal justice system in need of examination, with the burden of proof on the prosecution now set so high as to be in most prosecutions, almost unachievable and the search for truth being sacrificed in a web of

technicalities' (*Irish Times*, 23 March 2005, p. 4).

18 On Garda accountability, see Walsh (1998), (2004a) and (2004b).

19 Section 52 of the Children Act 2001 had provided a child under the age of 12 years of age benefited from the conclusive presumption that he or she was incapable of committing a criminal offence (prior to this the age of criminal responsibility had been set at seven years of age). The 2001 Act also provided for the rebuttable presumption of *doli incapax* between the ages of 12 and 14 (Walsh 2005b: 11–15). However, section 129 of the Criminal Justice Act 2006 reduces the age of criminal responsibility to 10 for children charged with murder, manslaughter, rape, or aggravated sexual assault. It also abolished the rebuttable presumption of *doli incapax* between 12 and 14. If, however a child under 14 is charged with an offence, the case can only go forward for trial with the consent of the DPP. Moreover, section 134 of the 2006 Act permits the court to dismiss a case against a child under 14 if, having regard to the child's age and level of maturity, it determines that the child did not have a full understanding of what was involved in the commission of the offence.

20 This provision transposed Ireland's obligations arising under article 5 of the UN Convention Against Transnational Organised Crime (Resolution A/res/55/25) and the EU Joint Action of 21 December 1998 (98/733/JHA).

21 In circumstances where the offence is to be committed outside the state, an offence under the section will only occur if the participation occurs in the Irish state, on board an Irish ship, or an aircraft registered in the state.

22 ICCL Submission on Criminal Justice Bill 2004 (March 2006), available at http://www.iccl.ie/DB_Data/publications/ICCLSubmissionCJB2004.pdf.

23 See *People v. O'Callaghan* [1966] IR 501.

24 [1989] IR 399 at 407.

25 See article 40.4.1 of the Irish Constitution. See also section 2(2) of the Bail Act 1997.

26 [1995] ILRM 259. See also *Hardy v Ireland* [1994] 2 IR 550 and Ni Raifeartaigh (1995). Ashworth (2006) suggests that there are currently four specific threats to the presumption of innocence: '*confinement*, by defining offences so as to reduce the impact of the presumption; *erosion*, by recognizing more exceptions; *evasions*, by introducing civil law procedures in order to circumvent the rights conferred on accused persons; and, *side-stepping*, by imposing restrictions on the liberty of unconvicted persons [such as restrictions on telephone and internet use, and meetings with other people]'.

27 See also section 2 of the Criminal Justice Act 1990 which provides that a person convicted of murder shall be sentenced to life imprisonment. See O'Malley (1995).

28 For the ways in which the Irish courts have interpreted these provisions, see Kilcommins *et al.* (2004: 185–90). See also Ennis (2003) and McEvoy (2005).

29 See section 27 of the Misuse of Drugs Act 1977, as amended by section 84 of the Criminal Justice Act 2006.

30 The notification periods are: (i) 12 years if the sentence imposed was life imprisonment; (ii) 7 years if the sentence imposed was greater than 10 years' imprisonment; (iii) 5 years if the sentence imposed was one of imprisonment between 5 and 10 years; and (iv) 3 years if the sentence imposed was one of

imprisonment between 1 and 5 years. The notification periods are halved for persons under the age of 18 at the time the sentence is imposed.

31 There is a presumptive minimum sentence of 10 years for possession or control of firearms or ammunition with intent to endanger life; or for the use or production of a firearm or imitation firearm while resisting arrest or aiding an escape from custody. There is a presumptive 5-year sentence for offences such as the possession of a firearm or imitation firearm while taking a vehicle or carrying a firearm or imitation firearm with intent to commit an indictable offence, or for shortening the barrel of a shotgun or rifle. For persons over 18 who commit a subsequent firearms offence, the court must specify a mandatory minimum sentence to be served. For repeat offenders to whom the presumptive 10-year minimum originally applied, the mandatory minimum is set at 10 years for the repeat offence. In all other cases, the mandatory minimum for the repeat offence is set at 5 years. See O'Malley (2006b).

32 Similarly, the recent Criminal Justice Act of 2006 doubled the periods of detention without charge for arrestable offences on the grounds that previous limits were too onerous on the Gardaí. No independent evidence was put forward justifying this extension.

33 The issue of security is now also increasingly being addressed at an EU level. See Regan and O'Mahony (2002). For more recent developments see, for example, the speeches of Michael McDowell on the Hague Programme on strengthening freedom, security and justice in Europe, which was adopted by the European Council on 5 November 2004 (available at http://www.iiea.com/eventsx.php?event_id=44) and on the changes a European Constitution will have for criminal justice in Ireland, which was delivered at a National Forum on Europe Seminar held on 12 May, 2005 (available at http://www.foreignaffairs.gov.ie/Press_Releases/20050512/1756.htm).

34 The Gardaí are now making similar arguments. The President of the Association of Garda Sergeants and Inspectors recently noted: 'The overwhelming feeling of members is that the criminal justice system has swung off balance to such an extent that the rules are now heavily weighted in the favour of the criminal, murderer, drug trafficker and habitual offender. At the same time, the system is oppressive on the victims of crime, the witness who comes to the defence of the victim and the juror whose role it is to ensure justice is done and seen to be done. Much of the blame for this can be laid at the door of the system. The State has an equal duty of care to the victim, witness and juror as to the accused.' (Joint Committee on Justice, Equality, Defence, and Women's Rights, 8 December 2003, *per* Mr Dirwan). James Hamilton, the Director of Public Prosecutions, also stated that Ireland's laws are heavily weighted against the prosecution: 'I sometimes feel that the criminal law in Ireland can be like a game of football with very peculiar rules. The prosecution can score as many goals as they like but the game goes on. As soon as the defence scores a goal the game is over and the defence is declared the winner' (*Irish Times*, 14 May 2006).

35 See Rebalancing Criminal Justice – Remarks by Tanaiste in Limerick, 20 October 2006, available at http://www.justice.ie/80256E01003A02CF/vWeb/

pcJUSQ6UTMDB-en. For the Interim Report of the Balance in the Criminal Law Review Group (13 February 2007), see http://www.justice.ie/en/JELR/Pages/PB07000268. For the Final Report, see http://www.justice.ie/en/JELR/Pages/PB07000527. A new Criminal Justice Bill proposes *inter alia* to provide prosecution authorities with more effective means of challenging bail applications, to make further provisions for mandatory sentencing, to introduce crime prevention orders for certain offenders after release from prison, to impose further restrictions on the right to silence, and to increase Garda powers of detention without charge.

36 As the Minister noted (as note 35): 'Has the time come to consider broadening the circumstances in which an inference can be drawn from the failure of an accused to respond to fair questioning duly recorded not as sufficient proof of guilt but as corroboration of other evidence of guilt?'

37 As the Minister noted (as note 35): 'why should the fact that a person has been convicted of serious offences in the past be concealed from those that have to decide on the credibility of his evidence?'

38 As Garland (2001: 181–2) notes: 'We allow ourselves to forget what penal welfarism took for granted: namely that offenders are citizens too and their liberty interests are our liberty interests. The growth of a social and cultural divide between "us" and "them", together with new levels of fear and insecurity, has made many complacent about the emergence of a more repressive state power.'

39 On the extent to which risk thinking is a neutral phenomenon, see O'Malley (2004b) and Garland (2003).

40 On the paradoxes of security, see Zedner (2003).

41 For example, the total value of property stolen in burglaries, larcenies and robberies in Ireland in 2002 was €97 million; in the same year, the Revenue Commissioners collected over €600 million from DIRT and bogus non-resident account investigations, €43 million for unauthorised offshore investments sold by National Irish Bank, and €21 million for Ansbacher Deposits. The DIRT inquiry itself related to 35,000 non-resident accounts that had Irish addresses associated with them. See Kilcommins *et al.* (2004: 131).

42 Indeed it can be also argued that those putting forward a civil libertarian agenda in Ireland have often not teased it out, preferring instead to rely on broad, often abstract, liberalist arguments about the need to restrain state power and protect the privacy rights of individuals. Such arguments, which though necessarily qualitative rather than quantitative in nature, often miss their intended public audience, not least because they do not engage with the social, cultural and political realities of crime in late modern society.

43 See also Simon (2002). In more parochial terms, this has been referred to as the need not to be part of the 'can't do anything, won't do anything brigade'. See Dáil Debates, 30 January 2002, vol. 547, col. 113, *per* Mr O'Donoghue.

44 Throughout the twentieth century, a clear divergence became evident in most western countries between the algebraic perceptions of the individual as presented in law, and the causal/social perceptions as presented by correctionalist criminology. The trial stage, for the most part, adopted the former; the sentencing stage, the latter. More recently, a reconvergence is

taking place as criminological discourse jettisons the 'biographical' individual in favour of the 'abiographical' individual or 'rational choice actor'. Classical legalism and the contemporary criminologies are *at idem* once again in coding responsibility to focus solely on the wrongdoer. The one-dimensional, one-size, *homo juridicus*, increasingly fits all criminological and legal representations of the 'Individual'.

45 See section 16 of the Criminal Justice Act 2006.

46 See, for example, *People (Attorney General) v Cradden* [1955] IR 130.

47 On the violence of law more generally, see Cover (1986). See also Sarat and Kearns (1991) and Sarat (2001).

48 See O'Connell (2001) and Coulter and Coleman (2003).

49 The politicised image of the victim is also important in this context. As Garland (2001: 200–1) noted: 'Why is the image of the suffering victim now so central to the crime issue and our responses to it? Because in the new morality of market individualism, public institutions lack compelling force and the state's laws lack independent authority. Whatever mutuality and solidarity exists is achieved through the direct identification of individuals with one another, not with the polity or the public institutions to which they each belong. In a world in which moral sentiments are increasingly privatised along with everything else, collective moral outrage more easily proceeds from an individualised basis than from a public one. A declining faith in public institutions now means that only the sight of suffering "individuals like us" can be relied upon to provoke the impassioned responses needed to supply the emotional energy for punitive policies and a war upon crime.'

50 On the positive capacity of punishment to forge solidarity, see Durkheim (1997).

51 But as Zedner (2006: 9) suggests: 'moves to pursue matters properly belonging to the criminal process to a different legal context … is liable to result in the application of inappropriate standards, principles, and values. It follows that the placing of a measure in a particular legal context or procedural channel should not be permitted to determine jurisprudential principle without asking the normatively prior question of whether the choice of context is defensible.' More generally, see Castells (1997: 243–308).

52 In *Hayes v Duggan* [1929] IR 406, the Irish Supreme Court had held that profits derived from a criminal enterprise could not be supposed to be within the contemplation of income tax legislation. See also *Collins v Mulvey* [1956] IR 223. Section 19 of the Finance Act 1983, however, permitted the state to assess and collect tax on profits that arose from unlawful sources or activities. Section 19 has since been replaced by section 58 of the Taxes Consolidation Act 1997.

53 The DPP should not, however, profit from any such disclosure for the purpose of any future criminal prosecution. See *M v D* (Unreported, High Court, 10 December 1996).

54 There is also considerable provision for the exchanges of information between the Revenue Commissioners, CAB and the Gardaí.

55 See section 933(1)(a) of the Taxes Consolidation Act 1997.

56 See section 957(2)(a) of the Taxes Consolidation Act 1997. See also *Keogh v Criminal Assets Bureau* [2004] 2 IR 159.

57 See sections 965(1)(b) and 966(5)(a)(i) of the Taxes Consolidation Act 1997.
58 See section 1078 of the Taxes Consolidation Act 1997.
59 See also Burke (2004: 252) and Hunt (2001).
60 See *United States v Salerno* 481 U.S. 739 107 S.Ct. 2095, 95, L.Ed. 2d, 697 (1987). For judicial determinations that the Proceeds of Crime Act, 1996 passes constitutional muster, see *Michael Murphy v GM, PB, PC, GH; John Gilligan v CAB, Revenue Commissioners, The Garda Commissioner, Ireland and the Attorney General* [2001] 4 IR 113. See also *Gilligan v Criminal Assets Bureau* [1998] IR 326. As McCutcheon and Walsh (1999: 131) noted: 'the classification of criminal asset proceedings as being non-criminal is not without difficulty. Could it not be argued that the deprivation of property that is involved in criminal asset proceedings coupled with the moral opprobrium implicit in a finding that the property represents the proceeds of crime, is equivalent to a finding of criminal guilt.'
61 As Sayre (1933: 35) presciently asked some 70 years ago: 'Does the modern conception of criminality, which seems to be shifting from a basis of individual guilt to one of social danger, presage the abandonment of the classic requirement of *mens rea* as an essential element of criminality? Are we to look forward to a day when criminality will be based upon external behaviour alone irrespective of intent?'
62 As Walsh suggests (2006: 10): 'The restraint can be imposed through an exercise of low visibility discretion on the street by an executive agent of the state. By any standards that reflects a significant transfer of power in criminal matters from the courts to the Garda. It is further evidence of the emergence of a second tier criminal process operated by the police.' A similar provision now exists for children under section 257A of the Children Act 2001, as amended by the Criminal Justice Act 2006.
63 See section 113(2) of the Criminal Justice Act 2006.
64 Section 89 of the Criminal Justice Act 2006 makes such orders mandatory for all persons convicted of drug-trafficking offences after the commencement of the relevant part (part 9) of the Act. Section 89(3), however, applied to persons who had been convicted on indictment of drug-trafficking offences prior to the commencement of the Act. The provision enables Gardaí to apply to the Circuit Court to have such a person made subject to the notification obligations, and the court could approve the application if it considered that 'the interests of the common good so require and that it is appropriate in all the circumstances of the case'. The application had to be made within two months of the commencement of the Act.
65 Those from the labelling school of criminology would argue that this reflects the fact that deviance is created by society. As Becker noted (1963: 9): 'Social groups create deviance by making the rules whose infraction constitutes deviance, and by applying those rules to a particular people and labelling them as outsiders.' See also McCullagh (2002) and Nelken (2002: 866–7).
66 On the rise of administrative justice through boards, inspectors and commissions, see Pound (1933: 1) who noted : 'In the case of factory acts, housing laws, pure food laws, laws for protection against fire and sanitary laws, today we commonly remove the whole subject in substance from the

domain of judicial prosecution and turn it over to boards and commissions, to be dealt with by inspectors and secretaries and agents.' See also Sayre (1933). The nature of the distinction between the criminal and administrative functions of the police has, however, been oversimplified. In Ireland, for example, the Gardaí continued to carry out a range of administrative duties, including the collection of agricultural statistics and the delivery of old-age pension books, for much of the twentieth century. See Kilcommins *et al.* (2004: 205).

67 See also section 8(6) of the Competition Act 2002, which makes the directors of an undertaking, its management or anyone acting in a similar capacity liable for criminal wrongdoing under the Act. Indeed section 8(7) makes a presumption that such a person has consented, *until the contrary is proved*, to the doing of the acts by the undertaking that infringe sections 6 (the prevention, restriction or distortion of competition in trade in any goods or services) and 7 (any abuse of a dominant position in trade for any goods or services) of the Act. The system of justice that applies in the regulatory realm is thus more exculpatory in orientation than its ordinary criminal counterpart. Moreover, any defences that might exist in the regulatory area are also more specialised than might be the case in the general defences that apply in criminal law. For example, in competition law, it is a specific defence to show that the agreement, decision or concerted practice complained of benefited from a declaration from the Competition Authority that the practice complained of contributes to improvement in the production or distribution of goods and services; or promotes technical or economic progress.

68 Section 80 of the Health and Safety Act 2005.

69 It provides: 'Where, in the course of, and by virtue of, their carrying out an audit of the accounts of the company, information comes into the possession of the auditors of a company that leads them to form the opinion that there are reasonable grounds for believing that the company or an officer or agent of it has committed an indictable offence under the Companies Acts, the auditors shall, forthwith after having formed it, notify that opinion to the Director [of Corporate Enforcement] and provide the Director with details of the grounds on which they have formed that opinion.' See also section 59 of the Criminal Justice (Theft and Fraud Offences) Act 2001.

70 See section 45(3) of the Competition Act 2002. In respect of Revenue powers, see, for example, section 905(2A) (the issue of search warrants) and section 908A (demands for information from financial institutions) of the Taxes Consolidation Act 1997. For the powers of the Office of Environmental Enforcement, see section 13 of the Environmental Protection Agency Act 1992, as amended.

71 If individuals start to incriminate themselves while being questioned in this manner, they should be cautioned.

72 See section 31 of the Competition Act 2002.

73 In relation to company law, section 20(2) of the Companies Act 1990, as amended, provides that a search warrant may be issued to authorise the Director of Corporate Enforcement to enter and search premises and seize and retain any material information found on the premises or in the custody or

possession of any person found on the premises. See also part II of the Companies Act 1990, as amended, which provides powers to the Director of Corporate Enforcement to require individuals to give information in relation to a company and to appoint inspectors to carry out investigations and to report on findings.

74 The Law Reform Commission (2006) recently published a report on corporate killing and called for the introduction of two new offences: a statutory offence of corporate manslaughter for corporate entities; and a secondary offence (grossly negligent management causing death) for corporate officers who play a role in the commission of the offence. See also Ahern (2004) and Brady (2006).

75 See section 8 of the Competition Act 2002. For increases in company law offences, see, for example, section 104 of Company Law Enforcement Act 2001. For the offences of fraudulent trading, furnishing false information, and insider dealing, see section 297 of the Companies Act 1963, as amended, section 242 of the Companies Act 1990, and section 114 of the Companies Act 1990 respectively.

76 [2001] 3 IR 390.

77 See Breen and Rottman (1985), O'Connell and Whelan (1994), Kirwan and O'Connell (2001), Watson (2000) and McGee *et al.* (2002).

78 In Ireland, these groups include, *inter alia*, Advic, Amen, the Commission for the Support of Court Support Services, National Crime Victims' Helpline, Rape Crisis Centres, Support after Homicide, Irish Centre for Parentally Abducted Children, Irish Tourist Assistance Service, One in Four, Sexual Violence Centre Cork, and Survivors of Child Abuse.

79 A Victims' Bill was also introduced in 2002 which, if enacted, would have made greater provision for the treatment and rights of victims of crime. It also provided a statutory definition of who constitutes a victim.

80 See Office of the DPP (2006: para 12.3).

81 EU member states are required *inter alia* to provide victims with the following rights: to furnish evidence in proceedings; be given access to relevant information from law enforcement agencies; to participate in the procedure as a victim; to be compensated for the crimes committed; to have legal costs refunded; and to be suitably protected.

82 In *A v Governor of Arbour Hill Prison* [2006] IESC 45, Hardiman J quoted the following passage from *State (Healy) v Donoghue* [1976] IR 325 where it was noted: 'In the first place the concept of justice, which is specifically referred to in the preamble in relation to the freedom and dignity of the individual appears again in the provisions of Article 34 which deals with the Courts. It is justice which is to be administered in the Courts and this concept of justice must import not only fairness and fair procedures, but also regard to the dignity of the individual. No court under the Constitution has jurisdiction to act contrary to justice.' Hardiman J went on to note 'that the "individual" referred to in the penultimate sentence of this quotation includes the applicant [a person accused and found guilty of unlawful carnal knowledge] ... or a person in his position but is not limited to such a person. The phrase certainly includes others who have become involved in the facts which give rise to this case and in particular the victim [of a crime].' The European Court of Human

Rights has also upheld the rights of victims of crime. See, for example, *X and Y v The Netherlands* (1985) 8 EHRR 235.

83 As the Minister for Justice, Equality and Law Reform recently noted (2006): 'However, along the way … concerns and rights of victims of crime may have unintentionally become secondary to the rights and protections for the criminal. Somehow it seems that we may now have arrived at a situation where on occasions the scales of justice are tilted too heavily on one side. Unfortunately when that occurs, that imbalance is likely to favour the criminal rather than the innocent victim all too often … What is interesting to note if one stands back from the development of the law in this area and considers the bigger picture, the focus is almost exclusively on the rights of the accused. Of itself, there is absolutely nothing wrong in that of course. But where do the rights of victims stand in such cases? Surely we need to ask questions as to why the focus seems to be always on the rights of the accused almost to the point of exclusion of the victim's rights or indeed anybody else who might be adversely effected. Is this desirable? Surely at least it must prompt us to raise questions about what the justice system seeks to achieve.'

84 See, for example, *People Attorney General v Williams* [1940] IR 195 at 200–1.

85 The attrition rates in the prosecution of sexual offences remains alarmingly high. We should therefore continue to remain alive to law's capacity to 'mask and legitimate conditions of social existence that are harmful and damaging to women' (Olsen 1984: 412). As Fennell (1993b: 182) notes: 'The partisan nature of the system is informed by a series of stereotypical assumptions and myths with regard to male and female roles, and the nature of sexuality which operate to disproportionately disadvantage women.'

86 But see also *People (DPP) v Molloy* (Unreported, CCA, 28 July 1995. See also Hanly (2001), McGrath (1999), and Fennell (1987).

87 [1999] 2 IR 25.

88 *People (DPP) v McGuinness* [1978] IR 189.

89 See section 28 of the Criminal Evidence Act 1992.

90 See sections 21 and 22 of the Criminal Evidence Act 1992. See also *People (DPP) v JT* (1988) 3 Frewen 141.

91 See *People (DPP) v DR* [1998] 2 IR 106. See also Ni Raifeartaigh (1994).

92 See, for example, section 3(4) of the Domestic Violence Act 1996.

93 See section 9 of the Criminal Law (Rape) (Amendment) Act 1990.

94 See section 27 of the Criminal Evidence Act 1992.

95 On the potential dangers of restorative justice including the usurpation of due process rights, the over-intrusion by the victim in the determination of an offender's punishment, net widening and power imbalances, see Ashworth (2002).

96 On the use of restorative justice in Ireland, see Joint Committee on Justice, Equality, Defence and Women's Rights (2007: 22–33), Lockhart (2002), Consedine (1999), Kilkelly (2006: 77–84), Bresnihan (1999) and O'Dwyer (2001).

## Chapter 7

1 The term is a deliberate allusion to Woodworth's (2001) *Dirty War, Clean Hands*. His account of how the Spanish socialist government enlisted the use of death squads to diminish the threat of the Basque separatist group ETA puts the Garda tactics in a relatively moderate light. However, the inception of Irish democracy in the 1920s witnessed extensive use of extra-judicial killings.

2 In the Criminal Justice Bill (2004), the government had proposed granting Gardaí, not below the rank of superintendent, the power to issue search warrants for any arrestable offence if it proved impractical to apply to a judge despite the protestations of many. In the light of Morris (2006), this proposal was withdrawn from the final legislation.

3 Judgements in the cases of *Hugh Jordan v the United Kingdom; McKerr v the United Kingdom; Kelly and others v the United Kingdom; Shanaghan v the United Kingdom*. Available at http://www.echr.coe.int/Eng/Press/2001/May/N%20Ireland%20cases.htm.

4 Following the signing of the Belfast Agreement, republicans were worried about its implications for the Irish Republican Army (IRA). At a rally, a heckler shouted 'What's happened to the IRA?', to which Adams responded, 'Well, they haven't gone away, you know'.

# References and further reading


Agamben, G. (2005) *State of Exception*. Chicago: University of Chicago Press.
Aherne, D. (2004) 'Corporate Killing in Ireland – A New Paradigm', *Irish Law Times*, 22: 235–9.
Allan, T. R. S. (2001) *Constitutional Justice: A Liberal Theory of the Rule of Law*. Oxford: Oxford University Press.
Allen, C. (1931) *Legal Duties and other Essays in Jurisprudence*. Oxford: Clarendon Press.
An Garda Síochána (1997) *Annual Report on crime*. Dublin: Stationery Office.
Anderson, M., den Boer, M., Cullen, P., Gilmore, W., Raab, C. and Walker, N. (1995) *Policing the European Union*. Oxford: Clarendon Press.
Archer, M. (1995) *Realist Social Theory: The Morphogenetic Approach*. Cambridge: Cambridge University Press.
Arditti, B. (2003) 'Populism, or, Politics at the Edges of Democracy?', *Contemporary Politics*, 9(1): 18–31.
Ashworth, A. (1977) 'Excluding Evidence as Protecting Rights', *Criminal Law Review*, 723–35.
Ashworth, A. (1996) 'Crime, Community and Creeping Consequentialism', *Criminal Law Review*, 43: 220–30.
Ashworth, A. (1999) 'Article 6 and the Fairness of Trials', *Criminal Law Review*, 261–99.
Ashworth, A. (2000) 'Is the Criminal Law a Lost Cause?', *Law Quarterly Review*, 116: 225–56.
Ashworth, A. (2001) 'Victims' Rights, Defendants' Rights and Criminal Procedure', in A. Crawford and J. Goodey (eds), *Integrating a Victim Perspective within Criminal Justice*. Aldershot: Ashgate.
Ashworth, A. (2002) 'Responsibilities, Rights and Restorative Justice', *British Journal of Criminology*, 42(3): 578–95.
Ashworth, A. (2004a) 'The Criminal Justice Act 2003: Criminal Justice Reform: Principles, Human Rights and Public Protection', *Criminal Law Review*, 516–32.
Ashworth, A. (2004b) 'Social Control and Anti-social Behaviour: The Subversion of Human Rights', *Law Quarterly Review*, 120: 263–91.
Ashworth, A. (2005) 'Four Threats to the Presumption of Innocence' Ben Beinart

Memorial Lecture, University of Cape Town.
Ashworth, A. (2006) 'Four Threats to the Presumption of Innocence', *South African Law Journal*, 123(1) 62–96.
Ashworth, A. and Pattenden, R. (1986) 'Reliability, Hearsay Evidence and the English Criminal Trial', *Law Quarterly Report*, 102: 292–331.
Ashworth, A. and Redmayne, M. (2005), *The Criminal Process*, 3rd edn. Oxford: Oxford University Press.
Atiyah, P. (1979) *The Rise and Fall of Freedom of Contract*. Oxford: Clarendon Press.
Austin, A. and McClean, E. (2004) 'Detention', in U. Kilkelly (ed.), *ECHR and Irish Law*. Bristol: Jordan Publishing.

Bache, I. and Flinders, M. (eds) (2004) *Multi-level Governance*. Oxford: Oxford University Press.
Bacik, I. (2004) 'Criminal Law', in U. Kilkelly (ed.) *ECHR and Irish Law*. Bristol: Jordan Publishing.
Baker, J. H. (1977) 'Criminal Courts and Procedure at Common Law 1550–1800' in J. S. Cockburn (ed.), *Crime in England 1550–1800*. London: Methuen.
Baldwin, R. (2004) 'The New Punitive Regulation', *Modern Law Review*, 67(3): 351–83.
Barrington, D. (1987) 'The Constitution in the Courts', *Administration*, 35(4): 110–27.
Bartrip, P. W. J. and Burman, S. B. (1983) *The Wounded Soldiers of Industry: Industrial Compensation Policy, 1833–1897*. Oxford: Oxford University Press.
Beattie, J. (1986) *Crime and the Courts in England, 1660–1800*. Princeton: Princeton University Press.
Beattie, J. (1991) 'Scales of Justice: Defence Counsel and the English Trial in the Eighteenth and Nineteenth Centuries', *Law and History Review*, 9(2): 221–67.
Beccaria, C. (1995, first published 1764) *On Crimes and Punishment*. Cambridge: Cambridge University Press.
Beck, U. (2000) 'The Cosmopolitan Perspective: Sociology of the Second Age of Modernity', *British Journal of Sociology*, 51(1): 79–105.
Beck, U. (2005) 'How Not to Become a Museum Piece', *British Journal of Sociology*, 56 (3): 335–43.
Becker, H. (1963) *The Outsiders*. New York: The Free Press.
Bellamy, R. (1992) *Liberalism and Modern Society: An Historical Argument*. London: Polity Press.
Bellamy, R. (2001) 'Constitutive Citizenship versus Constitutional Rights: Republican Reflections on the EU Charter and the Human Rights Act', in T. Campbell, K. D. Ewing and A. Tomkins (eds) *Sceptical Essays on Human Rights*. Oxford: Oxford University Press.
Bennett, D. (1988) 'Are They Always Right? Investigation and Proof in a Citizen Anti-Heroin Movement', in M. Tomlinson, T. Varley and C. McCullagh (eds) *Whose Law and Order? Aspects of Crime and Social Control in Irish Society*. Belfast: Sociological Association of Ireland.
Bentham, J. (1907, first published 1781) *An Introduction to the Principles of Morals and Legislation*. Oxford: Clarendon Press.
Bentham, J. (1830) *The Rationale of Punishment*. London: University of London Press.
Berlin, I. (1969) 'Two Concepts of Liberty', in I. Berlin (ed.), *Four Essays on Liberty*. Oxford: Oxford University Press.
Bigo, D. (2002) 'Security and Immigration: Toward a Critique of the Governmentality of Unease', *Alternatives*, 27: 63–92.
Black, J. (2005) 'The Emergence of Risk Based Regulation and the New Public

Management in the UK', *Public Law*, 512–49.
Black, J. (2006) 'Tensions in the Regulatory State', *Public Law*, 58–73.
Blackstone, W. (1765) *Commentaries on the Laws of England, Vol IV*. Boston, MA: Beacon Press.
Blick, A. and Weir, S. (2005) *The Rules of the Game: The Government's Counter-Terrorism Laws and Strategy*. Democratic Audit, University of Essex.
Bohan, G. (2002) 'Radical Change – Some Key Features of the Company Law Enforcement Act, 2001', *Irish Tax Review* 15(1): 63–8.
Boies, H. M. (1901) *The Science of Penology*. London: GP Putnam's.
Börzel, T. and Risse, T. (2003) 'Conceptualizing the Domestic Impact of Europe', in K. Featherstone and C. Radelli (eds) *The Politics of Europeanization*. Oxford: Oxford University Press.
Bottoms, A. E. (1995) 'The Philosophy and Politics of Punishment and Sentencing' in C. Clarkson and R. Morgan (eds) *The Politics of Sentencing Reform*. Oxford: Oxford University Press.
Bowyer Bell, J. (1989) *The Secret Army*, 3rd edn. Dublin: Poolbeg Press.
Boyce, D. (2005) *Nineteenth Century Ireland: The Search for Stability*. Dublin: Gill and Macmillan.
Boyle, K. (1972) 'Police in Ireland before the Union I', *Irish Jurist*, VII: 115–37.
Brady, A. (2006) 'Corporate Killing – The Law Reform Commission's Proposals', *Irish Law Times*, 15: 235–40.
Brady, C. (1974) *Guardians of the Police*. Dublin: Gill and Macmillan.
Braithwaite, J. (2000) 'The New Regulatory State and the Transformation of Criminology', *British Journal of Criminology*, 40: 222–38.
Braithwaite, J. (2003) 'What's Wrong with the Sociology of Punishment?' *Theoretical Criminology*, 7(11): 5–28.
Braithwaite, J. (2005) *Neoliberalism or Regulatory Capitalism*. Canberra: Regulatory Institutions Network.
Braithwaite, J. and Drahos, P. (2003) *Global Business Regulation*. Cambridge: Cambridge University Press.
Braudel, F. (1973) *The Mediterranean and the Mediterranean World in the Age of Philip II*. London: Collins.
Breen, R. and Rottman, D. B. (1985) *Crime Victimisation in the Republic of Ireland*. Dublin: ERSI.
Bresnihan, V. (1999) 'Restorative Justice in Ireland', in M. Barry, O. Burke, J. Connolly and J. Curran (eds) *Children, Young People and Crime in Britain and Ireland: From Exclusion to Inclusion*. Edinburgh: Scottish Executive Central Research Unit.
Brewer, J. (1980) 'Law and Disorder in Stuart and Hanoverian England', *History Today*, 30: 18–27.
Brewer, J. and Styles, J. (1981) 'Popular Attitudes to Law in the Eighteenth Century', in M. Fitzgerald, G. Mclennan and J. Pawson (eds) *Crime and Society: Readings in History and Theory*. Milton Keynes: Open University Press.
Bridgeman, I. (2003) 'The Constabulary and the Criminal Justice System in Nineteenth Century Ireland', in F. McAuley and I. O'Donnell (eds) *Criminal Justice History: Themes and Controversies from Pre-Independence Ireland*. Dublin: Four Courts.
Brodeur, J. P. (1983) 'High Policing and Low Policing: Remarks about the policing of Political Activities', *Social Problems*, 30(5): 507–20.
Broeker, G. (1970) *Rural Disorder and Police Reform in Ireland 1812–1836*. London: University of Toronto Press.

Brown, M. (2005) 'Liberal Exclusions and the New Punitiveness', in J. Pratt, D. Brown, M. Brown, S. Hallsworth and W. Morrison (eds) *The New Punitiveness: Trends, Theories, Perspectives.* Cullompton: Willan Publishing.

Burke, J. (2004) 'Revenue Powers – The Need for Adequate Statutory Safeguards', *Irish Tax Review*, 17(3): 252–56.

Butler, A. (1993) 'The Right to be Informed of the Right to a Lawyer – The Constitutional Dimension', *Irish Criminal Law Journal*, 3: 173–89.

Buxton, T. (1818) *An Enquiry, Whether Crime and Misery and Produced or Prevented by our Present System of Prison Discipline.* London: Arch, Butterworth and Hatchard.

Cairns, D. A. (1998) *Advocacy and the Making of the Adversarial Criminal Trial, 1800–1865.* Oxford: Clarendon Press.

Campbell, C. (1994) *Emergency Law in Ireland, 1918–25.* Oxford: Clarendon Press.

Carey, G. (1999) 'Recognition and Visual Identification Warnings, Provisos and Exceptional Circumstances', *Irish Law Times*, 17: 69–73.

Carey, T. (2000) *Mountjoy: The Story of a Prison.* Cork: Collins Press.

Carney, P. (2007) 'The Role of the Victim in the Irish Criminal Process', *Judicial Studies Institute Journal*, 7: 7–17.

Carroll Burke, P. (2000) *Colonial Discipline: The Making of the Irish Convict System.* Dublin: Four Courts Press.

Casey, J. (1987) *Constitutional Law in Ireland.* Dublin: Sweet and Maxwell.

Casey, J. (2000) *Constitutional Law in Ireland*, 3rd edn. Dublin: Sweet and Maxwell.

Cassidy, F. and Law Society of Ireland (2003) *Money Laundering and the Criminal Assets Bureau.* Dublin: Law Society.

Castells, M. (1997) *The Power of Identity.* Oxford: Blackwell.

Cerny, P. (1999) 'Reconstructing the Political in a Globalizing World: States, Institutions, Actors and Governance', in F. Buelens (ed.) *Globalization and the Nation-State.* Cheltenham: Edward Elgar.

Checkel, J. (2001) 'The Europeanization of Citizenship' in M. G. Cowles, J. Caporaso and T. Risse (eds) *Transforming Europe: Europeanization and Domestic Change.* Ithaca, NY: Cornell University Press.

Christie, N. (1977) 'Conflicts as Property', *British Journal of Criminology*, 17: 1–15.

Coen, D. and Thatcher, M. (2005) 'The New Governance of Markets and Non-Majoritarian Regulators', *Governance*, 18(3): 329–46.

Coleman, R. and Sim, J. (2005) 'Contemporary Statecraft and the "Punitive Obsession": A Critique of the New penology', in J. Pratt, D. Brown, M. Brown, S. Hallsworth and W. Morrison (eds) *The New Punitiveness: Trends, Theories, Perspectives.* Cullompton: Willan Publishing.

Connolly, J. (2002) *Community Policing and Drugs in Dublin.* Dublin: North Inner City Drugs Task Force.

Connolly, S. J. (1988) 'Albion's Fatal Twigs: Justice and Society in Scotland and Ireland, 1500–1939' in R. Mitchinson and P. Roebuck (eds), *Economy and Society in Ireland, 1500–1939.* Edinburgh: Edinburgh University Press.

Considine, J. (1999) 'Restorative Justice: Could Ireland Lead the Way?', *Studies: An Irish Quarterly Review*, 88(350): 132–37.

Considine, J. and Kilcommins, S. (2006) 'The Importance of Safeguards on Revenue Powers: Another Perspective', *Irish Tax Review*, 19(6): 49–53.

Cornish, W. R. and de N. Clark, G. (1989) *Law and Society in England 1750–1950.* London: Sweet and Maxwell.

Costello, K. (1988) 'A Constitutional Antiquity? The Habeas Corpus (Ireland) Act 1782 Revisited', *Irish Jurist*, XXIII: 240–54.

Costelloe, S. (2001) 'Detention for Questioning and Oppressive Interrogation', *Irish Criminal Law Journal*, 11(1): 12–17.

Coulter, C. and Coleman, S. (2003) *The End of Irish History: Critical Reflections on the Celtic Tiger*. Manchester: Manchester University Press.

Council of Europe (1995) *Report to the Irish Government on the visit to Ireland carried out by the European Committee for the Prevention of Torture and Inhuman or Degrading Treatment or Punishment (CPT) from 26 September to 5 October 1993*. Available at http://www.cpt.coe.int/documents/irl/1995-14-inf-eng.pdf.

Council of Europe (1999) *Report to the Irish Government on the visit to Ireland carried out by the European Committee for the Prevention of Torture and Inhuman or Degrading Treatment or Punishment (CPT) from 31 August to 9 September 1998*. Available at http://www.cpt.coe.int/documents/irl/1999-15-inf-eng.pdf.

Cover, R. M. (1986) 'Violence and the Word', *Yale Law Journal*, 95: 1601–29.

Damaska, M. (1975a) 'Presentation of Evidence and Fact Finding Precision', *University of Pennsylvania Law Review*, 123(5): 1083–106.

Damaska, M. (1975b) 'Structures of Authority and Comparative Criminal Procedure', *Yale Law Journal*, 84(3): 480–544.

Damaska, M. (1986) *The Faces of Justice and State Authority*. New Haven, CT: Yale University Press.

Delaney, V. T. H. (1979) *The Administration of Justice in Ireland*, 4th edn. Dublin: Institute of Public Administration.

Dicey, A. V. (1959, first published 1885) *Introduction to the Study of the Law of the Constitution*, 10th edition. London: Macmillan.

Dickinson, H. T. (1997) 'Irish Radicalism in the Late Eighteenth Century', *History*, 82: 266–84.

Douzinas, C. (2000) *The End of Human Rights: Critical Legal Thought at the Turn of the Century*. Oxford: Hart.

Dobson, M. J. (1987) *A Chronology of Epidemic Diseases and Mortality in South East England, 1601–1800*, Historical Geography Series No. 19. Oxford: Oxford University Press.

Dubber, M. D. (2002) 'Policing Possession: The War on Crime and the End of Criminal Law', *Journal of Criminal Law and Criminology*, 91(3): 1–151.

Durkheim, E. (1997, first published 1893) *The Division of Labour in Society*. London: The Free Press.

Driver, A. (1993) *Power and Pauperism: The Workhouse System, 1834–1884*. Cambridge: Cambridge University Press.

Dworkin, R. (1977) *Taking Rights Seriously*. Cambridge, MA: Harvard University Press.

Dworkin, R. (1981) 'Principle, Policy and Procedure', in C. Tapper (ed.) *Crime, Proof and Punishment*. London: Butterworths.

Dworkin, R. (1982) 'Law as Interpretation', *Texas Law Review*, 60: 527–50.

Dworkin, R. (1988) *Law's Empire*. Cambridge, MA: Harvard University Press.

Dwyer, P. (1993) 'The Duty of Disclosure in Criminal Proceedings', *Irish Criminal Law Journal*, 3(1): 66–81.

Dyzenhaus, D. (1999) *Legality and Legitimacy: Carl Schmitt, Hans Kelsen and Hermann Heller in Weimar*. Oxford: Oxford University Press.

Dyzenhaus, D. (2006a) *The Constitution of Law: Legality in a Time of Emergency*. Cambridge: Cambridge University Press.

Dyzenhaus, D. (2006b) *States of Exception*. Available at http://ptw.uchicago.edu/Dyzenhaus01.pdf.

Elias, N. (1978) *What is Sociology?* London: Hutchinson.
Elias, N. (1994) *The Civilising Process*. Oxford: Blackwell.
Ellis, H. (1890) *The Criminal*. The Contemporary Science Series. New York: Scribners and Welford.
Ennis, K. (2003) 'Mandatory Minimum Sentences in Section 15A Drugs Cases', *Bar Review*, 8(1): 30–5.
Esping-Andersen, G. (1990) *The Three Worlds of Welfare Capitalism*. Cambridge: Polity Press.

Farmer, L. (1996) 'The Obsession with Definition: The Nature of Crime and Critical Legal Theory', *Social and Legal Studies*, 5: 57–73.
Farrell, M. (1998) *Paper on the Offences against the State (Amendment) Act 1998*. Dublin: Irish Council for Civil Liberties.
Feeley, M. (2003) 'Crime, Social Order and the Rise of Neo-Conservative Politics', *Theoretical Criminology*, 6: 217–26.
Feeley, M. (2006) 'Origins of Actuarial Justice in Practice', in S. Armstrong and L. McAra (eds) *Perspectives on Punishment: The Contours of Control*. Oxford: Oxford University Press.
Feeley, M. and Levine, K. (2001) 'Assaults on the Adversarial Process: Rethinking American Criminal Justice', *Punishment and Society*, 3(4): 537–45.
Fennell, C. (1987) 'Differential Treatment of Sexual Complaints by the Law of Evidence: A Case for Reform', *Irish Jurist*, XXII: 228–50.
Fennell, C. (1993a) Crime *and Crisis in Ireland: Justice by Illusion*. Cork: Cork University Press.
Fennell, C. (1993b) 'Criminal Law and the Criminal Justice System: Women as Accused', in A Connolly (ed.) *Gender and the Law in Ireland*. Dublin: Oak Tree Press.
Fennell, C. (2001) 'The Culture of Decision-Making: A Case for Judicial Defiance Through Evidence and Fact Finding', *Judicial Studies Institute Journal*, 2(1): 25–68.
Fennell, C. (2003) *The Law of Evidence in Ireland*, 2nd edn. Dublin: Butterworths.
Ferriter, D. (2004) *The Transformation of Ireland 1900–2000*. London: Profile Books.
Fletcher, A. J. and Stevenson, J. (eds) (1985) *Order and Disorder in Early Modern England*. Cambridge: Cambridge University Press.
Foucault, M. (1972) *The Archaeology of Knowledge*. London: Tavistock.
Foucault, M. (1979) *The History of Sexuality*. Harmondsworth: Penguin.
Foucault, M. (1991) *Discipline and Punish: The Birth of the Prison*. Harmondsworth: Penguin.
Friedland, M. (1989) 'Controlling the Administration of Criminal Justice', *Dublin University Law Journal*, 11: 10–39.
Friedman, L. M. (1993) *Crime and Punishment in American History*. New York: Basic Books.

Gallagher, L. (2003) 'The Criminal Assets Bureau and Taxation – More Recent Developments', *Irish Tax Review*, 16(4): 391–4.
Garland, D. (1981) 'The Birth of the Welfare Sanction', *British Journal of Law and Society*, 8(1): 19–45.
Garland, D. (1985) *Punishment and Welfare: A History of Penal Strategies*. Aldershot: Gower.
Garland, D. (1990) *Punishment and Modern Society: A Study in Social Theory*. Oxford: Clarendon Press.
Garland, D. (1996) 'The Limits of the Sovereign State: Strategies of Crime Control in

Contemporary Societies', *British Journal of Criminology*, 36(4): 445–71.
Garland, D. (2001) *The Culture of Control: Crime and Social Order in Contemporary Society*. Oxford: Oxford University Press.
Garland, D. (2002) 'Of Crime and Criminals: The Development of Criminology in Britain', in M. Maguire, R. Morgan, R. Reiner (eds) *The Oxford Handbook of Criminology*, 3rd edn. Oxford: Oxford University Press.
Garland, D. (2003) 'The Rise of Risk', in R. Ericson and A. Doyle (eds) *Risk and Morality*. Toronto: University of Toronto Press.
Garland, D. (2005) 'Beyond the Culture of Control', in M. Matravers (ed.) *Managing Modernity: Politics and the Culture of Control*. London/New York: Routledge.
Gatrell, V. A. C. (1994) *The Hanging Tree: Execution and the English People, 1770–1868*. Oxford: Oxford University Press.
Gearty, C. (2006) *Can Human Rights Survive*. Cambridge: Cambridge University Press.
Gearty, M. R. (2004) 'Video Recording of Accused Persons in Custody', *Bar Review*, 65–6.
Goldstein, A. (1974) 'Reflections on Two Models: Inquisitorial Themes in American Criminal Procedure', *Stanford Law Review*, 26: 1009–28.
Goldstein, A. (1992) 'White Collar Crime and Civil Sanctions', *Yale Law Journal*, 101(8): 1895–99.
Gordon, R. (1997) 'Critical Legal Histories', *Stanford Law Review*, 36: 57–125.
Gorecki, P. and McFadden, D. (2006) 'Criminal Cartels in Ireland: The Heating Oil Case', *European Competition Law Review*, 11: 631–40.
Graveson, R. H. (1941) 'The Movement from Status to Contract', *Modern Law Review*, IV: 261–72.
Gray, G. (2006) 'The Regulation of Corporate Violations: Punishment, Compliance and the Blurring of Responsibility', *British Journal of Criminology*, 46(5): 875–92.
Gray, J. (1986) *Liberalism*. Milton Keynes: Open University Press.
Green, T. A. (1988) *Verdict According to Conscience: Perspectives on the English Criminal Trial Jury 1200–1800*. Chicago: University of Chicago Press.
Greer, D. (1969) 'Legal Services and the Poor in Ireland', *Irish Jurist*, IV: 270–92.
Greer, S. (1986) 'Supergrasses in the Legal System in Britain and Ireland', *Law Quarterly Review*, 102: 198–249.
Griffiths, J. (1970) 'Ideology in Criminal Procedure or A Third Model of the Criminal Process', *Yale Law Journal*, 79(3): 359–417.
Gwynn-Morgan, D. (2003) *A Judgment Too Far? Judicial Activism and the Constitution*. Cork: Cork University Press.

Hale, M. (1971, first published 1736) *The History of the Pleas of the Crown, Vol II*. Abingdon: Professional Books.
Hamilton, J. (2004) 'The Summary Trial of Indictable Offences', *Judicial Studies Institute Journal*, 4(2): 154–81.
Hanly, C. (2001) 'Corroborating Rape Charges', *Irish Criminal Law Journal*, 11(4): 2–11.
Hanly, C. (2006) *An Introduction to Irish Criminal Law*, 2nd edn. Dublin: Gill and Macmillan.
Harding, C. (1988) 'The Inevitable End of a Discredited System: The Origins of the Gladstone Committee Report on Prisons, 1895', *Historical Journal*, 31(3): 591–608.
Harvey, C. (2004) 'Talking about Human Rights', in T. Murphy (ed.) *Western Jurisprudence*. Dublin: Thomson Round Hall.
Hay, D. (1977) 'Property, Authority and the Criminal Law', in D. Hay, P. Linebaugh,

J. G. Rule, E. P. Thompson and C. Winslow (eds) *Albion's Fatal Tree: Crime and Society in Eighteenth Century England*. London: Allen and Unwin.
Hay, D. (1983) 'Controlling the English Prosecutor', *Osgoode Hall Law Journal*, 21(2): 165–86.
Hay, D. (1984) 'The Criminal Prosecution in England and its Historians', *Modern Law Review*, 47(1): 1–24.
Hay, D. and Snyder, F. (1989) 'Using the Criminal Law, 1750–1850: Policing, Private Prosecution and the State', in D. Hay and F. Snyder (eds) *Policing and Prosecution in Britain, 1750–1850*. Oxford: Clarendon Press.
Healy, J. (2004) *Irish Laws of Evidence*. Dublin: Thomson Round Hall.
Henderson, L. N. (1985) 'The Wrongs of Victims' Rights', *Stanford Law Review*, 37: 937–1021.
Henry, B. (1994) *Dublin Hanged: Crime, Law Enforcement and Punishment in the Eighteenth Century*. Dublin: Irish Academic Press.
Herrup, C. (1989) *The Common Peace: Participation in the Criminal Law in Seventeenth Century England.* Cambridge: Cambridge University Press.
Hillyard, P. (1987) 'The Normalisation of Special Powers: From Northern Ireland to Britain', in P. Scraton (ed.) *Law, Order and the Authoritarian State.* Milton Keynes: Open University Press.
Hobbes, T. (1651) *Leviathan*. New York: P.F. Collier & Son Co. 1909–14, Harvard Classics.
Hobsbawm, E. (1962) *The Age of Revolution: Europe 1789–1848.* London: Weidenfeld and Nicolson.
Hobsbawm, E. (1968) *Industry and Empire: An Economic History of Britain since 1750.* London: Weidenfeld and Nicolson.
Hobsbawm, E. (1975) *The Age of Capital 1848–1875.* London: Weidenfeld and Nicolson.
Hobsbawm, E. (1987) *The Age of Empire 1875–1914.* London: Weidenfeld and Nicolson.
Hogan, G. (1999a) 'Constitutional Law – The Right to Silence after National Irish Banks and Finnerty', *Dublin University Law Journal*, 21: 176–89.
Hogan, G. (1999b) 'The Belfast Agreement and the Future Incorporation of Human Rights in the Republic of Ireland', *Bar Review*, 4(4): 205–11.
Hogan, G. (2004) 'Incorporation of the ECHR: Some Issues of Methodology and Process', in U. Kilkelly (ed.) *ECHR and Irish Law*. Bristol: Jordan Publishing.
Hogan, G. and Walker, C. (1989) *Political Violence and the Law in Ireland*. Manchester: Manchester University Press.
Hogan, G. and Whyte, G. (2003) *J. M. Kelly: The Irish Constitution*. Dublin: Butterworths.
Holdsworth, W. (1902) 'Martial Law Historically Considered', *Law Quarterly Review*, XVIII: 117–32.
Holdsworth, W. (1908) *A History of English Criminal Law, Vol III*. London: Methuen.
Holmes, S. (2003) 'Lineages of the Rule of Law,' in J. M. Maravall and A. Przeworski (eds), *Democracy and the Rule of Law*. Cambridge: Cambridge University Press.
House of Lords European Union Committee (2006) *European Arrest Warrant – Recent Developments*. London: Stationery Office.
Hudson, B. (2001) 'Punishment, Rights and Difference: Defending Justice in the risk Society', in K. Stenson and R. Sullivan (eds) *Crime, Risk and Justice: The Politics of Crime Control in Liberal Democracies*. Cullompton: Willan Publishing.
Hudson, B. (2003) *Justice in the Risk Society: Challenging and Reaffirming Justice in Late Modernity*. London: Sage.

Hunt, A. (1986) 'The Theory of Critical Legal Studies', *Oxford Journal of Legal Studies*, 6(1): 1–29.

Hunt, A. (1998) 'Evaluating Constitutions – The Irish Constitution and the Limits of Constitutionalism in T. Murphy and P. Twomey (eds) *Ireland's Evolving Constitution: 1937–1997*. Oxford: Hart.

Hunt, P. (2001) 'The Criminal Assets Bureau and Taxation – Recent Developments', *Irish Tax Review*, 14(6): 573–8.

Hutton, N. (2006) 'Sentencing as a Social Practice', in S. Armstrong and L. McAra (eds) *Perspectives on Punishment: The Contours of Control*. Oxford: Oxford University Press.

ICCL (Irish Council for Civil Liberties) (1993) *Police Interrogation Endangers the Innocent*. Dublin: Irish Council for Civil Liberties.

Ignatieff, M. (1978) *A Just Measure of Pain: The Penitentiary in the Industrial Revolution, 1750–1850*. London: Macmillan.

Inglis, T. (2003). *Truth, Power and Lies*. Dublin: University College Dublin Press.

Irish Government (1999) *Response of the Irish Government to the report of the European Committee for the Prevention of Torture and Inhuman or Degrading Treatment or Punishment (CPT) on its visit to Ireland from 31 August to 9 September 1998*. Available at http://www.cpt.coe.int/documents/irl/1999-16-inf-eng.htm.

Irish Human Rights Commission (2002) *A Proposal for a New Garda Complaints System*. Available at http://www.ihrc.ie/_fileupload/publications/A_Proposal_for_a_New_Garda_Complaints_System.doc.

Jackson, J. (1989) 'Evidence Competence and Compellability of Spouses as Prosecution Witnesses', *Dublin University Law Journal*, 11: 149–58.

Jackson, J. (1993) 'Competence and Compellability of Spouses to Give Evidence', *Dublin University Law Journal*, 15: 202–11.

Jackson, J., Quinn, K. and O'Malley, T. (1999) 'The Jury System in Contemporary Ireland: In the Shadow of a Troubled Past', *Law and Contemporary Problems*, 62: 203–32.

Jessop, B. (2004) 'Multi-level Governance and Multi-level Metagoverance', in I. Bache and M. Flinders (eds) *Multi-level Governance*. Oxford: Oxford University Press.

Johnston, L. (2000) *Policing Britain: Risk, Security and Governance*. Harlow: Longman.

Joint Committee on Justice, Equality, Defence and Women's Rights (2003) *Review of Criminal Justice System: Presentations*. Dublin: Houses of the Oireachtas.

Joint Committee on Justice, Equality, Defence and Women's Rights (2005) *Report on Community Policing*. Dublin: Houses of the Oireachtas.

Joint Committee on Justice, Equality, Defence and Women's Rights (2007) *Report on Restorative Justice*. Dublin: Houses of the Oireachtas.

Keane, D. (1997) 'Detention without Charge and the Criminal Justice (Drug Trafficking) Act, 1996', *Irish Criminal Law Journal*, 7: 1–21.

Kelly, J. M. (1980) *The Irish Constitution*. Dublin: Jurist Publishing.

Kennedy, D. (1982) 'The Ideological Content of Legal Education', in D. Kairys (ed.) *The Politics of Law*. New York: Pantheon Books.

Kilcommins, S. (1998) 'Context and Contingency in the Historical Penal Process: the Revision of Revisionist Analysis Using the Twelve Judges' Notebooks as One Tool of Analysis', *Holdsworth Law Journal*, 19(1): 1–54.

Kilcommins, S. (2003) 'Reconstructing the Image of the Habitual Drunkard', in S.

Kilcommins and I. O'Donnell (eds) *Alcohol, Society and Law.* Chichester: Barry Rose Law Publishers, pp. 60–103.

Kilcommins, S. (2004) 'Historical Jurisprudence', in T. Murphy (ed.) *Western Jurisprudence*. Dublin: Round Hall, Sweet and Maxwell.

Kilcommins, S. and Vaughan, B. (2004) 'A Perpetual Sense of Emergency: Subverting the Rule of Law in Ireland', *Cambrian Law Review*, 35: 55–80.

Kilcommins, S., O'Donnell, I., O'Sullivan, E. and Vaughan, B. (2004) *Crime, Punishment and the Search for Order in Ireland.* Dublin: Institute of Public Administration.

Kilkelly, U. (2006) *Youth Justice in Ireland: Tough Lives, Rough Justice*. Dublin: Irish Academic Press.

King, P. (1984) 'Decision-Makers and Decision-Making in the English Criminal Law, 1750–1800', *Historical Journal*, 27(1): 25–58.

King, P. (2000) *Crime, Justice, and Discretion in England, 1740–1820*. Oxford: Oxford University Press.

Kirwan, G. and O'Connell, M. (2001) 'Crime Victimisation in Dublin Revisited', *Irish Criminal Law Journal*, 11(2): 10–13.

Klein, S. R. (1999) 'Redrawing the Criminal-Civil Boundary', *Buffalo Criminal Law Review*, 2: 681–723.

Komarek, J. (2007) *European Constitutionalism and the European Arrest Warrant In Search of the Contrapunctal Principles Limits*. Available at http://users.ox.ac.uk/~some2134/publ.html.

Kumm, M. (2005) 'The Jurisprudence of Constitutional Conflict: Constitutional Supremacy in Europe before and after the Constitutional Treaty', *European Law Journal*, 11(3): 262–307.

Lacey, N. (1998) 'Contingency, Coherence and Conceptualism: Reflections on the Encounter between Critique and the Philosophy of the Criminal Law', in P. Duff, (ed.) *Philosophy of the Criminal Law*. Cambridge: Cambridge University Press.

Lacey, N. (2001), 'In Search of the Responsible Subject: History, Philosophy and Social Sciences in Criminal Law', *Modern Law Review*, 64(3): 350–71.

Lacey, N. (2002) 'Legal Constructions of Crime' in M. Maguire, R. Morgan and R. Reiner (eds) *The Oxford Handbook of Criminology*, 3rd edn. Oxford: Oxford University Press.

Lacey, N. (2004) 'Criminalisation as Regulation: The Role of Criminal Law', in C. Parker, C. Scott, N. Lacey and J. Braithwaite (eds) *Regulating Law*. Oxford: Oxford University Press.

Lacquer, T. W. (1989) 'Crowds, Carnival and the State in English Executions, 1604–1868', in A. L. Beier, D. Cannadine, D. and J. M. Rosenheim (eds) *The First Modern Society: Essays in English History in Honour of Lawrence Stone*. Cambridge: Cambridge University Press.

Laird, H. (2005) *Subversive Law in Ireland, 1879–1920: From 'Unwritten Law' to the Dáil Courts*. Dublin: Four Courts Press.

Lambert, P. (2000) 'Swearing Blind with Pointed Fingers', *Irish Criminal Law Journal*, 10(3): 11–14.

Landsman, S. (1990) 'The Rise of the Contentious Spirit: Adversary Procedure in Eighteenth Century England', *Cornell Law Review*, 75: 498–609.

Langbein, J. H. (1973) 'The Origins of Public Prosecution at Common Law', *American Journal of Legal History*, 17(4): 313–35.

Langbein, J. H. (1983) 'Shaping the Eighteenth Century Criminal Trial: A View from the Ryder Sources', *University of Chicago Law Review*, 50(1): 1–135.

Langbein, J. H. (1994) 'The Historical Origins of the Privilege Against Self Incrimination at Common Law', *Michigan Law Review*, 92(5): 1047–85.
Langbein, J. H. (1996) 'Historical Foundations of the Law of Evidence: A View from the Ryder Sources', *Columbia Law Review*, 96: 1168–202.
Langbein, J. H. (1999) 'The Prosecutorial Origins of Defence Counsel in the Eighteenth Century: The Appearance of Solicitors', *Cambridge Law Journal*, 58(2): 314–65.
Langbein, J. H. (2003) *The Origins of Adversary Criminal Trial*. Oxford: Oxford University Press.
Law Reform Commission (1985) *Competence and Compellability of Spouses as Witnesses*. Dublin: Law Reform Commission.
Law Reform Commission (1990) *Report on Child Sexual Abuse*, Report No. 32. Dublin: Law Reform Commission.
Law Reform Commission (2006) *Report on Corporate Killing*, LRC 77-2006. Dublin: Law Reform Commission.
Lea, J. (2001) *Crime Control and Civil Liberties*. Available at http://www bunker8.pwp.blueyonder.co.uk/.
Lea, J. (2002) *Crime and Modernity*. London: Sage.
Lea, J. (2004a) 'Law, Ideology and the Gallows in 18th and 19th Century England'. Available at http://www.bunker8.pwp.blueyonder.co.uk/hisrory/36804.htm.
Lea, J. (2004b) 'Hitting Criminals Where it Hurts: Organised Crime and the Erosion of Due Process', *Cambrian Law Review*, 35: 81–96.
Lea, J. (2005) 'Terrorism, Crime and the Collapse of Civil Liberties', Lecture to Criminology Society at Middlesex University in April 2005.
Leibniz, G. (1998, first published 1714) 'Monadology', in *Philosophical Texts*. Oxford: Oxford University Press.
Lewis, A. (1990) 'Bentham's View of the Right to Silence', *Current Legal Problems*, 43: 135–57.
Llewellyn, K. (1940) 'The Normative, the Legal, and the Law-Jobs: The Problem of Juristic Method', *Yale Law Journal*, 49(8): 1355–400.
Lloyd-Bostock, S. (2000) 'The Effects on Juries of Hearing about the Defendant's Previous Criminal Record: A Simulation Study', *Criminal Law Review*, 734–55.
Loader, I. (2002) 'Policing, Securitization and Democratization in Europe', *Criminal Justice*, 2(2): 125–53.
Loader, I. (2006) 'Fall of the "Platonic Guardians": Liberalism, Criminology and Political Responses to Crime in England and Wales', *British Journal of Criminology*, 46(4): 561–86.
Loader, I. and Walker, N. (2007) *Civilizing Security*. Cambridge: Cambridge University Press.
Lockhart, B. (2002) 'Restorative Justice', in P. O'Mahony (ed.) *Criminal Justice in Ireland*. Dublin: Institute of Public Administration.
Lyder, A. (2005) *Pushers Out: The Inside Story of Dublin's Anti-Drugs Movement*. Cheshire: Trafford Publishers.
Lyons, F. S. L. (1982) *Ireland since the Famine*. London: Collins/Fontana.

MacDonagh, O. (1960) 'The Nineteenth Century Revolution in Government: A Reappraisal Reappraised', *Historical Journal*, 3(1): 17–37.
MacDonagh, O. (1976) 'Ideas and Institutions', in W. E. Vaughan (ed.) *A New History of Ireland, Vol V*. Oxford: Clarendon Press.
Maine, H. (1927, first published 1861) *Ancient Law*. London: Dent.
Maher, I. (2006) *The Rule of Law and Agency*, IEP WP 06/01. London: Chatham House.

Majone, G. (1998) 'Europe's "Democratic Deficit": The Question of Standards', *European Law Journal*, 4(1): 5–28.
Mann, K. (1992) 'Punitive Civil Sanctions: The Middle-Ground between Criminal and Civil Law', *Yale Law Journal*, 101: 1795–1871.
Martin, F. (1992) 'The Rationale of the Exclusionary Rule of Evidence', *Irish Criminal Law Journal*, 2: 1–18.
Matthews, R. (2005) 'The Myth of Punitiveness', *Theoretical Criminology*, 9(2): 175–201.
May, A. (2003) *The Bar and the Old Bailey, 1750–1850*. London: University of North Carolina Press.
McAuley, F. (1993) *Psychiatry and Criminal Responsibility*. Dublin: Round Hall.
McAuley, F. and McCutcheon, J. P. (1981) 'The People v Shaw: An Analysis', *Dublin University Law Journal*, 3: 63–75.
McAuley, F. and McCutcheon, J. P. (2000) *Criminal Liability: A Grammar*. Dublin: Round Hall, Sweet and Maxwell.
McCormick, J. P. (1997a) *Carl Schmitt's Critique of Liberalism*. Cambridge: Cambridge University Press.
McCormick, J. P. (1997b) 'The Dilemmas of Dictatorship: Schmitt and Constitutional Emergency Powers', *Criminal Justice Law Journal*, 10: 167–88.
McCrudden, C. (2000) 'Common Law of Human Rights?: Transnational Judicial Conversations on Constitutional Rights', *Oxford Journal of Legal Studies*, 20(4): 499–532.
McCullagh, C. (2002) 'Robbing the Revenue: Accounting for Deviant Behaviour', in M. Corcoran and M. Peillon (eds) *Ireland Unbound: A Turn of the Century Chronicle*. Dublin: Institute of Public Administration.
McCutcheon, J. (1987) 'Arrest, Investigation and Section 30', *Dublin University Law Journal*, 9: 46–63.
McCutcheon, J.P. and Walsh, D. (1999) 'Seizure of Criminal Assets: An Overview', *Irish Criminal Law Journal*, 9(2): 127–132.
McDermott, P. (1999) *Res Judicata and Double Jeopardy*. Dublin: Butterworths.
McDowell, R. B. (1979) *Ireland in the Age of Imperialism and Revolution, 1760–1801*. Oxford: Clarendon Press.
McEldowney, J. (1977) 'The Case of the Queen v McKenna (1869) and Jury Packing in Ireland', *Irish Jurist*, 12: 339–54.
McEldowney, J. (1979) 'Stand by for the Crown: An Historical Analysis', *Criminal Law Review*, 272–83.
McEldowney, J. (1980) 'Policing and the Administration of Justice in Nineteenth Century Ireland', in C. Emsley and B. Weinberger (eds) *Policing Western Europe: Politics, Professionalism and Public Order, 1850–1940*. London: Greenwood Press.
McEldowney, J. (1989) 'Crown Prosecution in Nineteenth Century Ireland', in D. Hay and F. Snyder (eds) *Policing and Prosecution in Britain, 1750–1850*. Oxford: Clarendon.
McEvoy, P. (2005) *Research for the Department of Justice on the Criteria Applied by the Courts in Sentencing Under Section 15A of the Misuse of Drugs Act, 1977 (as amended)*. Dublin: Department of Justice, Equality and Law Reform.
McFadden, N. (2002) 'The Right to a Solicitor: Recent Developments', *Bar Review*, 7: 390–2.
McGee, H., Garavan, R., de Barra, M., Byrne, J. and Conroy, R. (2002) *The SAVI Report: Sexual Abuse and Violence in Ireland*. Dublin: Liffey Press.
McGowen, R. (1983) 'The Image of Justice and Reform of the Criminal Law in Early Nineteenth Century England', *Buffalo Law Review*, 32: 89–125.

McGowen, R. (1986) 'A Powerful Sympathy: Terror, the Prison and Humanitarian Reform in Early Nineteenth Century', *Journal of British Studies*, 25 312–34.

McGrath, D. (1999) 'Two Steps Forward, One Step Back: The Corroboration Warning in Sexual Cases', *Irish Criminal Law Journal*, 9(1): 22–46.

McGrath, D. (2001) 'Legal Professional Privilege', *Irish Jurist*, 36: 126–52.

McGrath, D. (2005) *Evidence*. Dublin: Thomson Round Hall.

McGrath, D. (2006) 'The Evidential Implications of the Criminal Justice Act, 2006', Round Hall Criminal Law Conference 2006, Royal College of Surgeons, 25 November 2006.

McGuckian, S. (1999) 'Recent Developments in the Law Governing the Admissibility of Confessions in Ireland', *Irish Criminal Law Journal*, 9: 8–21.

McKendrick, N. (1961) 'Josiah Wedgwood and Factory Discipline', *Historical Journal*, IV: 40–52.

McLaughlin, P. (1981) 'Legal Constraints in Criminal Investigation', *Irish Jurist (ns)*, XVI: 217–27.

McNiffe, L. (1997) *A History of the Garda Síochána: A Social History of the Force 1922–52, with an Overview for the Years 1952–97*. Dublin: Wolfhound Press.

Mead, G. H. (1918) 'The Psychology of Punitive Justice', *American Journal of Sociology*, 23(5): 577–602.

Meade, J. (2000) 'Organised Crime, Moral Panic and Law Reform: The Irish Adoption of Civil Forfeiture', *Irish Criminal Law Journal*, 10(1): 11–16.

Moran, M. (2003) *The British Regulatory State: High Modernism and Hyper-innovation*. Oxford: Oxford University Press.

Morris, F. (2004) *Report of the Tribunal of Inquiry set up Pursuant to the Tribunal of Inquiry (Evidence) Acts 1921–2002 into Certain Gardaí in the Donegal Division: Report on 'Explosive' Finds in Donegal: Term of Reference (e)*. Dublin: Stationery Office.

Morris, F. (2005) *Report of the Tribunal of Inquiry set up Pursuant to the Tribunal of Inquiry (Evidence) Acts 1921–2002 into Certain Gardaí in the Donegal Division: Report on the investigation into the death of Richard Barron and the extortion calls to Michael and Charlotte Peoples, Term of Reference (a) and (b)*. Dublin: Stationery Office.

Morris, F. (2006) *Report on the arrest and detention of seven persons at Burnfoot, County Donegal on the 23rd of May 1998 and the investigation relating to same, Term of Reference (i)*. Dublin: Stationery Office.

Morth, U. (2003) 'Europeanization as Interpretation, Translation and Editing of Public Policies', in K. Featherstone and C. Radelli (eds) *The Politics of Europeanization*. Oxford: Oxford University Press.

Mulcahy, A. (2002) 'The impact of the Northern "Troubles" on Criminal Justice in the Irish Republic', in P. O'Mahony (ed.) *Criminal Justice in Ireland*. Dublin: Institute of Public Administration.

Mulcahy, A. (2005) 'The "Other" Lessons from Ireland? Policing, Political Violence and Policy Transfer', *European Journal of Criminology*, 2(2): 185–209.

Mulcahy, A. (2006) *Policing Northern Ireland: Conflict, Legitimacy, Reform*. Cullompton: Willan Publishing.

Mulcahy, A. and O'Mahony, E. (2005) *Policing and Social Marginalisation in Ireland*. Dublin: Combat Poverty.

Mullally, S. (2006) *Gender, Culture and Human Rights: Reclaiming Universalism*. Oxford: Hart.

Mullan, G. (2000) 'The Duty to Disclose in Criminal Proceedings', *Bar Review*, 5(4): 174–8.

Murphy, P. (1998) 'Character Evidence: The Search for Logic and Policy Continues', *International Journal of Evidence and Proof*, 2: 71–108.

Murphy, F. and Galvin, B. (1999) 'Targeting the Financial Wealth of Criminals in Ireland', *Irish Criminal Law Journal*, 9(2): 133–59.
Murphy, P. (2003) *Murphy on Evidence,* 8th edn. Oxford: Oxford University Press.
Murphy, S. (1999) 'Tracing the Proceeds of Crime', *Irish Criminal Law Journal*, 9(2): 165–75.
Murphy-Lawless, J. (2002) *Fighting Back: Women and the Impact of Drug Abuse on Families and Communities*. Dublin: Liffey Press.
Mythen, G. and Walklate, S. (2006) 'Criminology and Terrorism: Which Thesis? Risk Society and Governmentality?', *British Journal of Criminology*, 46: 379–98.

National Crime Council (2001) *Crime in Ireland: A Review of Crime Levels and Trends; 1950 to 1998*. Dublin: Stationery Office.
Nelken, D. (2002) 'White Collar Crime', in M. Maguire, R. Morgan and R. Reiner (eds) *The Oxford Handbook of Criminology*, 3rd edn. Oxford: Oxford University Press.
Ni Raifeartaigh, U. (1994) 'The Doctrine of Fresh Complaint in Sexual Cases', *Irish Legal Times*, 12: 160–2.
Ni Raifeartaigh, U. (1995) 'Reversing the Onus of Proof in a Criminal Trial', *Irish Criminal Law Journal*, 5(2): 135–55.
Ni Raifeartaigh, U. (2001) 'The ECHR and the Irish Criminal Justice System', *Bar Review*, 7(2): 111–16.
Nietzsche, F. (1956) *The Genealogy of Morals*. New York: Anchor Books.
Nolan, B., O'Connell, P. and Whelan, C. (eds) (2000) *Bust to Boom? The Irish Experience of Growth and Inequality*. Dublin: Institute of Public Administration.
Norrie, A. (2001) *Crime, History and Reason: A Critical Introduction to Criminal Law*, 2nd edn. London: Butterworths.

O'Connell, D. (2000) 'The Irish Constitution and the ECHR: Belt and Braces', in D. Driscoll (ed.) *Irish Human Rights Review*. Dublin: Round Hall.
O'Connell, D. (2004) 'The ECHR Act 2003: A Critical Perspective', in U. Kilkelly (ed.) *ECHR and Irish Law*. Bristol: Jordan Publishing.
O'Connell, D., Cummiskey, S. Meeneghan, E. and O'Connell, P. (2006) *ECHR Act, 2003 A Preliminary Assessment of Impact*. Dublin: Law Society of Ireland and Dublin Solicitor's Bar Association.
O'Connell, M. (2001) *Changed Utterly: Ireland and the New Irish Psyche*. Dublin: Liffey Press.
O'Connell, M. and Whelan, A. (1994) 'Crime Victimisation in Dublin', *Irish Criminal Law Journal*, 4(2): 85–112.
O'Connor, P. (1980) 'Observations on the Voluntariness Test in Irish Law', *Gazette of the Law Society of Ireland*, 74: 198.
O'Connor, P. (1982a) 'The Admissibility of Unconstitutionally Obtained Evidence in Irish Law', *Irish Jurist*, 17: 257–94.
O'Connor, P. (1982b) 'Corroboration and the Testimony of Accomplices in the Irish Law of Evidence', *Dublin University Law Journal*, 4: 12–24.
O'Connor, P. (1985) 'Competence and Compellability of Spouses for the Prosecution', *Irish Law Times*, 3: 208–12.
O'Connor, P. and Cooney, P. (1980) 'Criminal Due Process, the Pre-Trial Stage and Self-Incrimination', *Irish Jurist* (ns), 15: 219–36.
O'Donnell, I. (2000) 'A Comment on Sentencing', *Irish Criminal Law Journal*, 10(4): 2–3.
O'Donnell, I. and McAuley, F. (eds) (2003) *Criminal Justice History: Themes and*

*Controversies from Pre-Independence Ireland*. Dublin: Four Courts Press.
O'Dwyer, K. (2001) *Restorative Justice Initiatives in the Garda Siochana: Evaluation of the Pilot Programme*, Research Report 4/01. Templemore: Garda Research Unit.
Office of the Director of Public Prosecutions (DPP) (2006) *Guidelines for Prosecutors*. Dublin: Office of the Director of Public Prosecutions.
O'Halpin, E. (1999) *Defending Ireland: The Irish State and its Enemies since 1922*. Oxford: Oxford University Press.
O'Higgins, M. (1998) 'Bail – A Privilege or a Right', *Bar Review*, 3: 318–21.
Ó Longaigh, S. (2006) *Emergency Law in Independent Ireland 1922–48* Dublin: Four Courts Press.
Olsen, F. (1984) 'Statutory Rape: A Feminist Critique of Rights Analysis', *Texas Law Review*, 63: 387–432.
Olsen, J. P. (2002) 'The many faces of Europeanization', *Journal of Common Market Studies*, 40(5): 921–52.
O'Mahony, P. (1998) 'The Constitution and Criminal Justice', in T. Murphy and P. Twomey (eds) *Ireland's Evolving Constitution: 1937–1997*. Oxford: Hart.
O'Malley, P. (1999) 'Volatile and Contradictory Punishment', *Theoretical Criminology*, 3(2): 175–96.
O'Malley, P. (2002) 'Globalising Risk: Distinguishing Styles of "Neo Liberal" Criminal Justice in Australia and the USA', *Criminal Justice*, 2(2): 205–22.
O'Malley, P. (2003) 'Penal Policies and Contemporary Politics', in C. Sumner (ed.) *The Blackwell Companion to Criminology*. Oxford: Blackwell.
O'Malley, P. (2004a) *Risk, Uncertainty and Government*. London: Glasshouse Press.
O'Malley, P. (2004b) 'The Government of Risks', in A. Sarat (ed.) *The Blackwell Companion to Law and Society*. Oxford: Oxford University Press.
O'Malley, T. (1994) 'The First Prosecution Appeal against Sentence', *Irish Criminal Law Journal*, 4: 192–204.
O'Malley, T. (1995) 'Sentencing Murderers: The Case for Relocating Discretion', *Irish Criminal Law Journal*, 5: 31–66.
O'Malley, T. (2000a) 'The Power to Punish: Reflections on Deaton (1963)' in E. O'Dell (ed.) *Leading Cases of the Twentieth Century*. Dublin: Round Hall: Sweet and Maxwell.
O'Malley, T. (2000b) *Sentencing Law and Practice*, 1st edn. Dublin: Round Hall, Sweet and Maxwell.
O'Malley, T. (2006a) *Sentencing Law and Practice*, 2nd edn. Dublin: Thomson, Round Hall.
O'Malley, T. (2006b) 'The Criminal Justice Act, 2006: Sentencing Provisions', Thomson Round Hall Criminal Law Conference, Royal College of Surgeons, 25 November.
Osborne, P. (1993) 'Private Prosecutions: A Comparative Perspective', *Irish Criminal Law Journal*, 3: 119–44.
Osborough, W. N. (1975) *Borstal in Ireland: Custodial Provision for the Young Adult Offender, 1906–1974*. Dublin: Institute of Public Administration.
O'Sullivan, E. (1997) 'Restored to Virtue, to Society and to God: Juvenile Justice and the Regulation of the Poor', *Irish Criminal Law Journal*, 7(2): 171–94.
O'Sullivan, E. and O'Donnell, I. (2007) 'Coercive Confinement in Ireland: The Waning of a Culture of Control', *Punishment and Society*, 9(1): 27–48.

Packer, H. (1964) 'Two Models of the Criminal Process', *University of Pennsylvania Law Review*, 113(1): 1–68.
Packer, H. (1968) *The Limits of the Criminal Sanction*. Palo Alto, CA: Stanford

University Press.
Paley, R. (1989) 'Thieftakers in London in the Age of the MacDaniel Gang, c. 1745–1754', in D. Hay and F. Snyder (eds) *Policing and Prosecution in Britain, 1750–1850*. Oxford: Clarendon Press.
Paley, W. (1833) *The Works of William Paley DD Archdeacon of Carlisle, With A Life of the Author*. London: Thoemmes Continuum.
Palmer, S. (1988) *Police and Protest in England and Ireland, 1780–1850*. Cambridge: Cambridge University Press.
Palmer, S. (2003) 'The Irish Police Experiment: The Beginnings of Modern Police in the British Isles, 1785–1795' in I. O'Donnell and F. McAuley (eds) *Criminal Justice History: Themes and Controversies from Pre-Independence Ireland*. Dublin: Four Courts Press.
Pasquino, P. (1991) 'Criminology: The Birth of the Special Knowledge', in G. Burchell, C. Gordon and P. Miller (eds) *The Foucault Effect*. Chicago: Chicago University Press.
Patten Report (1999) *A New Beginning: Report of the Independent Commission on Policing*. Belfast: Stationery Office.
Pattenden, R. (1991) 'Should Confessions be Corroborated?', *Law Quarterly Review*, 107: 317–39.
Perkins, H. (1989) *The Rise of Professionalised Society: England since 1880*. London: Routledge.
Philips, D. (1980) 'A New Engine of Power and Authority: The Institutions of Law Enforcement in England, 1780–1830', in V. A. C. Gattrell, B. Lenman and G. Parker (eds) *Crime and Law: The Social History of Crime in Western Europe since 1500*. London: Europa.
Philips, D. (1983) 'A New Engine of Power and Authority: The Institutionalisation of Law Enforcement in England 1780–1830' in V. Gatrell, B. Lenman and G. Parker (eds) *Crime and the Law: The Social History of Crime in Western Europe since 1500*. London: Europa Publications.
Philips, D. (1989) 'Good Men to Associate and Bad Men to Conspire: Associations for the Prosecution of Felons in England, 1760–1860' in D. Hay and F. Snyder (eds) *Policing and Prosecution in Britain, 1750–1850*. Oxford: Clarendon Press.
Posner, R. (1999) 'An Economic Approach to the Law of Evidence', *Stanford Law Review*, 51: 1477–1546.
Pound, R. (1912/1913) 'The Administration of Justice in the Modern City', *Harvard Law Review*, 26: 303–28.
Pound, R. (1933) 'The Future of the Criminal Law', *Columbia Law Review*, 21: 1–15.
Pratt, J. (2000) 'Emotive and Ostentatious Punishment: Its Decline and Resurgence in Modern Society', *Punishment and Society*, 2(4): 417–40.
Pratt, J. (2002) *Punishment and Decivilisation*. London: Sage.
Pratt, J. (2005) 'Elias, Punishment and Decivilisation' in J. Pratt, D. Brown, M. Brown, S. Hallsworth and W. Morrison (eds) *The New Punitiveness: Trends, Theories, Perspectives.* Cullompton: Willan Publishing.
Pratt, J. (2007) *Penal Populism*. London: Routledge.

Radin, M. (1936) 'Enemies of Society', *Journal of Criminal Law and Criminology*, 27(3): 328–56.
Radzinowicz, L. (1956) *A History of English Criminal Law and its Administration from 1750*, Vol. 2. London: Stevens.
Rawlings, P. (1999) *Crime and Power: A History of Criminal Justice, 1688–1998*. London: Longman.

Rawls, J. A. (1999) *A Theory of Justice*. London: Belknap Press.
Redmayne, M. (2002) 'The Relevance of Bad Character', *Criminal Law Journal*, 61: 684–714.
Regan, E. and O'Mahony, P. (2002) 'The Third Pillar of the European Union: The Emerging Structure of EU Police and Judicial Cooperation in Criminal Matters, and its Impact on Irish Criminal Justice and Civil Liberties', in P. O'Mahony (ed.) *Criminal Justice in Ireland*. Dublin: Institute of Public Administration.
*Report from the Departmental Committee on Prisons* (1895) [c. 7702], Vol. LVI.
*Report of the Committee to Review the Offences against the State Acts, 1939–1998, and Related Matters* (2001). Dublin: Stationery Office.
*Report of the Expert Group on Changes to the Criminal Law* (1998). Dublin: Stationery Office.
*Report of the Human Rights Committee, Official Records of the General Assembly, 48th Session, Supplement No. 40* (1993) (A/48/40), Part 1.
Revenue Powers Group (2003) *Report to the Minister for Finance*. Dublin: Stationery Office.
Ring, M. (1997) 'The Right to Silence: Rock v Ireland and Others', *Bar Review*, 3(5): 225–8.
Risse, T. and Ropp, S. (1999) 'International Human Rights Norms and Domestic Change: Conclusions', in T. Risse, S. Ropp and K. Sikkink (eds) *The Power of Human Rights Norms*. Cambridge: Cambridge University Press.
Roberts, P. and Zuckerman, A. (2004) *Criminal Evidence*. Oxford: Oxford University Press.
Rock, P. (2004) 'Victims, Prosecutors and the State in Nineteenth Century England and Wales', *Criminal Justice*, 4(4): 331–54.
Rogan, M. (2006a) 'The Role of Victims in Sentencing – The Case of Compensation Orders', *Irish Law Times*, 13: 202–8.
Rogan, M. (2006b) 'Victims' Rights: Theory and Practice Part II', *Irish Law Times*, 10: 151–5.
Rogers, P. (2006) *Into the Long War*. London: Pluto Press.
Rosanvallon, P. (2006) *La contre-démocratie: La Politique a l'Âge de la Defiance*. Paris: Seuil.
Rothman, D. J. (1979) *Incarceration and its Alternatives in Twentieth Century America*. New York: US Department of Justice.
Rothman, D. J. (1983) 'Sentencing Reforms in Historical Perspective', *Crime and Delinquency*, 29: 631–47.
Rottman, D. (1986) 'Crime and the Criminal Justice System', in K. Kennedy (ed.) *Ireland in Transition*. Dublin: Mercier Press.
Ruff, J. (2001) *Violence in Early Modern Europe, 1500–1800*. Cambridge and New York: Cambridge University Press.
Ryan, A. (2000) 'Arrest and Detention: A Review of the Law', *Irish Criminal Law Journal*, 10(1): 2–10.
Ryan, E. and Magee, P. (1983) *The Irish Criminal Process*. Dublin: Mercier Press.

Saleilles, R. (1968, first published 1911) *The Individualisation of Punishment*. New Jersey: Patterson Smith.
Sands, P. (2005) *Lawless World*. London: Penguin.
Sarat, A. (ed.) (2001) *Law, Violence and the Possibility of Justice*. Princeton, NJ: Princeton University Press.
Sarat, A. and Kearns, T. R. (1991) 'A Journey through Forgetting: Toward a Jurisprudence of Violence' in A. Sarat and T. R. Kearns (eds) *The Fate of Law*.

Michigan: University of Michigan Press.
Sayre, F. B. (1933) 'Public Welfare Offences', *Columbia Law Review*, 55: 35–68.
Scheureman, B. (1993) 'The Rule of Law under Siege: Carl Schmitt and the death of the Weimar Republic', *History of Political Thought*, 14(2): 265–80.
Schmidt, V. and Radaelli, C. (2004) 'Policy Change and Discourse in Europe: Conceptual and Methodological Issues' *West European Politics*, 27(2): 183–210.
Schmitt, C. (1985, first published 1922) *Political Theology: Four Chapters on the Theory of Sovereignty*. Cambridge, MA: MIT Press.
Scraton, P. (2004) 'Regulating Anti-Social Behaviour: A Critical Perspective', Irish Association for the Study of Delinquency Conference, Cavan, November.
Shapiro, I. (1986) *The Evolution of Rights in Liberal Theory*. Cambridge: Cambridge University Press.
Shipan, C. (2003) *Independence and the Irish Environmental Protection Agency: a comparative assessment*, Working Paper 08. TCD, Dublin; Policy Institute.
Shubert, A. (1981) 'Private Initiative in Law Enforcement: Associations for the Prosecutions of Felons, 1744–1856', in V. Bailey (ed.) *Policing and Punishment in Nineteenth Century Britain*. London: Croom Helm.
Simon, J. (1997) 'Governing Through Crime', in L.M. Friedman and G. Fisher (eds) *The Crime Conundrum: Essays on Criminal Justice*. Boulder, CO: Westview Press, pp. 171–89.
Simon, J. (1998) 'Managing the Monstrous: Sex Offenders and the New Penology', *Psychology, Public Policy and Law*, 4: 452–67.
Simon, J. (2000) 'Megan's Law: Crime and Democracy in Late Modern America', *Law and Social Inquiry*, 25: 111–48.
Simon, J. (2002) 'Visions of Self-Control: Fashioning a Liberal Approach to crime and Punishment in the Twentieth Century', in A. Sarat, G. Bryant and R. Kagan (eds) *Looking Back at Law's Century*. Ithaca, NY: Cornell University Press.
Simon, J. (2007) *Governing Through Crime: How the War on Crime Transformed American Democracy and Created a Culture of Fear*. Oxford: Oxford University Press.
Slaughter, A. M. (2004). *A New World Order*. Princeton, NJ: Princeton University Press.
Smith, B. A. (1989) 'Ireland's Ennis State Reformatory: A 19th Century Example of Failed Institutional Reform', *Federal Probation*, 53(1): 53–64.
Smith, J. C. (1987) 'The Presumption of Innocence', *Northern Ireland Legal Quarterly*, 38 (3): 223–43.
Smyth, J. (1992) *The Men of No Property: Irish Radicals and Popular Culture in the Late Eighteenth Century*. London: Palgrave Macmillan.
Sparks, R. (2006) 'Ordinary Anxieties and States of Emergency: Statecraft and Spectatorship in the New Politics of Insecurity', in S. Armstrong and L. McAra (eds) *Perspectives on Punishment*. Oxford: Oxford University Press.
Stephen, J. F. (1863) *A General View of the Criminal Law of England*. London: McMillan.
Stephen, J. F. (1883) *A History of the Criminal Law of England, Vol I*. London: Routledge/Thoemmes Press.
Stone, L. (1987) *The Past and Present Revisited*. London: Routledge.
Storch, R. D. (1980) 'Crime and Punishment in Nineteenth Century England', *History Today*, 30: 32–7.
De Swaan, A. (2001) 'Dyscivilisation, Mass Extermination and the State', *Theory, Culture and Society*, 18(2–3): 265–76.

Tarde, G. (1912) *Penal Philosophy*. London: Heinemann.
Temkin, J. (1982) 'Towards a Modern Law of Rape', *Modern Law Review*, 45: 399–419.

Thompson, E. P. (1963) *The Making of the English Working Class*. London: Gollancz.
Thompson, E. P. (1967) 'Time, Work Discipline and Industrial Capitalism', *Past and Present*, 38: 56–97.
Thompson, E. P. (1971) 'The Moral Economy of the English Crowd in the Eighteenth Century', *Past and Present*, 50: 76–136.
Thompson, E. P (1977) *Whigs and Hunters: The Origins of the Black Act*. Harmondsworth: Penguin.
Thompson, F. M. L. (1981) 'Social Control in Victorian Britain', *Economic History Review*, 34: 189–208.
Tilly, C. (2004) *Contention and Democracy in Europe 1650–2000*. Cambridge: Cambridge University Press.
Townshend, C. (1982) 'Martial Law: Legal and Administrative Problems of Civil Emergency in Britain and the Empire, 1800–1940', *Historical Journal*, 25(1): 167–95.
Townshend, C. (1983) *Political Violence in Ireland: Government and Resistance since 1848*. Oxford: Clarendon Press.

Vaughan, B. (2000) 'Punishment and Conditional Citizenship', *Punishment and Society*, 2(1): 23–39.
Vaughan, B. (2005) 'A New System of Police Accountability', *Irish Criminal Law Journal*, 15 (4): 18–22.
Vaughan, B. (2007) 'The Provision of Policing and the Problem of Pluralism', *Theoretical Criminology*, 11(3): 347–66.
Vaughan, B. and Kilcommins, S. (2007) 'The Europeanization of Human Rights and the limits of authoritarian policing in Ireland', *European Journal of Criminology*, 4(4): 437–59.
Vaughan, W. E. (1976) 'Ireland c. 1870' in W. E. Vaughan (ed.) *A New History of Ireland, Vol V*. Oxford: Clarendon Press.
Vibert, F. (2007) *The Rise of the Unelected: Democracy and the New Separation of Powers*. Cambridge: Cambridge University Press.
Vink, M. (2003) 'What is Europeanisation? And Other Questions on a New Research Agenda', *European Political Science*, 3(1) 63–74.

Walker, C. (2001) 'The Patten Report and Post-Sovereignty Policing in Northern Ireland', in R. Wilford (ed.) *Aspects of the Belfast Agreement*. Oxford: Oxford University Press.
Walker, N. (2002) 'The Idea of Constitutional Pluralism', *Modern Law Review*, 65: 317–59.
Walker, R. B. J. (2006) 'Lines of Insecurity: International, Imperial, Exceptional', *Security Dialogue*, 37: 65–82.
Wallace, H. (2000) 'Europeanisation and Globalisation: Complementary or Contradictory Trends', *New Political Economy*, 5(3): 369–82.
Walsh, D. (1989) 'The Impact of Anti Subversive Laws on Police Powers and Practice in Ireland: The Silent Erosion of Individual Freedom', *Temple Law Review*, 62(4): 1099–110.
Walsh, D. (1998) *The Irish Police: A Legal and Constitutional Analysis*. Dublin: Round Hall, Sweet and Maxwell.
Walsh, D. (2002) *Criminal Procedure*. Dublin: Thomson, Round Hall.
Walsh, D. (2004a) 'The Proposed Garda Siochana Ombudsman Commission: A Critique', *Irish Criminal Law Journal*, 14(1): 2–12.
Walsh, D. (2004b) 'The Proposed Garda Complaints Procedure: A Critique', *Irish Criminal Law Journal*, 14(4): 2–26.

Walsh, D. (2005a) 'The Criminal Justice Bill: Completing a Crime Control Model of Justice', Conference on the Criminal Justice Bill: Implications for Human Rights and Legal Practice, Trinity College Dublin, 20 April.

Walsh, D. (2005b) *Juvenile Justice*. Dublin: Thomson, Round Hall.

Walsh, D. (2006) 'Police Powers in the Criminal Justice Act, 2006: The Triumph of Executive Convenience over Judicial Checks and Balances', Thomson Round Hall Criminal Law Conference, Royal College of Surgeons, 25 November.

Walsh, D. (2007) 'The Criminal Justice Act, 2006: A Crushing Defeat for Due Process Values', *Judicial Studies Institute Journal*, 7(1): 44–59.

Watson, D. (2000) *Victims of Recorded Crime in Ireland: Results from the 1996 Survey*. Dublin: Oak Tree Press.

Whelan, K. (1996) *The Tree of Liberty: Radicalism, Catholicism and the Construction of Irish Identity, 1760–1830*. Cork: Cork University Press.

White, J. (2000a) 'The Confessional State – Police Interrogation in the Irish Republic I', *Irish Criminal Law Journal*, 10(1) 17–20.

White, J. (2000b) 'The Confessional State – Police Interrogation in the Irish Republic II', *Irish Criminal Law Journal*, 10(2): 2–6.

Wiener, M. J. (1990) *Reconstructing the Criminal: Culture, Law, and Policy in England: 1830–1914*. Cambridge: Cambridge University Press.

Wincott, D. (2004) 'Policy Change and Discourse in Europe: Can the EU make a "Square Meal out of a Stew of Paradox"?', *West European Politics*, 27(2): 354–63.

Woodiwiss, A. (2005) *Human Rights*. Routledge: London.

Woodiwiss, A. (2006) 'What Could it Mean to Take Human Rights Seriously?', Human Rights and Global Justice Conference, University of Warwick, 29–31 March.

Woodworth, P. (2001) *Dirty War, Clean Hands. ETA, the GAL and Spanish Democracy*. Cork: Cork University Press.

Wouters, C. (1999) 'Changing Patterns of Social Controls and Self-controls: On the Rise of Crime since the 1950s and the Sociogenesis of a "Third Nature"', *British Journal of Criminology*, 39(3): 416–32.

Zedner, L. (2002) 'Dangers of Dystopia in Penal Theory', *Oxford Journal of Legal Studies*, 22(2): 341–66.

Zedner, L. (2003) 'Too Much Security', *International Journal of the Sociology of Law*, 31(3): 155–84.

Zedner, L. (2005) 'Securing Liberty in the Face of Terror: Reflections from Criminal Justice', *Journal of Law and Society*, 32(4): 507–33.

Zedner, L. (2006) 'Security for Whom? Reducing Risk by Eroding Rights?', British Criminology Conference Glasgow, 5–7 July.

# Index